THE
INSTINCTIVE
SHOT

THE INSTINCTIVE SHOT

THE PRACTICAL GUIDE TO MODERN GAME SHOOTING

Chris Batha

Quiller

First published in the UK in 2012
by Quiller, an imprint of Quiller Publishing Ltd

British Library Cataloguing-in-Publication Data
A catalogue record for this book
is available from the British Library

ISBN 978 1 84689 111 3

Printed in China

Quiller

An imprint of Quiller Publishing Ltd
Wykey House, Wykey, Shrewsbury, SY4 1JA
Tel: 01939 261616 Fax: 01939 261606
E-mail: info@quillerbooks.com
Website: www.countrybooksdirect.com

Contents

Acknowledgements

The contents of *The Instinctive Shot* are not only my thoughts and ideas but are a distillation of all that I have learned from a variety of sources – from every instructor that I have worked with, every client I have coached, every article and book I have read and every video I have watched. I would like nothing better than to list and credit each and every one of you, but it would take another book in its own right to do so!

Just let me offer a big "Thank you" to you all and recognize that if it were not for your willingness to share your knowledge, in person or on paper, I could have not have written this book. I hope you recognize a little of your input in my interpretation of how to shoot straight.

My grateful thanks go to the many editors, writers and authors (living and deceased) whose works have helped build the knowledge to write this book and to my fellow coaches and associates who have helped create the experience to know what works:

Cyril Adams, Dolph Adams, Bob Allen, Gil and Vicki Ash, Lionel Atwill, Lanny Bassam, Fred Baughan, Paul Bentley, John Batley, John Bidwell, Guy Bignell, Bryan Bilinski, Chris Bird, Stephen A. Blumenthal, Bruce Bowlen, Robert Braden, John Brindel, Bob Brister, Bruce Buck, Nash Buckingham, Louise Burke, Pat Burridge, Major Sir Gerald Burrard, Adam Calvert, Chris Cantrell, Dan Carlisle, G.L. Carlisle, Ed Carroll, Andy Castle, Robert Churchill, Charles Conger, George Conrad, Chris Cradock, Fred Neal David, Ken Davies, Bob Decot, Steve Denny, Chuck DeVinne, George Digweed, Andy Duffy, George Evans, Julian Murray-Evans, Richard Faulds, Alister Ferguson, Marty Fischer, Rex Gage, Chuck Gaskin, John Goesslin, Rob Gray, Les Greevy, John Gregson, B.C., Peter Harris, Robert R. Hartman, Macdonald Hastings, John Hawley, Arthur Hearn, Gene Hill, Roger Hill, Charles Hillman, Tony Hoare, Michael Kayes, Bill Kempffer, John King, Mike King, Richard Alden Knight, Frank Kodl, Charles Lancaster, David Leathart, Ernie Lind, John R. Linn, Frank Little, David Lloyd, Tom Mack, Dennis Macnab, Robin Marshall-Ball, Dr. Wayne F. Martin, E.S. McCawley, Jr., Michael McIntosh, Jerry Meyer, E. Migdalski, Tom Migdalski, Chris Miles, Brian Miller, Fred Missildene, Jack Mitchell, Peter Munday, Andrew A. Montague, Bob Nichols, Tony Norman, Steve Nutbeam, Jack O'Connor, George G. Oberfell, Tom Payne, Michael Pearce, Tom Penman, Neal Phillips, Richard Rawlingson, Mike Reynolds, Alan Rose, Michael Rose, Mickey Rouse, Bob Rotella, Major J.E.M. Ruffer, Ed Scherer, Charles Schneible, Dan Schindler, Bruce Scott, Robin Scott, Roger Silcox, A. J. Smith, Ronald W. Stadt, Percy Stanbury, Jackie Stewart, Ralph Stuart, Dale Tate, Douglas Tate, John Taylor, Mark H. Taylor, Charles E. Thompson, John Topliss, David Trevallion, Vic Venters, Doug Vine, Billy Walker, Roland Watson, Sam Wilkinson, Mike Williams, John Wooley, Mike Yardley, Claire Zamboni and Don Zutz.

I am grateful for the help given to me by a number of people and companies in the writing of this book:

For their permission to use original artwork illustrations, tables and reference materials from their publications: *Black's Wing and Clay*, Eley Hawk Ltd., Remington Arms Company and Winchester Firearms (Olin Corporation).

For their assistance and providing their original photographs: Terry Allen, Arrow Laser Shots, Barbour Ltd, Beretta USA, The Dallas Divas – Judy Rhodes, Bettws Hall Sporting – Gwynn and Anne Evans and Will Criddle, Luciano Bosis, Charles Boswell Gunmaker, E.J. Churchill Shooting Grounds, Jeff Coates, Electronic Shooters Protection (ESP), FAMARS di Abbiatico & Salvinelli, Paul Fievez, Forest City Gun Club, David Grant, Griffin and Howe Shooting Grounds at Hudson Farm, GripSwell Gloves, G.R.I.T.S. – Elizabeth Lanier, Grulla Srl., Holland & Holland – Robert Pearson, Holland & Holland Shooting

Grounds, Krieghoff International, Le Chameaux Boots, The Orvis Company, Inc., Orvis Sandanona – Brian and Peggy Long, James Purdey & Sons, Randolph Ranger Shooting Glasses, Rizzini USA, Russell Boots, Charles, Margaret and Gavin Schneible, Schoffel, Shot Spots, Sporting Targets, John C. Sullivan, Jr., John Taylor, Teague Chokes, West London Shooting Grounds, Kim and Niles Wheeler.

Trudie Abadie for her excellent work in transforming ordinary photographs into handsome photo illustrations.

Jason Fox for his exceptional graphic illustrations.

Jeff Love for his outstanding cover design.

Sara Gump of Redfield & Associates for original photography, editing and never flagging help and support – without her this book would never have been written.

And finally, my thanks go to Andrew Johnston of Quiller Publishing for his foresight and confidence in making the decision to publish *The Instinctive Shot*.

New Charles Boswell .410 Over and Under. (DAVID GRANT)

Foreword
Mike Barnes Editor, *Fieldsports* Magazine

Having known Chris for more years than I care to remember, and handled a variety of his work during that time, when he called to ask if I would write this foreword, saying yes was a given.

Chris's knowledge and dexterity never cease to surprise me. He can talk about practically any given subject, which, regardless of its previous mileage he will give a new and added twist. Which for a shooting instructor and columnist is a rare gift.

Chris has been a regular writer for *Fieldsports* Magazine since it was launched. Each quarter we discuss his proposed subject for the forthcoming issue. Never a problem, and we agree a date for delivery.

An editor's joy! It arrives on time (or early), word perfect and while it covers the agreed topic, there is always a different and unexpected slant.

It helps that he knows what he is talking about. Great knowledge of guns too. A vastly experienced instructor, he can also shoot a bit, as I'm sure those who have stood next to him in the shooting line will have discovered. He has shot game on at least three continents, and yet his heart remains in the English countryside. This is the place where he is probably most at home, certainly in the autumn and winter. His love of great sport and the heritage that goes with it fuels his imagination to the point that he never, ever tires of it.

So, as a truly first-rate coach and highly experienced and widely travelled game shot, and a good writer, there could be no one better to deliver a book such as this. I'm sure you will enjoy it.

(TERRY ALLEN)

Foreword
Ralph Stuart Editor in Chief, *Shooting Sportsman*

We all wish that we could shoot better. Whether we are new to the sport, have become competent with a shotgun, or are consistently on the leader board at clays tournaments, none of us are completely satisfied with our performances every time.

The fact that you have cracked the cover of this book shows that you don't feel that you know everything about shotgunning. And that's a good thing. A willingness to learn and an openness to new ideas are big first steps in improving your abilities.

Another big step is finding the right teacher – and you've found him in Chris Batha. I have known Chris for going on 15 years, and he never ceases to impress. He is one of the most knowledgeable, skilled, enthusiastic shotgunners I have ever met. He pretty much lives to pull the trigger. You've heard people say, "Been there, done that", well when it comes to Chris and shooting, truer words were never spoken. Chris is an international clays shooter, a globetrotting game shooter, an award-winning instructor, a host of television shows and videos, a writer, a trip host, a gunfitter, a gun salesman and even the owner of two gunmaking companies. He knows shooting inside out.

But more importantly, Chris is passionate about sharing what he's learned with others and helping grow their enjoyment of the sport. I remember when we were looking for a Sporting Clays Editor for *Shooting Sportsman* Magazine, Chris's name is the one that popped up time and again as someone who would connect with readers and be able to present technical information in an accessible manner.

Having shot all over the world, Chris is familiar with almost every type of situation and environment likely to be encountered by shotgunners. Whether it's upland hunting over dogs, waterfowling in a blind or shooting driven birds on the moors, Chris has experienced it and can offer sound advice in a clear, concise way.

The same goes for clay shooting. Chris is so familiar with the various presentations – having shot them as well as set them – that he knows the best methods and techniques for breaking them.

Which is the true beauty of this book: it bridges the gap between the range and the field, applying to both the clays enthusiast and the keen game shot.

In all honesty, when I first heard about this project, I thought, *Really? Another clay-shooting book?* But after Chris began explaining the details, I started thinking, *finally, someone is going to address the specifics on how shooting targets relates to shooting game. It's about time.*

Because when you really think about it, all of today's clay-shooting disciplines have their roots (buried though they may be) in game shooting. Successfully taking clays or game still comes down to mastering the fundamentals, establishing the right technique, and then practising until a particular shot becomes second nature.

For hunters, even if the shots presented on a clays course don't bear much resemblance to those seen in the field, they can only benefit from shooting during the off-season. As Chris said in his first Sporting Clays column in *Shooting Sportsman*, "A well-practised sporting clays shooter who likes to hunt birds will be a better and far more consistent shot than the stalwart hunter whose only practise for live quarry is the quarry itself."

In other words, if a hunter bangs away enough at clays, not only will he fine-tune the fundamentals such as footwork, stance, posture and gun mount, but he also will improve his hand-eye co-ordination, which is a key to good wingshooting. With enough practise at the range, his reactions to birds in the field will become purely instinctive and he will stand a much better chance of connecting. After all, there's no asking Mother Nature, "May I see that grouse again?"

So whether you shoot clays, birds or both, you have done well to pick up *The Instinctive Shot*. Chris's on-target advice will put more Xs on your scorecard and birds in your bag. Not only that, but it will give you another excuse to get out and shoot.

Now who could wish for more?

Charles Boswell .410 Over and Under. (TERRY ALLEN)

Introduction

Over my thirty years as a shooting instructor, the one question that I am most often asked is: "How does one shoot the *Instinctive Technique*?" To answer, I first must define *Instinctive*. It is an inherent, spontaneous and unthinking reaction to stimulus. When shooting a shotgun, the *Instinctive Shot* is one made without conscious thought – a pure reaction to the bird's speed and line of flight. Everyone has experienced that split-second chance at a pheasant over a rise, or a quail unexpectedly exploding from cover – we simply react to the stimuli and, more often than not, make a clean shot.

Yet when standing on a peg in a driven shoot or sitting in a dove field, the bird appears as a distant smudge in the sky, and seems to take an age to arrive into range. This gives ample time to read the bird's speed and line of flight and to make any last-second adjustments to successfully execute the shot. With all that time to prepare, why are these shots so often missed?

The difference lies in the two scenarios. The first shot is made by harnessing our natural eye–hand co-ordination to make an *Instinctive Shot*. See bird, shoot bird. With the second shot, there is toomuch time to think. Making a conscious effort to place the shot cloud on a collision course with the bird all too easily morphs into aiming. Referencing the bead and measuring the lead is known to shooting instructors as the "*Poke and Hope*" style of shooting.

The core skill in consistent shooting is to match the muzzle speed to the target speed, developing both speed and line of flight. This is achieved by harnessing one's innate ability to point at an object.

In shooting, as in any sport, there will be the so-called *Natural* – those blessed with better reflexes and visual acuity than the rest of the population. It is possible for an athlete like this who has never had a shooting lesson or any formal training to become an accomplished shot, but they are a rarity. However, it is absolutely true that any less-gifted shooter who is prepared to work hard on the fundamentals of straight shooting, can match and often surpass the more naturally gifted shots.

The word *modern* in the dictionary, when applied to art or medicine, is defined as "of or relating to, a recently developed or advanced style, technique, or technology". Seeing the Olympian heights at which pheasant and partridge are shot today is testimony to the "*modern*" improvements in shotguns, ballistics and technique. Those on the annual list of the country's top shots are all capable of taking high birds that lesser mortals would consider out of reach.

There is not one top athlete in any sport, amateur or professional, who has not received professional coaching. They then practise the lessons taught until the movements or actions are grooved into their muscle memory. All sports require mastery of the fundamental mechanics to be successful, and shooting a shotgun is no different. To be a consistently good shot requires practice and that practice must be perfect – how well you practise is how well you will shoot.

This book is written to explain what to practise and how to practise so you can improve your skills and consistency in the field. To make an *Instinctive Shot* you need to groove those fundamentals, to create the correct muscle memory to be able to make a shot without consciously thinking about it.

In the late 1890s, the German psychologist Herman Ebbinghaus conducted experiments to attempt to understand how the human mind stores memory. He discovered that if an act is repeated in practice or repeated beyond the point required for mastery of the task, a long-term muscle memory was created for that task. This eventually allowed the task to be performed without conscious effort. He referred to this process as *overlearning*.

It takes time for the body to *overlearn* a movement. A single motion must be repeated thousands of times for three to four weeks before it becomes "learned" by the muscles. During the martial artist's practice of *Kata (Exercises)*, he practises blocking a punch *(Wax On!)*. When this movement is *over-*

learned it becomes a reflex. If he is punched, he reflexively blocks the punch without conscious thought!

Making an *Instinctive Shot* is just like blocking a punch. You do not have time to think about all of the movements involved. If you have practised the movements until they are a reflex, you will simply "*See Bird, Shoot Bird*".

The fundamentals are just one side of the Trinity of Straight Shooting. The correct well-fitted gun and sound technique complete the *Triangle* of the *Instinctive Shot*. This book is structured so that chapter by chapter your understanding and application of the information contained herein will start the beginner out right, improve the intermediate and, if you're an experienced shot, there are still some insights that will help you shoot straighter still!

Chapter 1
History

There are more than sufficient books on the history of hunting and the evolution of the shotgun. So, in keeping with the theme of this book, the focus here is on the 1800s, where the development of the shotgun and the introduction of competitive and driven shooting, hand in glove, created the modern shotgun and the shooting techniques that are used today.

To survive, humans have hunted for food since the dawn of time, but the sport of shooting birds on the wing is a relatively modern pursuit. Until the middle of the seventeenth century, snares, traps, nets, dogs and even predatory birds were commonly used to catch birds in the air or on the ground.

Though gunpowder was introduced into Europe from China in the 13th Century, actual firearms are relatively recent inventions. The French are credited with shooting birds on the wing in the 1600s, but the slow lock times of matchlock and wheellock guns made this type of shooting a lottery, with little consistency. The successful construction of Damascus steel barrels and the perfecting of the flintlock ignition system in the late 1700s enabled the manufacture of double barrel shotguns which made shooting birds on the wing a more viable and consistent option.

One could say that these advancements in gunmaking were the result of the various military actions taking place during this period and, to some degree, that would be correct. However, it was when King Charles II returned from forced exile in France in 1660, bringing with him the new art of "shooting flying", that court followers and landed gentry embraced this new sport with enthusiasm. It was their wealth and passion for this new sport that pushed and encouraged the gunmakers of the period to make significant advances in the development of the sporting guns. The likes of Joseph

The Halcyon Days of Driven Game Shooting.

Manton and Henry Nock picked up the baton, taking the double flintlock into the 1800s.

The French nobility continued to refine shooting birds on the wing and in the 1820s, introduced "Battue" (To Beat) Shooting. At first, birds were driven from cover with the Guns walking in the beating line, but this practice quickly morphed so that the birds were driven towards a waiting line of Guns. This became the Driven Shooting subsequently introduced into Britain. This new sport was adopted by royalty, the court and the upper classes, taking its place alongside fox hunting and horse racing, as one of the Sports of Kings. The older practice of shooting birds over dogs, with its simple straight-away shot, was ultimately considered far too easy.

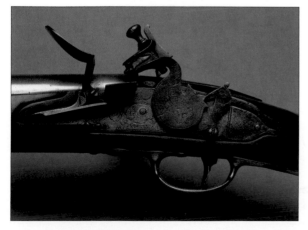

Late 1700s Flintlock. (David Grant)

Money was no object! Bigger and bigger bags were demanded and better guns were required to shoot them. The gunmakers bent to the task. The double flintlock shotguns lasted from approximately 1790 through 1820 – a mere 30 years. These were replaced during the 1820s by the double barrel muzzle loader with its new percussion ignition system – the design in widespread use for about forty years. But beginning in the 1860s, the muzzle loading shotgun began to be replaced by the new breech loading shotguns. These allowed much swifter loading, ushering in the Halcyon Days of Driven Game Shooting.

The development and perfection of the modern sporting shotguns as we know them today occurred between 1860 and 1909. This was a time of extreme self-indulgence during which those with extraordinary wealth created a demand for game shooting where success was measured in the number of birds killed in a day or, in the extremely popular sport of competitive live pigeon shooting, the number shot in succession.

The essential requirements of the game gun are speed and ease of firing and reloading plus the robust reliability to stand up to a prodigious amount of cartridges being fired in quick succession. The live pigeon competitions depended as much on the gun as the shooter as the huge purses being contested could be won or lost on a simple shotgun malfunction. The arduous tests provided by Driven Shooting and Live Pigeon competitions were the proving grounds for the multiplying patents, constant innovations and improvements in the development of the modern shotgun.

These esoteric wingshooting events were not the pastimes of the hoi polloi but of the royalty and aristocracy. The fervour with which these aristocrats immersed themselves in every aspect of these new sports was matched with golden guineas and five pound notes which the gun trade was more than happy to accept. Estates were reshaped to accommodate the owners' new passion: cover crops, coppices and woods were cultivated and planted. But the great numbers of birds being shot meant the wild population needed to be supplemented by pen-raised birds, so the wild grouse moors were coveted above all.

There was great rivalry between estates, with the gamekeepers and gunmakers all striving to outdo each other – their efforts fuelled from the wallets of these affluent shooting enthusiasts! With the birds it was quantity, not quality, that was demanded and with the Guns, it was quality not quantity – and the estate lords were more than happy to pay in full for both. The London newspapers carried weekly reports of record driven bags and the results of live pigeon competitions. Advertisements were run offering sporting attire and equipment and not to have the very latest and very best was a social faux pas! And a London Best Gun was de rigueur!

The Edwardian Shooting Party was a high society event – elaborate dinners and entertainment revolved around the game and pigeon shooting. Non-shooting guests were invited into the field to admire the marksmanship of the Guns, especially of their host. The greatest shot of the period was acknowledged to be Lord Ripon, formerly the Earl De Grey. In his lifetime of shooting, his Game Book records his having shot some 550,000 pheasants, grouse, partridge, ground-game

Monte Carlo, the Mecca of live pigeon shooting.

The who's who of British aristocracy and their passion for game shooting created the "Best London Shotgun".

Lord Ripon, the Earl De Grey, considered by many to be one of the best shots of all time. His record books reveal that he shot 556,813 fur and feathered game. Born in 1867, he fell dead on the grouse moor after a day's shooting in 1923.

and wildfowl. His other astonishing accomplishments included shooting 28 pheasants in one minute and having seven birds dead in the air at one time! These feats could not be achieved without a dedicated team of loaders – it was the norm to have two loaders, one cartridge boy and a triumvirate of shotguns!

As a result of the fierce competition among the estates, their owners and their teams of Guns, a record-breaking number of birds and game were shot during this period. The participants were, to all purposes, professional shots. They could afford to and they did practise constantly, averaging 30,000 plus cartridges per person, per season. Colonel Peter Hawker, Lord Ashburton, Lord De Grey, Marquess of Ripon, Lord Walsingham, Maharajah Prince Duleep Singh and the Prince of Wales (later to become Edward the Seventh) are some of the names that appear repeatedly, credited with the incredible record bags for that period and the frequent sales in the gunmakers' record books.

Throughout Europe, live pigeon shooting was so popular that the head-to-head matches were reported in the daily papers. Pigeons were released from sprung boxes in the centre of a fenced ring and the object was to see who could shoot the most pigeons. This was made more difficult by the random release and the rule that, to count, the dead

The World live pigeon shooting Championships in Italy, 1930.

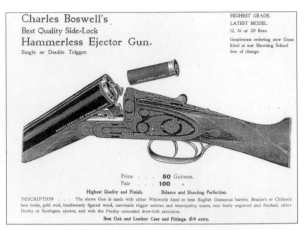

Charles Boswell Live Pigeon Gun.

Charles Hellis built on The Boss Action. (PAUL FIEVEZ)

pigeon had to fall within the ring. The participants were eliminated once they missed two birds in a row. The winner's purse at these games was as much as £40,000.00! The sport was held in such high esteem that live pigeon shooting was an event included in the 1900 Olympic Games.

London had several clubs devoted to live pigeon shooting. The Hurlingham Club in Fulham opened in 1867 as a pigeon-shooting club and the blue rock dove can still be seen on its flag today. This Club was a favourite location for over forty years, until shooting ceased there in 1906. The National Gun Club at Hendon, however, did not close its live pigeon rings until 1920.

In Monaco, The Live Pigeon International Competitions and Sweepstakes were held in a 20 yard ring instead of the standard 31 yard – testing even the best of shots! Those taking part chose their guns, cartridges and chokes with the same care as did their game-shooting peers. Because of the "Miss and Out" rule and the requirement to drop the bird within the ring, many larger gauges were used.

Eventually, a rule change was made to level the playing field and gauges bigger than 12 were not allowed in competition. At that time, the standard game gun was chambered at 2½ inches, so competition shooters began to chamber their pigeon guns for 2¾ inch cartridges to increase the amount of shot that could be used. These larger loads created more pressure on the gun and barrels but gunmakers were quick to strengthen their guns' actions. A combination of weight, size and an extra third bite, doll's head extensions to the top rib, cross bolts and side clips to actions fine-tuned these specialized competition guns. The Pigeon Gun of the period could be compared to the modern clay target competition gun of today.

Luciano Bosis Trap Gun.

Live pigeon shooting was banned in England in 1920, but continued on the Continent for another half century, ceasing in Monaco in 1966 and in Italy in 1970. It may simply be that the Side by Side had effectively been perfected in the 1890s, with the Over and Under design finalized with the Boss Patent of 1909 and the Woodward Patent of 1913, but after the end of live pigeon shooting in England, followed by the World Wars and with the impact of a diminishing economy, there were very few new patents in shotgun design issued in England.

After the Second World War, the Italian gunmakers did continue to develop and innovate shotgun designs – in particular, with the Over and Under. The single sight plane and superior control of recoil made the Over and Under the configuration of choice for many of the live pigeon shooters still actively competing on the Continent. Italy's Over and Under designs have been utilized to produce some of the best known names in Competition Shotguns made today: Beretta and Perazzi have been proven in Olympic Competitions and Fabbri rules in the World's Pigeon Rings.

During the evolution of the European gun trade, a similar chain of events was occurring in America where the Live Pigeon and Trap Shooters were driving the development of the American shotgun. Eventually, their patents and improvements found their way into the shotguns used for hunting.

Hunting in America was mainly for food for the table rather than for sport. This was "shoe leather" hunting, where a dog to find, flush and retrieve the bird was as essential as a gun and cartridge. There were major differences in the requirements for a European Sporting Gun, where expense was no object in a fast and furious sport like Driven Shooting, and those of an American

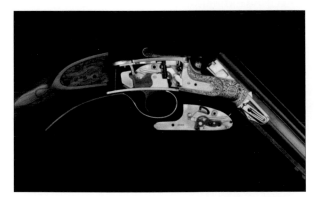

James Purdey and Sons Over and Under.

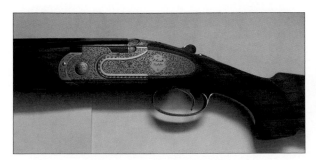

Beretta Over and Under.

Winchester Model 97. (PAUL FIEVEZ)

Working Gun, where the shotgun was a tool for the job of Walked-up Shooting. This difference created another gunmaking philosophy. The majority of the American gunmakers' clients were not the landed gentry, but farmers and sportsmen who considered the shotgun a functional necessity used to supplement their food sources.

Then, in America, came the commercial wild-fowl harvesters – the "market gunners". The expansion of the American railway system in the 1880s and the expanding urban populations created the demand for these commercial shooters' bags of wildfowl. There were no rules or restraints – birds could be shot night or day. Market gunners used punt guns and multiple-barrel battery guns, each harvesting hundreds of birds a day which were then freighted into the towns and cities around the country by rail.

The Club House at West London Shooting Grounds.

In the 1890s, Winchester introduced its first single barrel pump gun, the forerunner of its famous Model 12. In 1902, John Moses Browning introduced his Auto A5. Such was the efficiency of these new shotguns that when they came into use by the commercial gunners, by 1910 daytimes and limits had to be introduced to control the number of birds an individual could shoot in a day.

I am sure that the likes of Capt. Adam Bogardus in the pigeon ring and Fred Kibble, the Illinois market gunner, could have held their own in the line with the best of the European sportsmen. Further, the American-manufactured shotguns such as Parker, A.H. Fox and L.C. Smith could stand comparison to those of James Purdey & Son, Boss & Co. or Holland & Holland of the same period.

There can be no doubt that, at the turn of the 19th Century, skill with a shotgun was one of a

Wildfowling at Cowbit Wash, Spalding, January, 1907.

The high tower at Holland & Holland Shooting Grounds.

gentleman's essential qualities. Being recognized as a 'Good Shot' in this period was to be on a par with the top performers in any of the more traditional sporting activities. Shooting schools that taught sound fundamentals and sporting techniques were opened and became as popular as the schools for racquet sports or fencing.

The Churchill Shooting Grounds was established in 1925 by the renowned pigeon shooter, Robert Churchill. He developed a coaching style with some controversial ideas on the application of lead but his technique and method of instruction were without fault. After Churchill's death, his Chief Instructor Norman Clarke became the Chief Instructor at Holland & Holland Shooting Grounds (established in 1885). Where Norman Clarke modified the Churchill style of shooting to some degree, his understudy and eventual Chief Instructor, Ken Davies, refined the technique into the Churchill Shooting Style that is taught today.

West London Shooting Grounds, established in 1901 has always been closely associated with James Purdey & Sons, but perhaps more famously, was home to the legendary Percy Stanbury, one of the greatest shots of all time! One of his understudies, Alan Rose, still teaches The Master's Technique there today. In the United States, The Orvis Sandanona Shooting Grounds, established in1907 in Millbrook, NY, also champions the Stanbury Technique.

But which is the best – Churchill or Stanbury? Both are excellent, and it is up to the individual to find which works best for him or her. The techniques differ slightly but both emphasize the fundamentals and the grooving of the chosen technique by practice. There have been continuous evolutions in shooting techniques matched by the technical advances in shotguns and choke and cartridges. I consider the combination of these modern developments has raised the standard and consistency of shooting today to a level that far surpasses that of the Edwardian era.

I concede that, for the height and number of birds being pushed over the line, the Edwardian shots were as good as the birds presented. But, typically, the birds of that era were driven at a height that, today, would be considered low and unsporting, and would not be shot at by the modern sportsman. As a further example, grouse were driven repeatedly back and forth over the butts until exhausted, showing usually twenty drives a day, ten in each direction, with two teams of beaters.

The end of the World Wars and the end of The Empire saw the end of the huge bags and the time when a sportsman either belonged to a syndicate or was fortunate to receive an invitation to shoot from the owner of a Grouse Moor or a private estate. But driven game shooting, along with the shotguns, continued to evolve, and in the 1970s, the exclusive status began to change. This change was pioneered by David Hitchings with the Gurston Down Shoot, where he created one of the first commercial High Pheasant and Partridge shoots in the UK.

The availability and opportunity of the commercial shoot ignited a passion for birds presented at heights to test even the best of Guns. Now, driven shooting had come full circle and the participants demanded quality, not quantity. Today, the best Driven Shoots strive to present higher and higher pheasant and partridge which often fly well in excess of 40 yards above the Guns! Some are so high they seem to be out of range of a modern shotgun. The margin for error on these birds is so slim that those who can regularly knock down these skyscraper birds are very few – they are expert shots having the right combination of cartridge, choke and gun to do it. These sportsmen are as professional as their Edwardian predecessors. They shoot throughout the whole game season, visiting South America in the European off-season and continue to hone their skills on the high towers of the shooting schools, using the very best equipment they can find.

The history of all sports is that every one developed as it did for particular reasons that related to the social conditions of the time. Many of the sports we take part in today did not exist 120 years ago and those that did, would be barely recognizable to the modern participant. The history of shooting birds on the wing and the development of the modern shotgun is no exception. Shooting a shotgun is an athletic skill comparable to any other eye and hand sport and the early shooters laid the foundations that have been built upon by today's top shots.

Shooting driven grouse. (PAUL FIEVEZ)

Chapter 2
Safety

We all have a clear and unambiguous responsibility for safety while shooting. Nothing can ruin a day in the field more than an accident. Fortunately, they are a rare occurrence and it is every sportsman's responsibility to keep it that way. The experienced shot can become complacent and the beginner, young or old, is often never correctly instructed in the most essential of shooting skills: *'Safety'*!

It is no coincidence that the shot who demonstrates solid safety in his gun handling and awareness in the field usually shoots equally well.

I believe that safety and etiquette are inextricably entwined; safety covering the mechanics of safe gun handling and etiquette defining an awareness of one's position and that of others taking part in the shooting. A keen understanding of both enables a shot to fulfil his responsibility to himself, his fellow Guns, guides, beaters and dogs.

There are many mature shooters who enter hunting after first taking up clay target shooting – they may have attended a charity or corporate entertainment shoot and been bitten by the bug. Gaining proficiency with the shotgun, they are often invited by friends, family or clients to a day in the field. However, shooting in the field is totally unlike the sport of clay target shooting with its fixed parameters, safety zones and shooting cages, all controlling the safe direction of fire, where, if a shotgun should be accidentally discharged, it is always in a safe direction.

In the field, it is a completely different situation. The movement and activity can be very distracting to the uninitiated so I always recommend that an instructor/loader accompany a novice on his first two or three shoots. The presence of an experienced field shooter allows a beginner to relax and concentrate on his shooting. The instructor will explain the rules of safety and etiquette. He will explain the "fields of fire" created by the positioning of the beaters, pickers-up and fellow Guns, and, calling the shots, point out the birds that are a safe and sporting shot, and advise against the low and potentially dangerous shots and, of course, help the novice with his straight shooting.

First, we will cover safe gun handling:

Rule Number One: A shotgun is a lethal weapon. Though we use a shotgun in a recreational sport in the same manner as a golf club or tennis racquet, we must recognize and *never forget* its lethal qualities.

Rule Number Two: Always prove a gun is unloaded. When you take it from storage, put it in and take it out of a gunslip, or are handed one to inspect, check it is unloaded. Break and empty the gun and place it in its slip when leaving the field, cover or blind, between drives or when moving between hunts.

A gun out of its slip should always be open and proven empty.

A shotgun is safest when transported unloaded in a closed gunslip.

Rule Number Three: Every gun should be considered loaded, potentially dangerous and treated with the utmost respect at all times. There are only two safe guns: one that is broken and seen to be unloaded; one that is in a zipped and closed gunslip where access to the trigger is impossible.

Rule Number Four: Guns should be in a safe and sound condition. There should be no dents, bulges or pitting in the barrels; no loose ribs, cracked stocks or barrels "off the face" (loose action). The guns should have been nitro-proofed and be in proof. Barrel walls must be the correct and safe thickness, and the correct size cartridge *must* be used to match the chamber length and proof pressure.

All guns sold in the UK, by law, have to be submitted to proof-testing either by the London or Birmingham proof houses or their European counterparts. At the proof house, the guns are subjected to a pressure test and, if passed, stamped with the appropriate marks. Guns of modern manufacture will have the chamber size and gauge engraved or stamped on the gun. You should regularly maintain your shotguns. They should receive an annual strip, clean and inspection where any remedial work is carried out to make the gun safe to shoot. If in any doubt regarding the above information, contact a reputable gunsmith who can give you a report on the condition and safety of your gun.

The correct technique for placing a shotgun into a gunslip. Reverse the action to take the shotgun out of its slip.

LEFT: Barrels of open and empty gun are placed into slip.　　*RIGHT: Holding barrels, close gun and slide it into slip.*

Rule Number Five: You should familiarize yourself with your gun and how it works, especially the safety and barrel selector. The control of the safety catch and the sequence in which it is pushed "off safe" is an essential skill. When the decision to shoot is made, the gun is lifted to the cheek and shoulder, the safety is *removed* and as the gun is fully *mounted*, the trigger finger moves from the trigger guard to the trigger and the shot is taken. When the safety is pushed off, it is essential to roll the thumb over the grip from behind the top lever. If you do not place it in this position, the recoil on firing can cause the top lever to strike the thumb – a very painful event!

There are two types of safety mechanisms:

Automatic safety: On opening the gun, the top lever operates a sprung rod that pushes the safety *on*. Every game gun should be fitted with an automatic safety.

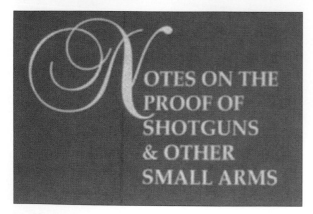

NOTES ON THE PROOF OF SHOTGUNS & OTHER SMALL ARMS

All shotguns should be in proof and in safe and sound condition. It is important that if steel shot is to be used the shotgun must be proofed for steel shot.

Manual safety: Competition, semi-automatic and pump guns are usually fitted with a manual safety. This needs to be manually pulled and pushed *on* and *off*. When using a pair of guns with a loader, guns should be exchanged with the safetys *on*, especially if only one cartridge has been fired. When using shotguns with manual safetys, practise is essential. I believe it was Sir Joseph Nickerson who said "The person most likely to shoot you during a day in the field is your loader."

Note: The "*safety*" should more correctly be named the "*trigger block*". It is actually a mechanical device that blocks the trigger from being pulled. However, the hammers are still cocked and, as with any mechanical device, it can fail. Slamming the gun shut, or placing it in such a way that it can fall over can cause an accidental discharge.

Rule Number Six: Before loading, always check the barrels for obstructions. Any blockage, no matter how small, can cause pressure to be generated in the barrels, with potentially dangerous results. On firing, the cartridge is literally a controlled explosion. The resulting pressure propels the shot charge down the barrel at extremely high speed. A shotgun's barrel is constructed to withstand the pressure generated in a straight line, breech to muzzle. Any obstruction will cause a pressure spike within the barrel for which the barrels are not designed. This sideways pressure can bulge or rupture the barrel.

An obstruction can be anything from a dent, a bulge or a piece of wadding left in the barrel after cleaning, to the muzzles being blocked with snow or mud – this can occur inadvertently, for example, when bending to pick up a dead bird or to take cartridges from a shell bag on the ground, as one balances by unconsciously putting the barrel muzzles in the ground.

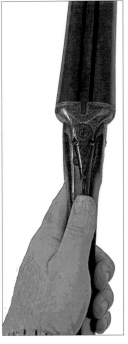

Do not leave your thumb on the safety: the force of recoil can drive the top lever back, splitting the thumb.

Rule Number Seven: Use only cartridges of the correct gauge and chamber length to match the gun you are shooting. Never mix different gauge cartridges in your shell bag or pockets. A 20 gauge cartridge can pass through the chamber of a twelve gauge shotgun and lodge in the barrel or, even worse, allow a 12 gauge cartridge to be loaded on top of it! The results can be disastrous! This scenario can also happen with the 16 gauge and 28 gauge cartridges.

Cartridges of different gauges should be stored separately, both at home and while hunting. With the exception of some foreign imports, all 20 gauge cartridges are yellow and other gauges can be assorted colours.

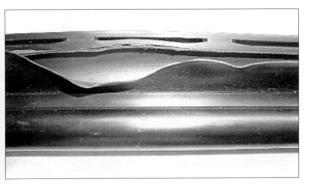

Burst barrels caused by a blockage.

Never mix cartridges of different gauges.

Mixing cartridges can have disastrous results.

Rule Number Eight: Never point or fire a gun at anything that you do not intend to shoot.

Rule Number Nine: Be aware of the three gun malfunctions possible while shooting.

First: You pull the trigger and the gun fails to discharge. Do not instantly open the gun! Keep it closed and pointed in a safe direction for 30 seconds before opening the gun and safely disposing of the cartridge. This failure is referred to as a "hang fire" – a slow ignition from faulty powder or primer may mean that the cartridge could still explode and the 30 second delay will allow it to do so safely. Opening the gun instantly could cause blowback and injury.

Second: You fire the gun and you get a strange discharge, i.e., a soft "ploof" sound instead of the normal loud crack. Stop and open the gun and check the barrels for blockage. The cartridge may have not had sufficient energy to push the wad clear of the muzzle. Both of these phenomena are, fortunately, rare occurrences with modern ammunition, but more often happen with home-loaded cartridges. However, you should be alert to this possibility if it should occur. Semi-automatic and pump shotguns can be difficult to check visually. In this case, the proprietary *"wad weasel"*, a small weight that can be dropped through the barrel of a shotgun, will remove an obstruction or prove it is clear. This is a recommended accessory when shooting with a fixed breech shotgun.

Third: If a gun is in poor condition, badly maintained or has developed a fault, closing the gun may cause the hammer to fall, accidentally discharging the gun. This discharge is caused by the bent and sear not seating correctly. Wear, corrosion, congealed powder residue or even dried oil can be to blame. Sidelocks and some boxlocks have a second intercepting sear designed to prevent the accidental discharge. This is just another one of the reasons a shotgun should never be slammed shut. An accidental discharge can happen to anyone, so it is important to have control of the gun, especially when opening and closing it.

The best way to open and close a shotgun: Hold the gun stock on your hip, your right hand gripping the stock, but your finger off the trigger and on the guard. The barrels which are pointing down are then brought closed to the action.

The correct way to open and close a shotgun.

This closing technique, with the gun pointed down, ensures that if the gun *should* discharge, it will do so harmlessly into the ground, some two yards in front of you. This hip and hand grip allows you to keep control of the gun at all times – especially important if two cartridges are loaded.

With the semi-automatic and pump shotgun, use the same grip and safe muzzle direction, just turning the gun on its side to access the breech, then close the action with the barrel pointing safely down and away from your feet.

I do not recommend the traditional method of lifting the stock to the barrels. A stiff action or a novice shot without much strength or co-ordination can cause the muzzles to pivot back and point at the feet as the gun is closed. If an accidental discharge were to occur, they would *"shoot themself in the foot"*. Also, lifting the stock to the barrels leaves little control of the gun and it could easily be dropped from the recoil generated on the first accidental discharge, followed by a potentially uncontrolled discharge of the second barrel.

Rule Number Ten: You are responsible for the safe handling of yourself and your gun at all times. You are also responsible for the behaviour of any family, guests and dogs when they are in your company. Set the best possible example for your children when it comes to safety. And, of course, no one should ever touch or handle another person's gun without the owner's consent.

Shotguns and ammunition should be stored separately in an approved and locked cabinet or safe. Do not leave your shotgun unattended, especially if there are children present. If you leave your shotguns or cartridges in a vehicle, be sure that they are out of sight and the vehicle is both locked and alarmed.

Horseplay is not tolerated and alcohol should never be consumed while shooting, only after the shoot is over. In Europe, it has long been traditional to have a *"bullshot"* (a game consommé) with a splash of sherry for flavour after the first drive and perhaps a glass of wine with the shoot lunch. However, many teams of Guns now prefer to "shoot through" and have a late lunch where they can enjoy the meal and partake of alcohol after the guns are safely put away.

We all have an obligation to both ourselves and others when it comes to gun safety. You need to demonstrate safe gun handling yourself, and if you see anyone violating any of the rules of safety, you need to ask them to cease in a diplomatic but firm manner and instruct them in the correct and safe methods of gun safety.

An open and unloaded shotgun is best carried over the crook of the arm.

Carrying the Shotgun in the Field

There are only two ways in which a gun can be carried safely.

1. Unloaded, in a closed gunslip, where it is impossible to access the trigger.

2. Open and seen to be empty.

The open gun should be carried over the crook of the arm and not, as is too often seen, over the shoulder. Though it is comfortable and easy to carry a gun over the shoulder, there is every chance of striking a fellow hunter with the stock of the gun as you turn around. You must *never* carry the gun with the barrels sticking backwards over your shoulders!

Semi-automatics and pump guns that cannot be broken open, should have a flag or a piece of cloth placed in the open breech to draw attention to the fact that the chamber is empty and a cartridge cannot be placed in it. The way to carry a semi-automatic is with the muzzles pointing up, with the open and flagged breech facing out.

An open and unloaded shotgun carried over the shoulder is comfortable, but beware of striking a fellow hunter with the stock.

Never carry the shotgun with its barrels pointing backwards over your shoulder.

Correct way to load a semi-automatic shotgun.

Correct way to load a semi-automatic in a hide or blind.

The best practice is to carry your shotgun in a gunslip. It is safe, comfortable, easier to manage and the slip protects the gun in transit.

Guns should only be loaded when you are ready to shoot – when you are on your peg, in the blind or ready to walk up over dogs. As soon as the drive is over or the hunt is finished, guns should be unloaded and placed in their slips.

Walking in the Field

When walking with a loaded gun, the correct carry is with the muzzles elevated, the stock placed between arm and chest, and the barrels pointed skyward. In addition to being safe, this position allows the most efficient gun mount.

Carrying a loaded gun correctly and safely requires muzzle awareness; if the gun is held across the body with the barrels lying across the forearm, every time one steps forward with the right foot, the muzzles will swing to the left, fanning fellow Guns, guides, beaters, pickers-up and their dogs – it is a recipe for disaster! Safe muzzle management means that the barrels must be pointed at the ground, clear of any dogs and feet, or upwards, at the sky.

When shooting in company or in a line of Guns, the safest carry for a loaded gun is skyward with the breech resting on the shoulder, trigger guard uppermost, the stock held so that the barrels are perpendicular. Many find that, when shooting alone, they prefer to carry the gun resting over the forearm with the

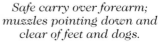

Correct carry when shooting over dogs.

Incorrect and dangerous carry when shooting in a line. Every time you step forward, you sweep the muzzles through the line.

Correct carry of loaded shotgun; muzzles vertical.

Safe carry over forearm; muzzles pointing down and clear of feet and dogs.

144 Inches of Hunter Orange is mandatory when Upland Bird Hunting.

Incorrect and dangerous carry.

stock between arm and chest, the barrels pointing down. This is a comfortable alternative carry, though personally, I do not recommend it as the muzzles are pointing at "dog height".

Note: In the USA, hunters are required to wear 144 square inches of Hunter Orange or high-visibility vests or clothing while hunting. Turkey, dove and waterfowl hunters are not, and usually wear camouflage.

Standing on a Peg or Sitting in a Blind

While standing on a peg waiting for the drive, the stock should be placed between the arm and chest, barrels safely elevated, with the arms allowed to relax, resting against the chest. This position minimizes the gun's weight and allows a smooth gun mount. If sitting on a shooting stick or in a blind, the butt of the stock should be placed on the thigh with the barrels elevated and forward. This position allows an easy rise into the correct stance and facilitates a smooth gun mount.

When shooting from a hide or blind, it should be of sufficient size to hold the occupants and, if needed, their dogs. When sharing a hide, the best advice is to take turns shooting, with one spotting while the other shoots. The biggest danger is that one occupant remains seated to shoot and the other rises to his feet and into his fellow Gun's line of fire.

If two people are going to shoot at the same time, be sure that there is an agreement that you will both stand or remain seated to shoot and agree on the safe *"arcs of fire"*. Imagine a clock, and the person on the left shoots from 12 o'clock through 9 o'clock and the person on the right shoots from 12 o'clock through 3 o'clock.

Never shoot into water. Something hard under the surface could deflect the shot in a dangerous direction.

Crossing an Obstacle

When crossing a fence, gate, fallen tree, or any other obstacle, you must unload your shotgun and place it safely where you can reach it after you have climbed over or ducked under the obstacle. Once safely over, retrieve the empty gun, open and check for obstructions that might have occurred and reload.

When shooting with a companion, you both unload your guns, then you hand your gun *butt first* to your companion and cross the obstacle without a gun. Once over, your companion passes both guns *butt first* to you and crosses the obstacle without a gun. When both are safely over, you hand him back his gun *butt first*. Both guns are then checked for obstructions before being reloaded.

Awareness in the Field

Your host, shoot captain or guide will brief you and go through safety procedures before any shooting takes place. It is important that you take note of any special instructions that are issued to the Guns during the briefing. Be sure to understand what signal or command starts and ends the shooting, what quarry can be shot and what is not

Safely passing a gun over an obstacle, always unloaded and butt first. Before reloading, check barrels for obstructions.

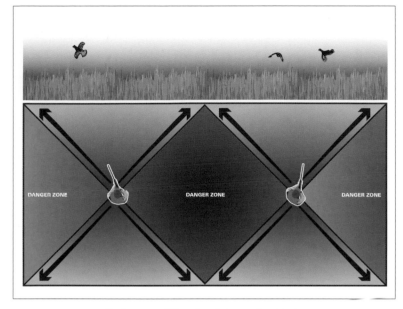

Safe arcs of fire for driven shooting.

to be shot, i.e. no ground game and no hen birds. Once on your peg, in the blind or beginning a hunt, use the time before shooting to look for the other shooters, beaters, guides and pickers-up and determine their position in relation to you and your hunting dogs. From this observation you can judge *"your safe arc of fire"*. Always shoot into a safe background and be aware of what's beyond the target. If you have any doubt, do not shoot.

Never fire at a low-flying bird! Beaters or pickers-up may be in close proximity. And never swing through the line!

Keep on your peg or in your blind or in the line walking up over dogs. Hold the line and check

When shooting behind the line, muzzles must be vertical.

Turn with muzzles vertical in a smart "about face".

Completing the turn, the muzzles are still vertical.

positions, cover and companions. Never wander away by yourself – you may be walking into the line of fire. If a walking Gun, never shoot in front of the line. If you are to shoot *behind* the line, always keep your muzzles elevated and turn to the rear with a smart "about face". *Never* swing through the line!

Shooting in grouse butts is particularly dangerous. Always be sure that the *safety frames* are in their proper position. This is especially important in round butts. Better to have a narrow *"arc of fire"* than one that allows you to swing too far, endangering the Guns in the adjacent butts. Butts or pegs in a curved line can exacerbate this situation and require greater awareness.

For example, here are three dangerous shooting scenarios:

A novice, concentrating on his shooting and caught up in the general excitement of the oncoming quarry, can become distracted and forget all considerations of safety. This is why safety should become an ingrained habit, so it becomes consistent behaviour at all times, even under pressure.

The greedy, competitive or aggressive shot can overreach the safe *arcs of fire* and his poaching actions can cause neighbouring Guns to match his behaviour, creating a very perilous situation.

When shooting ground game or birds with erratic flight patterns like woodcock, it is very easy to develop tunnel vision. Your peripheral vision shrinks and you experience a narrowing of focus, not recognizing what is behind the bird or hare you are attempting to shoot. Equally bad, is hunting in thick cover, shooting on sound alone without a clean sight of the bird. In any of these scenarios, accidents can easily happen.

Eye and Ear Protection

I believe that eye and ear protection should be mandatory in the field just as it is in the clay target sports. It always amazes me when I see fellow Guns shooting without one or the other and often without either! The report of a shotgun is louder than a jet engine at take off and repeated exposure to this level of noise will cause permanent hearing damage.

In regard to the need for safety shooting glasses, you are more at risk of being struck by an errant pellet in the field than on the shooting grounds. A low shot or pellet ricocheting off trees or water can penetrate the eye at great distances.

Remember, "Safe Shooting is No Accident"!

Eye and ear protection should be compulsory when shooting.

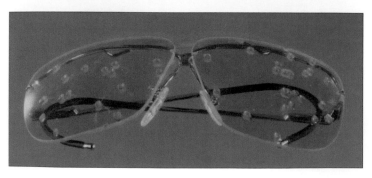

Your eyes are priceless.

Chapter 3
Etiquette

Apart from its important impact on safety, etiquette is simply good manners – treat others as you would like to be treated yourself and this good behaviour should be extended to all of the participants who are required to make a shooting day happen.

Driven Shooting in Europe

No successful shoot would happen without the keepers, guides, beaters and pickers-up, so as your paths cross during the day, be sure to thank them for their efforts. The keeper and the guide are full-time employees, but all the others are volunteers, working for the love of the sport rather than recompense, and acknowledgement of their efforts is always appreciated.

If you are a member of a syndicate, you will know your fellow members, the shoot and the rules of the day. However, if you have received an invitation to shoot, a short note of acceptance or a phone call to your host thanking him for his generosity not only confirms your attendance, but also gives you the opportunity to ask any questions that may have not been answered in the invitation. Would the ladies be joining the Guns for lunch? Is it permissible to bring your own dog? What species will the bag consist of? (This is important because if there is a duck drive, you will need to take non-toxic cartridges with you.) Is it a single gun day or will there be loaders and paired guns? Ask these and any other queries that you may have.

Always make your best effort to be prompt. Allow time for the unexpected and have all of your equipment, gun and sufficient cartridges for the day with you. Upon arrival, if you have brought your dog, leave it in the car or keep it on a leash. Find and greet your host or shoot captain and then introduce yourself to your fellow Guns.

Be prompt and have all of your equipment, gun and sufficent cartridges for the day. (TERRY ALLEN)

There is usually a breakfast of some sort, where old friends can catch up and the spark of new friendships can be ignited. Following breakfast, the team will gather their kit and guns for the captain's briefing on the rules of the day. This will always begin with a petition for safety and good sportsmanship; no low birds, no ground game, including foxes, and the careful attention to the position of beaters, pickers-up, any flankers and your fellow Guns. He will let you know what the signal will be for the start and cessation of the drives – it is usually a whistle or a horn. The old adage "The only safe shot is at a bird with sky all around it" is often the last sentence before pegs are drawn and you are told how many pegs to move up each drive.

Pegs can take many shapes, from playing cards to steel or ivory pins numbered 1 through 8. Pegs are numbered from the right, so on any drive number 1 will be on your right and if you have drawn 5, you would subsequently be 7, 1, and 3, if the day consists of four drives.

On some drives, the end Guns 1 and 8 will walk into position at the ends of the line and in line with the beaters to shoot the birds that break out of the sides of the drive. It is advisable to ask the beater nearest to you to work in sight of you to help you keep in line and to let you know the position of the beaters in the cover.

The peg system is designed to spread the shooting evenly among the Guns. So during the day, on one or two of the drives, you may find yourself defending the line as wave after wave of birds pass; while on another drive, you may be practically a spectator, watching your fellow Guns. On some shoots, the shooting positions are marked by numbered markers on sticks or stakes driven into the ground, while on other shoots, the Guns will be placed by the host or shoot captain in the best positions depending on the conditions of the day.

Picking pegs at the start of the day; they can be anything from playing cards, ivory pegs to stirrup cups. (TERRY ALLEN)

A typical peg. (TERRY ALLEN)

A good shot selects the most sporting shots, letting birds pass that are low but climbing towards your neighbour or over the line to a back Gun.
(BETTWS HALL SPORTING)

If there is firmer footing close to your peg, use it.
(BETTWS HALL SPORTING)

There are drives where there is insufficient width for the whole line of Guns and it is necessary to shoot in two reduced lines. The front line is usually 5 Guns and the rear line, referred to as the back Guns, usually 3, are placed 50 to 60 yards behind the front line. Your host controls everything on the shoot day with the exception of the birds and the weather – and the wind in the wrong direction or a fox running through the cover can turn a drive inside out. Your understanding and patience in such circumstances is always appreciated.

Many shoots have a special trailer or bus to transport the team of Guns to the drives; on other shoots, individuals use their own cars. If this is the case, once parked, collect your gun (in its slip) and cartridge bag and proceed to your designated peg. The team should attempt to get to the pegs with a minimum of noise. Slammed car doors and loud voices on the approach to the pegs can scare the birds and cause them to disperse, ruining the drive.

Once on your peg, your first job is to establish firm footing. If a firmer footing offers itself a few feet from the peg, it is perfectly acceptable to use it. Next, it is your duty to note the terrain and cover from which the birds will be driven. You need to ascertain where the beaters will appear as the drive progresses – also pay particular attention to the positioning of any flankers on the sides and the pickers-up behind you. Then look along the line of Guns and establish your safe "arcs of fire". If you do not have a loader, open your cartridge bag, place a handful of cartridges in your pocket and place the bag on the ground. Take your gun from its slip, open it and check the barrels for obstructions before loading it and then wait for the signal for the start of the drive.

A good shot is one who picks his birds carefully, noting the safe "arcs of fire" and, taking into consideration the dividing line between himself and his adjacent Guns, respecting which birds are rightfully theirs or his. If a low bird is climbing and according to its first position, rightfully his, a good shot will let it pass to his neighbour by which time it will have developed into a spectacularly high and sporting bird.

The same etiquette would apply when shooting in the front line of a double line of Guns; the good shot allows the easy birds to pass to become extremely sporting shots as they rise over the back Guns. The greedy Gun shoots every bird that passes over him, regardless of his fellow Guns behind who, much to their frustration, watch the easy birds being slaughtered. There is no more certain way to be excluded from a syndicate or taken off the invitation list than to be unsafe – shooting at low birds – or to be a game hog – poaching your neighbours' birds.

Judicious selection of his target is the mark of a good shot. He allows low and unsporting birds to pass, picking out the more challenging birds which test his shooting ability. However, if he lets a bird through to his neighbour who then fails to connect with both barrels or has his gun open loading, any good shot would take the opportunity to "*wipe his eye*". A good Gun recognizes the limits of his shooting ability and the sporting distance at which he can cleanly kill. It is distressing to see birds being pricked at distances nearly out of range or shot with not enough skill or gun for the job. Watching a wounded bird glide way behind the pickers-up to suffer a lingering death is not good sportsmanship to me.

The most dangerous time for the beaters is as they approach the end of the drive. The last of the birds will often hold at the edges of the cover and, as the beaters come into view and range, pushing these last birds, some will fly out, perilously low.

The hinge pin of a good shoot: the gamekeeper and his team of beaters. (FIELDSPORTS MAGAZINE)

Ensuring that every bird is retrieved is an essential task and a good team of pickers-up ensures this.
(BETTWS HALL SPORTING)

When the signal for the end of the drive is heard, you should unload your gun and place it in its slip, collect your spent cartridges and look for the picker-up nearest to you. Ask him if he has picked up all your felled birds. If his tally does not match yours, point out where the errant birds have fallen, and thank him for his assistance. It is the character of a good sportsman that he marks his birds and makes every effort to see them all retrieved.

After the last drive, take the opportunity to thank the beaters for their work. When you see the keeper, if you consider the day an excellent one, tell him. Tips are discretionary but at the time of writing, £20 per hundred birds is about right. The tip and your thanks should be passed while collecting your brace of birds from the day's bag.

Finally, take the time to write a short note of thanks to your host, commending him on his hospitality and generosity and the quality of the estate and birds presented. A safe, considerate and grateful sportsman is a welcome addition to any line of Guns.

Chapter 4
The Shotgun

It is said that a poor craftsman blames his tools, but I have never yet met a competent craftsman who did not have the very best tools for the job in hand.

Consistent shooting is a combination of technique, shotgun and ballistics; the fundamentals of technique, correctly applied, ultimately require the proper selection of shotgun and ballistics to match the quarry being hunted.

As using a fly rod for deep sea fishing would hamper even the best fly caster, so using a high pheasant gun to shoot woodcock over dogs would be the wrong tool for the job. Both could be made to work, but neither would be comfortable, practical or efficient.

What Defines a Sporting Shotgun?

A sporting shotgun is a smooth-bored weapon with a barrel not less than 24 inches (18 inches in the USA) in length and an overall length of 40 inches or more. It is the gun of choice for shooting a moving target. It fires a large number of projectiles (shot) instead of a single projectile (bullet or slug) through a barrel which is polished smooth on the inside.

When fired, the shot is propelled through the barrel by the gas pressure created by the powder in the cartridge. As the shot leaves the barrel, it is spread laterally and longitudinally by the effects of its collision with the air's pressure. This spreads the column of shot pellets, creating the pattern that gives the margin for error required to shoot a bird on the wing.

For sporting purposes, the minimum barrel length I would recommend would be 26 inches, but shotguns come in many types, shapes and gauges.

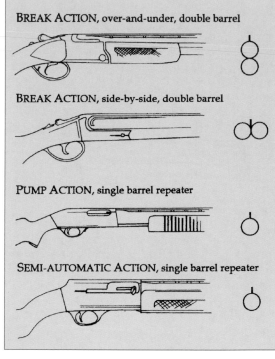

BREAK ACTION, over-and-under, double barrel

BREAK ACTION, side-by-side, double barrel

PUMP ACTION, single barrel repeater

SEMI-AUTOMATIC ACTION, single barrel repeater

ABOVE:
Various shotguns.

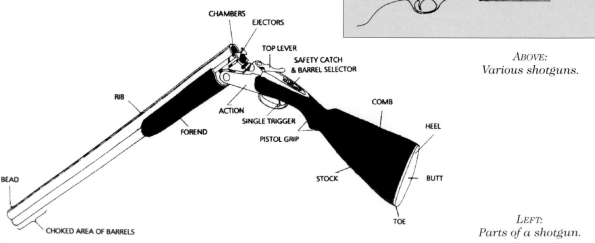

CHAMBERS
EJECTORS
TOP LEVER
SAFETY CATCH & BARREL SELECTOR
RIB
ACTION
COMB
SINGLE TRIGGER
FOREND
PISTOL GRIP
HEEL
BEAD
STOCK
BUTT
CHOKED AREA OF BARRELS
TOE

LEFT:
Parts of a shotgun.

Benelli Supernova Pump, in Realtree camouflage.

Shotgun Types are defined by their actions and barrel configuration:

Fixed Action: Semi-Automatic – Pump – Bolt Action

Break Action: Side by Side – Over and Under

Differences and Applications

Each type will have its proponents, but from a practical standpoint, each has advantages and disadvantages in their use and application. You could compromise and use one gun for all of your shooting but that would be at the expense of shooting to your full potential.

The following will outline the specific types of shotguns, describe their strengths and weaknesses, and match the gun to the bird being hunted.

Semi-Automatic The semi-automatic shotgun has a single barrel with a tube-shaped magazine attached below it. When fired, either inertia or gas pressure triggers the action mechanism, then extracts the spent cartridge from the chamber, ejects it, re-cocks the firing mechanism and loads a new cartridge into the chamber from the magazine. As the semi-auto is relatively inexpensive to manufacture (in comparison to a break-action shotgun), has comparatively low recoil and is fast handling, it is a very popular choice for certain types of bird hunting.

Advantages: Semi-automatic shotguns offer light recoil and fast handling characteristics and as they can be loaded without breaking the gun open, they are perfect for use in hides and blinds when room can be limited.

Though relatively inexpensive, their robust construction, using synthetic stocks and corrosion resistant finishes, the availability of improved recoil-reducing devices plus their ability to handle high velocity steel loads, make the semi-automatic shotgun the first choice for wildfowl and decoyed shooting.

Disadvantages: The fixed action on the semi-automatic means they cannot readily be seen to be unloaded and safe, particularly from a distance. They were also considered unreliable and prone to jamming, especially with fouling from hard use. However, with changes in design and improved manufacturing techniques, reliability has improved remarkably in recent years.

With a semi-automatic, the mechanism's movement/noise and spent cartridge ejection in the reloading cycle can be distracting. Unless spent shells are ejected from the bottom of the action, they can strike a partner sharing a blind or hide. Having only one barrel, they do not allow the selection of choke for near and far shots.

Pump Action The pump action has a single barrel with a tube-shaped magazine attached below it. Firing a pump shotgun is often compared to playing a trombone – the action is operated by sliding the forend. When pulled back, the forend opens the chamber, cocking the hammer, allowing a cartridge to be removed from the magazine and loaded into the firing chamber. Pushing the slide

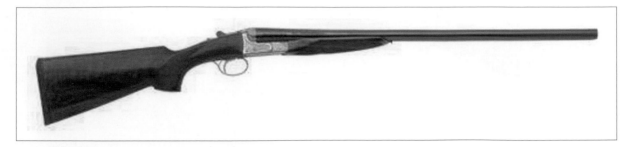

Beretta Silver Hawk Boxlock.

forward closes the action. On firing, the slide is pulled back, ejecting the fired cartridge. Pushing the slide forward loads a shell from the magazine into the chamber. As the shooter repeats this action, "pumping" the slide to reload the gun and eject fired cartridges, the action resembles a musician playing a trombone.

Advantages: The pump can be loaded without breaking the gun, a distinct advantage in tight quarters, like a hide or blind. Like the semi-automatic, the pump is available in durable synthetic and corrosion-resistant materials, has limited recoil and can handle steel shot in high velocity loads. The pump is also very inexpensive, making it a good choice for an entry-level wildfowler.

Disadvantages: Unless well-practised, operating the slide mechanism of the pump both takes time and moves the barrel off the target line. It is difficult for others to see if the fixed action is loaded or unloaded and safe. Spent shells ejected from the side are distracting and can hit another shooter if in close quarters, like a blind. The single barrel doesn't allow a selection of chokes for shooting at different distances.

Bolt Action Bolt action shotguns are relatively uncommon, usually found in the traditional 9mm or .410 Garden Guns. A single barrel shotgun, it is operated by a bolt handle which is twisted up and then pulled back to open the chamber and cock the firing mechanism. A single cartridge is placed in the chamber and the bolt is pushed forward and locked into place. The gun is then ready for firing. If the bolt action is fitted with a magazine, every time the bolt is pulled back and pushed forward, the fired cartridge is ejected and the next cartridge is loaded from the magazine.

Advantages: There really are no advantages to using a bolt-action shotgun. If a single barrel is wanted, the semi-automatic is a better choice.

Disadvantages: Again, because of the action configuration, it is difficult to see if the shotgun is loaded, or unloaded and safe. Unless it is kept meticulously clean, it is prone to jamming.

Side by Side The side by side shotgun can be either a sidelock or boxlock design, but both have two inline or side by side barrels.

The boxlock is the simplest design, consisting of three parts per barrel: *the tumbler* (also known as the hammer), *the cocking dog* and *the sear.* When the top lever is moved to the right, the gun is hinged open at the breech, the internal tumblers are cocked by the cocking dogs which are pushed

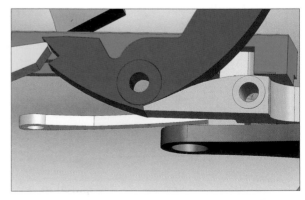

Side view of the bent and sear of a cocked gun.
(BOXHALL & EDMINSTON)

backwards by the dropping barrels, then held in place by the sprung sears. The gun can then be loaded and closed and the safety taken off.

When the trigger is pulled, the sear is tripped, releasing the tumbler that strikes the firing pin, detonating the cartridge.

The forward movement of the tumblers pushes the cocking dogs forward so when the top lever is moved to the right again, as the gun opens, and, depending on the type of gun, it either extracts the empty hulls or trips the ejectors expelling the empty shells from the gun and re-cocking the tumblers.

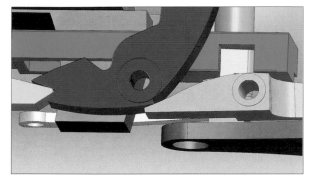

Side view of the bent and sear of a fired gun.
(BOXHALL & EDMINSTON)

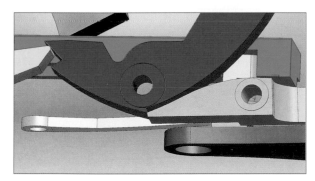

Side view of the bent and sear with the trigger pulled.
(BOXHALL & EDMINSTON)

Most side by side *boxlocks* are built on the *Anson & Deeley* patent – a simple and practical design with all of the cocking and firing mechanism contained inside of the frame or "box-shaped" action body. This design was suited to more modern manufacturing processes and, as the parts are all contained in the action body, the stocking process is simplified, reducing manufacturing time and costs.

Though considered more reliable because it has fewer parts, if any repair or regulation is required in a boxlock, the stock and sometimes the action floor plate needs to be removed. The cramped space offers little room for intercepting sears that can prevent an accidental discharge and the position and short length of the cocking dogs and sear lever arms can make trigger regulation difficult which can result in irregular trigger pulls.

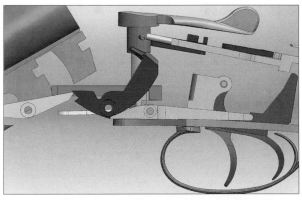

Side view of an open gun. (BOXHALL & EDMINSTON)

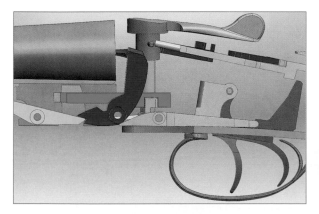

Side view of a closed gun.
(BOXHALL & EDMINSTON)

The boxlock action is hollow to accommodate the working parts.

The boxlock's short action body is hollow to accommodate the mechanics, so the action has to be larger, as does the head of the stock, giving the shotgun an overall bulkier appearance compared to a sidelock in the equivalent gauge.

Note: Vintage hammer shotguns require the manual cocking of the external hammers.

The sidelock, perfected circa 1870, is so-called because the cocking and firing mechanism is attached to *side plates* located on the sides at the rear of the action. This design has several benefits – first, it has a stronger, slimmer action body, with longer cocking dogs which ease cocking the gun, and locks that allow sufficient space to include "intercepting sears" to prevent accidental discharge. Second, the locks can be removed for inspection and maintenance without the necessity of removing the stock from the action. Finally, the extra room created by the sidelocks allows a more precise trigger regulation, giving positive, crisp trigger pulls.

It is generally believed that the *sidelock* shotgun has more elegant lines which give it an edge over the *boxlock* in balance and handling.

Advantages: The side by side's shallow gape or opening makes it very swift to open, eject and reload. Double triggers allow for the instant selection of choke for near or far shots and the break action, when open, is clearly seen to be safe. The combination of shape, light weight and excellent handling dynamics make the side by side the perfect choice for an upland bird gun.

Note: Side by side shotguns can be fitted with an "easy-opening" or "spring-opening" device that, when the top lever is operated, causes the barrels to "spring" open. This speeds ejecting and loading of cartridges, a valuable time-saver in driven shooting.

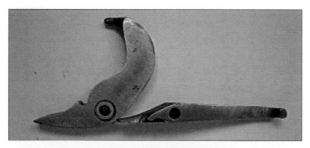

The bent and sear.

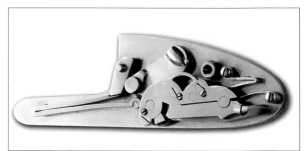

Grulla 7 pin sidelock.

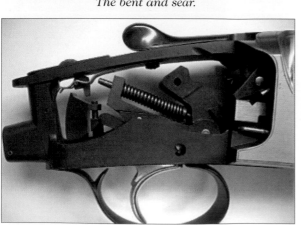

Boxlock over and under action. Note the coiled springs and captive strikers.

Easy opener: when the gun is closed, the piston is compressed and when the top lever is pushed it assists in opening the gun.

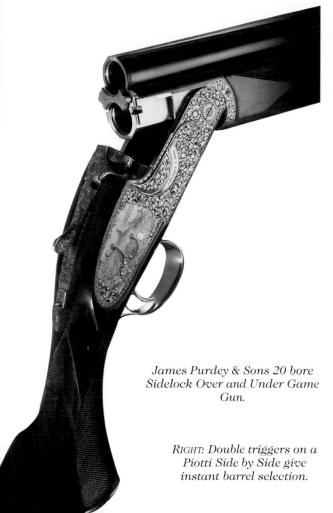

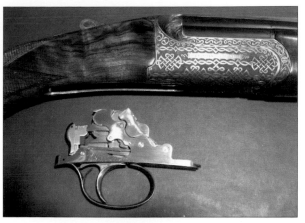

Detachable trigger group of an Abbiatico & Salvinelli Excalibur Over and Under.

James Purdey & Sons 20 bore Sidelock Over and Under Game Gun.

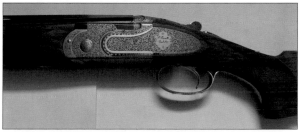

Single selective trigger on a Beretta Over and Under.

RIGHT: Double triggers on a Piotti Side by Side give instant barrel selection.

Disadvantages: The broad barrel configuration of the side by side can obstruct the view of the target. The second phase of recoil plus muzzle flip reduces muzzle control.

Over and Under *The over and under* with two barrels superposed, i.e., one stacked upon the other, can also be of either sidelock or boxlock design. The operating mechanism is similar to the side by side, with modifications to allow for the stacked barrels. When the top lever is moved to the right, the barrels hinge at the breech and move downwards, cocking the mechanism. The gun is then loaded, closed, the safety taken off and fired. Opening the shotgun trips the extractor/ejector mechanism and re-cocks the gun.

The over and under boxlock action differs from the side by side in that the firing mechanism is situated between the top and bottom straps, behind the action, concealed by the head of the stock. This design is an adaption of the *trigger plate* gun which had the firing mechanism fixed to the trigger plate within the stock head.

The trigger plate action was developed in the breech-loading era and is still used on Scottish Best Guns today. This action produces guns of extremely slim and pleasing lines. The modern Italian *over and unders* have incorporated a modified trigger plate design and many are detachable. The simple operation of a catch releases the trigger group from the bottom of the action and it is ready for cleaning or maintenance.

Note: Both *side by side* and *over and under* shotguns can have one or two triggers. Traditionally, the side by side has two triggers and the over and under, a single trigger. The over and under is fitted with a barrel selector allowing the choice of which barrel will be fired first, whereas with the side by side, it is simply a choice of which trigger is pulled first.

Advantages: The single sight plane of the over and under complements our natural pointing ability; placing both hands in line with the barrels creates a natural line and movement to the target. The rigid construction of the stacked barrels results in a single phase of recoil and reduced muzzle flip. When open, the break action is easily seen to be safe from a distance.

Disadvantages: The only disadvantage of the over and under is that it requires the largest amount of movement to facilitate ejecting and loading, particularly the bottom barrel.

Although the side by side and over and under can both be of boxlock or sidelock designs, there are many other differences between the side by side and the over and under.

Comparing the Side by Side and the Over and Under Shotgun

You need to consider the different characteristics of the two types of shotguns and choose the one that best matches the quarry you are hunting. Also, if I have been shooting either a side by side or an over and under exclusively for any period of time, changing from one to the other requires changes in handling and technique, plus a fair amount of practise to reinforce those adjustments. The following are some insights into the characteristics of these two types of shotguns and how these impact on straight shooting.

Weight

The first consideration in guns of either configuration is weight. The weight difference is created by the depth of the actions – the horizontal barrels of the side by side only need sufficient depth to accom-

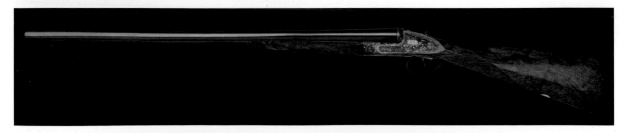

Holland & Holland Royal Side by Side. (ROBERT PEARSON)

Holland & Holland Sporting Over and Under. (ROBERT PEARSON)

modate the chopper lump and the depth of one barrel, while the stacked barrels of the over and under require a deeper, heavier action.

The early over and unders were very large and cumbersome, so the side by side reigned supreme until the early 1900s. Then the patents of John Robertson (Boss & Co.) in 1909 and James Woodward in 1913 allowed the locking system to be placed on the action walls, creating the modern lines of the over and under that we shoot today.

Still, the over and under requires a deeper action than the equivalent gauge in a side by side.

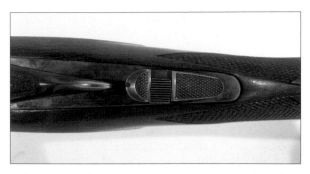

The barrel selector on a B. Rizzini Over and Under.

This deeper action has a domino effect – bigger locks require increased depth in the head of the stock and a deeper forend – and these factors combine to add size and weight. Gauge for gauge, the over and under is usually a pound heavier than the side by side. This weight difference really comes into play when you consider the type of shooting you are doing.

When shooting driven, decoyed or passing quarry, you carry the gun a little and shoot it a lot. In this case, weight is a bonus, helping to tame recoil and smooth the rhythm and timing of the swing.

When shooting rough or upland birds over dogs, you carry a gun a lot and shoot it a little. In this case, excessive weight is a negative, causing fatigue during long hunts and hindering your swing in those split-second chances when a bird explodes from cover.

Weight impacts in other ways. In swing characteristics, everyone loves the balance and handling of a svelte small gauge, however, a lighter gun is quick to start and equally quick to stop. While the heavier over and under may initially feel like a dead weight, requiring more effort to start the swing, it holds and sustains speed and line, creating a more consistent swing.

Recoil

Regardless of the barrel and action configuration, the combination of too light a gun and too heavy a load will create excessive recoil. However, the over and under will always have the advantage in recoil control. As the first phase of recoil is a backwards movement into the shoulder pocket, the shotgun pivots against the shoulder, rotating upwards. Because the stock of the over and under is lower than the line of the top barrel, the centre of gravity is in line with the bottom barrel and this upward movement is minimized.

In the side by side, both barrels are above the line of the stock and the upwards flip is more pronounced. As the barrels are unsupported, in guns with thinner walls or in small gauges with longer barrels, there can be an initial downward flex on firing. The second phase of recoil is upwards and left or right depending on which barrel is fired.

I use video in my instruction and when the tape is played back to my students, they are amazed at the amount of gun movement that happens between the first and second shots when shooting a side by side.

Because of the two phases of recoil, more control is required in the forend grip on a side by side than with an over and under. Excessive barrel movement occurs when the left arm is not properly extended. I believe this is exacerbated by the short splinter forends found on most side by sides. So, the correct extension of the arm should place the hand at the end of the forend, with part of the hand resting on the barrels. In this case, a hand guard or glove is required to protect the fingers from hot barrels, but this extended grip helps control recoil and unwanted barrel movement.

The over and under's superposed barrels, stacked one upon the other, are jointed with both side and top ribs. This design creates an "I" beam, giving the barrels great rigidity. The result is little vertical or horizontal movement and single, direct recoil into the shoulder pocket.

Double or Single Triggers

Double triggers on an over and under are still somewhat of a rarity as their makers prefer to opt for a barrel selector, which determines which barrel is fired first. Shotguns are usually choked with an open and tight degree of choke. This combination is used to match the gauge, ballistics, shot load and distance of the quarry being hunted. The two triggers allow instant selection of the right combination for the hunting opportunity that presents itself. Traditionally, the open choke is fired by the front trigger. The exception occurs in some driven grouse guns, where often the first barrel contains the most choke for that first shot at distance.

I do know a barrel selector on an over and under is nigh-on impossible to use with the same speed and dexterity as the double triggers on a side by side, in that split-second when a bird bursts from cover.

When it comes to loading, the side by side beats the over and under every time. The horizontal barrels of the side by side only have to hinge a small distance compared to the over and under. Again, no matter the quarry or type of shooting, you will always have the edge in speed when loading a side by side.

The shallow gape of the Side by Side will always beat the Over and Under in speed of loading.

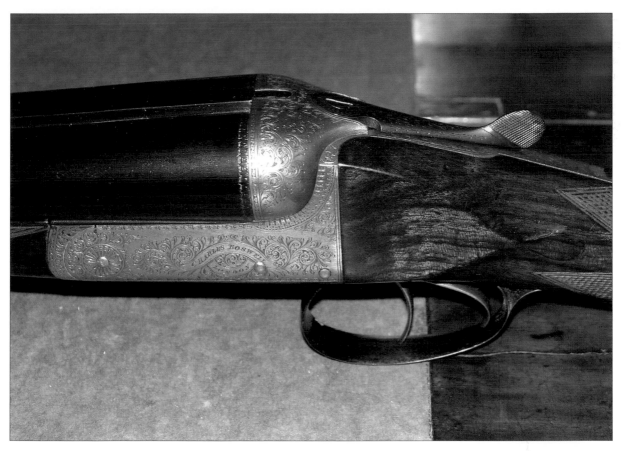

1930s Charles Boswell Side by Side.

Buying a Shotgun

The biggest decision and investment in game shooting is the purchase of a shotgun. For the novice, the choices are many and can be more than a little bewildering. As a shooting instructor, the mistake I most often observe is that people rush out and buy a shotgun with little, if any, consideration to its suitability for the type of shooting they plan to do or to its match to their build and height. The wrong choice is not only a handicap to better shooting, but if you spend a few hundred, or worse, a few thousand, on the wrong gun, you are either stuck with it or take a loss selling it to someone else.

Before you make the purchase, take your time, do some research – read the gun reviews in magazines and online, talk with more experienced shots and consider their opinions and suggestions.

Then visit gun shops, examine and handle the shotguns that fit your criteria and are a close fit and handle well. The gun shop owners are usually experienced shooting enthusiasts and can offer sound advice during this process. Whenever the opportunity is available to try a gun, do so. There is a world of difference between handling a gun in the store and live-firing it on the shooting ground. Actually shooting a gun allows you to get a true feel for its handling and dynamics, as well as its recoil characteristics.

This "go-slow" advice also applies to the intermediate and advanced shot who wants to change guns. Research will allow you to compile a list of guns that match your physical requirements, the quarry and your budget.

New or Pre-owned?

With proper maintenance, a shotgun will give decades of use. There are guns still being used today that were made in the late 1800s! Used shotguns can usually offer significant savings compared to buying new; however, if you are buying a new gun, it will come with a warranty and can be ordered specifically for the birds to be hunted – plus the type, gauge, barrel length and fit can all be included in the price.

If you are purchasing a shotgun second-hand, you should be aware that a gun is mechanical and just like your car, it requires regular cleaning and maintenance. If these aspects have been neglected, the gun could be in poor condition and, in some cases, unsafe to shoot.

Buying a second-hand or new gun through a dealer allows you to purchase with confidence. A registered firearms dealer has both legal responsibilities and a reputation to maintain. If you purchase a second-hand gun from a private party, you will need the knowledge and experience to carefully check the gun to ensure that it is nitro-proofed, in proof and in a safe condition to shoot. If you are unsure as to how to do this, ask a more experienced friend or consult a firearms dealer.

Evaluating a Pre-Owned Shotgun

First, check for overall signs of wear and tear – is the barrel bluing worn off, is the woodwork scratched, dinged or dented or the chequering worn smooth? Closely inspect the stock for any cracks, particularly around the head of the stock and through the grip. Inspect the head of the stock to see if it is soaked in oil, and then repeat the process with the forend.

Inspect the barrels by holding them up to a light. Check both inside and outside the bores – look for pitting, dents or bulges, paying particular attention to the chambers. Running your fingers gently along the barrels can often reveal dents and bulges as your fingertips are very tactile and sensitive.

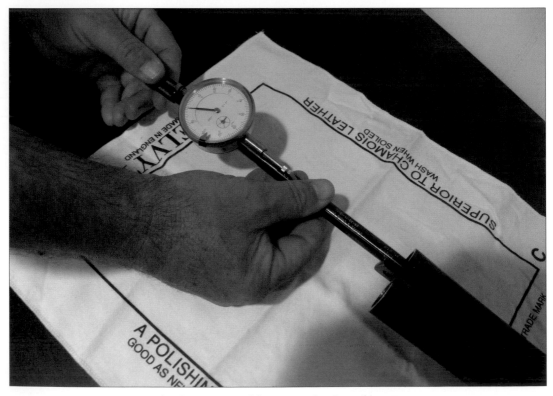

Checking nominal boring with a barrel gauge.

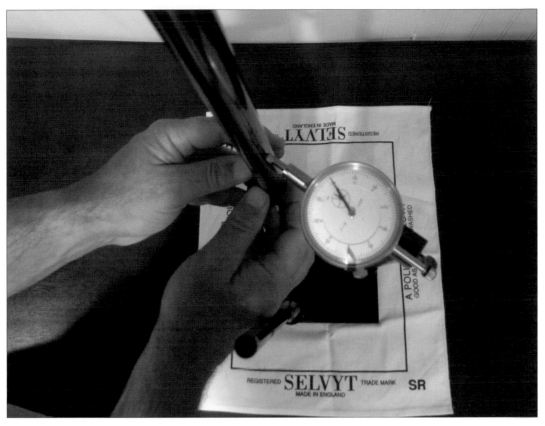

Checking barrel wall thickness with wall thickness gauge.

Hold the barrels by the lump and gently "ring" them, using the wooden handle of a screwdriver. The barrels should chime like a bell, indicating that the ribs are correctly attached. If there is a dull thud, it is indicative of loose ribs. Inspect the ventilated ribs of over and under barrels for dents and look for signs of any corrosion at the joint of the ribs and barrels on all guns.

Specialized equipment is required to check that the barrels are "in proof". A gun dealer or gunsmith will use a bore gauge to measure each barrel and compare the results to the nominal boring stamped on the action. They will also use a wall gauge to measure each barrel's wall thickness.

If multi-chokes are installed, check that they are easily removed and re-installed. Inspect the threads of the chokes and the barrels for wear or corrosion. If the shotgun has fixed chokes, measure them to see the degree of choke in each barrel. If it is a modern shotgun, check the choke measurements against the manufacturer's markings to see if they have been altered.

The serial numbers on barrels, receiver and forearm should match! If not, it could mean that one or more of these parts have been replaced or that the gun has been built from a collection of parts.

Look for chewed-up screws and pins and wear marks on the action hinge pin and knuckles. Inspect the forend iron for the same, as these areas can provide indications of good or poor maintenance.

Place the barrels on the action but leave the forend off. Grasp the action with both hands, barrels erect, and gently shake the gun. If there is even a slight movement of the barrels, it indicates that the gun requires re-jointing.

Check that the "Safety", whether automatic or manual, is working correctly and that the trigger pulls are crisp and of the correct poundage.

Selecting the Best Gun for You

There are four critical points to consider when selecting a gun, in addition to the fact that it is visually pleasing and a pleasure to own. Addressing these points will, hopefully, enable you to acquire a gun that will allow you to shoot the quarry of your choice to the best of your ability.

1: Your budget

2: Your height and build

3: The quarry and type of shooting

4: The shotgun as the sum of its parts

Your Budget

"You get what you pay for in life." Nowhere do these words ring more true than when applied to the selection of your first gun or when trading up. Always buy the best gun that your budget will allow. The differences between the entry grade and the top grade shotguns of any particular maker are nothing more than better-figured walnut and more elaborate engraving. Ballistically, they are the same and neither of these upgrades will help you take one more bird.

It is far better to buy a plain, entry grade shotgun from a quality maker than to buy an equally priced, but elaborately-engraved shotgun from a lesser-quality manufacturer. If you buy a shotgun made from quality components, it will be better balanced, with improved trigger pulls, reliable ejectors and give you years of good service.

Your Height and Build

It would seem obvious that if you are a petite lady or of a slight build, the choice of a heavy, long-barrelled gun would be inappropriate. Whereas, if you are a six foot-plus weight lifter, a light, fast gun would be a definite handicap. You want to find a shotgun that is a complement rather than a handicap to your shooting, to choose one of an overall length, correct length of pull and with a barrel length and weight to suit your physical size and strength.

While the old gunmakers' rule was that the barrel length should be twice the length of pull, the new lighter, longer barrels have allowed gunmakers to maintain balance and handling and push this envelope. But you should still find the barrel length that suits you best. Barrel length should be determined by your physical size and strength, not the bird being shot. While long barrels might help on the long passing shot, they are not going to help on the close, fast bird flushing from cover. Improved control is worth more than length any day and a compromise between barrel length and handling can often make the difference in how well a gun shoots for you.

The Quarry and the Type of Shooting

It amazes me how many people I see shooting a shotgun that is totally inappropriate to the type of shooting they do. Many are doing an adequate job, but I can only wonder how much better they might shoot with the right tool for the job. Different types of bird shooting require different characteristics and performance in a shotgun; these can be broken down into four types.

1. Driven shooting
2. Upland bird or walked-up shooting over dogs
3. Pass shooting
4. Wildfowl or decoyed shooting

Driven Shooting

There are three distinct types of driven shooting:

1. Partridge and pheasant, in the traditional presentation, are driven from cover crops over hedgerows and spinney to a waiting line of Guns.

2. Red grouse are driven low across the moors over a line of Guns, partly concealed in a line of "grouse butts".

3. Pheasant and partridge are driven from very high cover and moorland fringes, with many birds passing over the line of Guns at heights in excess of 50 yards.

The classic British Game Gun is the side by side. Weighing around six pounds, eight ounces, it is *the* shotgun for traditional driven shooting. Its combination of weight, balance, dynamic handling and speed of loading fulfil all the requirements needed when partridge explode from cover or when a covey of grouse sweep over the butts.

Though the 12 gauge is by far the most used, 16 and 20 gauge side by sides are becoming more popular. Occasionally a 28 gauge is used, but when a Gun arrives at a shoot with a 28 gauge, he is at risk of implying that the birds presented are not the most testing or that he is an exceptional shot and that it would be far too easy shooting with a 12 gauge.

I personally like the 28 gauge and have found that its ballistic performance is not that far short of the 20 gauge and, in the right hands, can be equally effective.

The over and under, once frowned upon by the traditionalists, is now commonplace in a line of Guns. The 20 gauge over and under is the most popular choice as it is of similar weight and handling characteristics to the classic 12 gauge side by side.

With the increased demand for higher, more challenging birds, guns are required to be able to shoot heavier loads. This has increased the "felt" recoil. The classic game gun's light weight is insufficient to control this increased recoil. The lighter gun is quick to start, and equally quick to stop, making it more difficult to hold the line and maintain the lead. These guns are often choked Improved Cylinder and Modified, but this (often insufficient) choke combination can be a real disadvantage at longer distances.

Some traditionalists have opted to shoot heavier 12 gauges – long-barrelled continental side by side guns weighing 7 pounds or more – while others have opted to use vintage live pigeon and wildfowl guns of similar dimensions. However, the majority of high bird specialists today choose the long-barrelled (30 or 32 inch) over and under, heavily choked with Improved Modified or Full, weighing 8 pounds plus.

Note: Driven grouse should always be shot with a pair of guns. A smaller day of pheasant and partridge shooting can be shot with a single gun, but any bag anticipated to be over 300 birds should be shot with a loader and pair of guns. Pairs can be composed or matched. A composed pair consists of two guns of similar design, gauge and specification. A true pair are made simultaneously, by the same team of craftsmen, have consecutive serial numbers, are numbered one and two, and are identical twins in weight and handling.

Upland Bird Shooting or Walked-up Shooting over Dogs

The small gauge side by side is the ultimate upland bird gun – it offers swift handling and three points of balance. It is balanced for carrying during long hunts, balanced for a one-handed carry when hunting in heavy cover and balanced for reactive (point and shoot) instinctive shooting when seconds count.

With the exception of some plains shooting, most upland birds are shot within 15 to 30 yards. The recommended choking for an upland bird gun is True Cylinder in the first barrel and Light Modified in the second barrel. With two triggers, the hunter has the ability to instantly select the choke that matches the range of the shooting opportunity.

The break-action allows the side by side to be easily opened and made safe, especially important when crossing fallen trees, fording streams or climbing fences.

The only argument against a small gauge over and under is, one with double triggers can be hard to find and most single trigger barrel selectors are impractical in the field. Otherwise, the over and under is a realistic option, especially for those weaned on a single sight plane.

Gauge is a practical consideration and an upland bird gun can be anything from a 12 gauge, for longer shots like pheasant shooting in the Dakotas, to a .410 for plantation quail in the South. You need to recognize your shooting skill and match it with the knowledge of the bird being hunted when considering gauge.

Pass Shooting

Dove, duck and flighted pigeon offer the most pass shooting opportunities, as all are migratory flock birds and follow established flight lines. Most pass shooting takes place from 25 to 40 yards. Choke with lead shot should be Light Modified and Modified, and with steel shot, Improved Cylinder and Light Modified.

You want a little weight in a shotgun for pass shooting, just as you do in driven shooting. This is a more deliberate style of shooting requiring lead and maintaining the line of flight. Passing birds can be

Shooting with a pair of guns and a loader. (BETTWS HALL SPORTING)

Walked-up shooting over dogs. (TERRY ALLEN)

shot with any style of shotgun – side by side or over and under. When shooting migratory waterfowl requiring the use of steel shot, you may choose semi-automatics and pump shotguns capable of handling steel shot.

For a gauge that can kill cleanly at 40 yards, 12, 16 or 20 gauges are the popular choices.

Decoyed Shooting

The first thing migratory birds do when they are ready to feed is to look for others of their own species doing exactly that. Nothing says safety louder than a large number of their cousins apparently feeding contentedly. A few encouraging calls will turn a passing shot into a head-on shot, as a bird sets its wings to make its approach run into the decoy pattern.

But any sudden movement can turn this certain incoming 20-yard head shot into a jinking, improbable going-away 40-yard shot in the blink of an eye. Ducks and geese are tough birds and they require tight chokes and large shot, well placed, to make a clean kill, especially at distance.

The guns of choice are 12 gauge semi-automatics or pump shotguns proofed for 3" and 3½" steel shot. But many choose to stick with tradition and still use a break-action in 10 gauge and larger. If birds are shot between 15 and 40 yards, a double barrel shotgun would allow a larger range of flexibility in matching choke to range. With the single barrel guns there are two choices – use either Improved Cylinder for the closer shots or Modified for the shots at greater distances and be prepared to compromise. With a two-barrelled gun, I would choke Improved Cylinder and Modified, to cover most eventualities.

The Gun is the Sum of its Parts

Barrel Length

Everyone will change guns several times during their shooting learning curve. As your shooting skills and knowledge of the differences in guns improve, you will change guns to better match your physique, your increase in skill and the discipline or quarry you are currently shooting.

There has been a recent trend towards longer and longer barrels, particularly when shooting high driven game. Modern metallurgy and manufacturing techniques give today's shotgun barrels superior strength and shooting qualities.

Better barrels and actions, barrel-boring and advances in choke systems have enabled the creation of longer-barrelled guns that shoot impressive patterns. The excellent distribution of weight throughout the whole shotgun means the extra length can be achieved without sacrificing handling. The modern over and under shotgun is 20% better balanced, 30% stronger and 40% more reliable than the guns made fifty years ago.

However, looking back over the years, the great shots of the day and many others are still shooting very well with 28 inch barrelled guns. While some of the top shots of today choose to shoot 32 and 34 inch guns, the debate goes on as to the degree of advantage in a couple of inches.

Shotguns can have a variety of barrel lengths, which should match the type of shooting in which you are participating.

Only you can make the decision on the correct barrel length for you, but here is a list of opinions on the advantages and disadvantages of using shotguns with longer barrels:

Advantages of Longer Barrels:

1. It is easier to point with a longer gun than a short one.

2. A little like a super tanker, once under way, the gun will hold its course and line, giving a good follow-through.

3. The length and balance help control recoil and muzzle flip.

4. They are better suited to high driven and longer pass shooting.

Disadvantages of Longer Barrels:

1. Overcoming the dead gun or inertia is required – it is slow to start.

2. Deliberate timing of swing and trigger pull is required.

3. The gun requires a more deliberate style.

4. At low driven presentations, the gun can be a disadvantage.

Matching the muzzle speed to the target speed, regardless of technique, requires timing! Rhythm and co-ordination are essential and must be applied with an understanding of, and a familiarity with, the gun's weight and dynamics. You must be able to shoot a gun without upsetting your timing, regardless of the gun's barrel length. I believe that those who struggle with a longer-barrelled gun do so because they aren't familiar with this fact.

Discover by experimenting and then shoot the longest-barrelled gun that is complementary to your build, technique and quarry and you will *always* have the advantage of pointability over the shorter-barrelled gun.

Patterns

Will a longer gun give you better patterns? The pattern of a shotgun is regulated at the muzzle, and is independent of the barrel length. It makes little difference if the gun has 26 or 34 inch barrels, as the velocity is minimally affected and the pattern quality is regulated by the choke present in the muzzles, not the length of the barrels.

Ribs, Beads and Optical Illusions

Your next consideration is the sight plane. Asked to point at a distant object you would do so with an extended arm and a single forefinger. You would not point with two or three fingers, but just one. The over and under offers a single sight plane as opposed to the side by side's broad barrels. If you have been weaned on the single sight plane of the single barrel or over and under, the view of the broad barrels of the side by side can be very hard to overcome. Many feel the broad barrels distract the eyes

from the bird, whereas others find their width helps with muzzle awareness, especially in poor light conditions or against dark backgrounds.

There are a myriad of rib configurations available for a side by side compared to the over and under. Swamped, concave, rib-less, Churchill, flat, all side by side ribs are designed to draw the eye out past the muzzles to the target. The combination of rib and bead can have a big impact on how the barrels affect your eye – bird relationship. It is worth the time and trials to find the one that works best for you.

Ribs and beads have a big impact on apparent barrel length as well. A narrow rib and small bead will make a short-barrelled gun look long when mounted, whereas a wide rib and large bead will make the long-barrelled gun look short. In fact, ribs and beads can create an optical illusion! They are a very personal addition, and you should experiment to find the combination that gives you good muzzle awareness while being minimally distracting while shooting.

There is a great variety in rib and bead configurations.

FLAT RIB CONCAVE RIB CHURCHILL STYLE RIB

Shotgun rib styles.

The purpose of the raised, ventilated ribs on the over and under is to dissipate heat and avoid the "mirage effect". Ribs are cross-filed to reduce distracting reflection. I have found that "one-eyed" shooters who tend to be "aimers" favour a narrower rib, while those shooting with both eyes open tend to be "pointers" and prefer a wider rib.

Choosing Choke

Choke is simply a constriction or thickening at the end of the barrel. As the shot column passes through the end of the barrel it is squeezed or shaped to a greater or lesser degree depending upon the amount of choke present.

Choke is measured in thousandths of an inch, from 0 to 40 thousand and it increases in increments of 10 thousandths starting with:

True Cylinder	=	0 thou
Skeet	=	5 to 8 thou
Quarter or Improved Cylinder	=	10 thou
Half or Modified	=	20 thou
Three Quarter or Improved Modified	=	30 thou
Full	=	40 thou

There is an English choke measurement also called Improved that is 3 to 8 thou of choke and can be compared to Skeet.

A rough guide to choke selection would be for birds at these yardages:

0 to 25 yards	=	True Cylinder, Skeet
25 to 35 yards	=	Improved Cylinder, Modified
35 to 45 yards	=	Modified, Improved Modified
45 yards plus	=	Full

I would always use less choke rather than more. The modern shotgun cartridge is far more efficient than those that were in use when these basic tables were compiled. For the average shot, after Modified or Half-choke, there is little advantage to be gained by going to tighter chokes.

The option of using multi-chokes, whether factory-installed or installed after-market, is an individual choice. Multi-chokes do offer greater flexibility, especially when one gun is to be used for several different hunting scenarios.

If multi-chokes are fitted by the manufacturer, or if fitting after-market thin wall chokes, replacement chokes can be ordered in any constriction. For example, chokes in 12 thou and 18 thou would translate to a tight quarter and a loose half and allow greater flexibility in choke options.

Triggers

The dynamics involved in shooting a moving target with a shotgun are complex and the timing of the shot is essential; this is impossible without properly regulated and well-shaped triggers. Often taken for granted, triggers are a very important part of the gun and their effect on timing is immense.

Too light a trigger pull and there is every chance of an involuntary or accidental discharge, especially on cold days when gloves may be worn. Too heavy a trigger pull and the effort of pulling the trigger can create loss of timing, breaking that all-important connection to the bird.

In some cases, a too-heavy trigger pull can create a flinch, which, in turn, causes two consistency-wrecking faults – the gun will be jerked violently low and left off the bird's line of flight or the swing will be either too slow or stop completely, resulting in a miss behind.

The shape and position of the trigger is another aspect worthy of consideration. If your length of pull is correct, but the trigger is too far back in the guard, your finger will have to extend too far, forcing you to pull the trigger with the first joint of your finger, rather than the pad. Regardless of the weight of trigger pulls, this position will cause you to jerk the trigger, jerking the gun off the target when you pull the trigger. If the trigger is too far forward in the guard, you have to stretch to place your finger on the trigger, which forces your hand into an unnatural position. This awkward placement of your hand interferes with the efficiency of and impairs the timing of the trigger being pulled.

Proper hand position is a combination of the grip configuration and trigger placement and should be an important consideration when having your gun fit. The curvature and width of the trigger blade is a personal matter, but I would try to avoid a too-straight or too-narrow trigger configuration. I find that the broader, curved shape gives more consistent finger placement and a better feel or touch when taking the shot.

Single triggers are complex in design. When you open the gun to load it, rods running through the action "cock" or compress the main springs and they are held "cocked" by a simple device known as the "bent and sear". When you pull the trigger, it hinges around its axis and the rear portion lifts and disengages the bent and sear, releasing the main spring that powers the hammer through the striker, igniting the cartridge.

After the first shot, the trigger must be released to allow the engagement of the second lifter. This is referred to as the "dead pull". Without this "dead pull", the recoil from the first shot would cause an involuntary firing of the second barrel.

The correct regulation or setting of the triggers is essential. A gun with "crisp pulls" and the correct poundage will allow unconscious firing of the gun with minimum lock-time. Weights of trigger pulls are a personal choice, and my personal preference is three and a half pounds on the front and four pounds on the back. The ideal trigger pull could be compared to a stem of fine-spun glass snapping crisply, with no drag or sponginess. The regulation and setting of trigger pulls is skilled work, and should only be done by a competent gunsmith.

Adjustable triggers are a good addition to any gun. They can be adjusted to the grip to achieve that all-important correct finger placement. Double triggers can be twisted and curved to allow for better fit and feel and offer instant barrel selection. With double triggers, if one should malfunction, you still have a gun that shoots, albeit with only one barrel.

Stocks, Grips and Forends

Manufacturers differ greatly in their standard stock dimensions. You may be lucky and find one that fits right out of the box, but the odds are against it. Many shooters struggle unnecessarily for years with a poorly fitting gun, when a good gun fit could easily put matters right.

The most crucial measurement on a shotgun is the drop at face (where the cheek bone rests approximately 3 inches from the nose of the comb). If the drop is too low, it will cause head-lifting or worse, cross dominance. If the gun is too high in the comb, the result will be misses over the target.

The correct eye–rib alignment is very important and the comb "at face" should be as parallel as possible, reducing the chance of involuntary head movement when taking shots at different angles. The Monte Carlo stock (named after the famous city in Monaco which was once the "Mecca" of live pigeon shooting) has a parallel stock and though not to the liking of traditionalists, is the best choice for people with long necks – women, in particular.

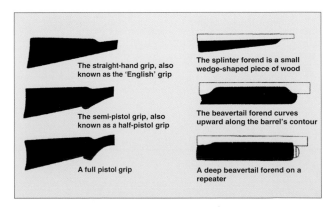

The straight-hand grip, also known as the 'English' grip

The semi-pistol grip, also known as a half-pistol grip

A full pistol grip

The splinter forend is a small wedge-shaped piece of wood

The beavertail forend curves upward along the barrel's contour

A deep beavertail forend on a repeater

Basic shotgun stock grips and forend styles.

There are several stock and forend shapes from which to choose. The classic straight hand or "English" grip, usually accompanied by the splinter forend, is particularly advantageous when using a gun with double triggers.

The semi-pistol grip can be cut flat to a grip cap or rounded – the differing radiuses are known as The Woodward or Prince of Wales grip and are often paired with a semi-beavertailed forend. On a side by side, this wider forend offers a little more protection from hot barrels.

The full pistol grip is used mostly on the over and under in combination with a deep beavertail forend which can be of the Schnabel design or grooved, with finger channels.

The shape of the grip on the stock and forend requires careful consideration. They must be of a shape and size that allows a natural, relaxed hand position while permitting full articulation throughout the shooting action. If the radius of the grip is too sharp, it places the hand in an unnatural position with the hand under tension and its movements constricted.

Stocks come in all shapes and sizes. (PAUL FIEVEZ)

The thickness of both grip and forend should be comfortable while placing the hands in the correct shooting position and enhancing gun control. The distance between the comb nose and breech face affects hand placement. If this distance is too small, it forces the hand forward into an awkward position which, combined with too large a grip, causes poor grip control and forces the trigger finger into a poor position on the trigger.

Balance

A gun's handling dynamics are created by the centre of balance and its position along the length of the gun. This centre is directly proportional to the gun's overall length and weight distribution. Traditional

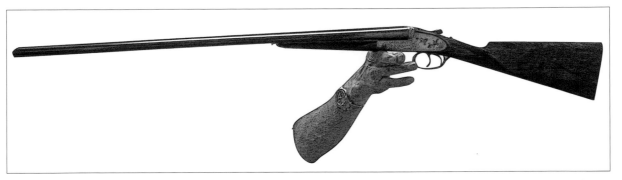

A shotgun's centre of balance should be on or just in front of the hinge pin, placing the weight correctly between the hands.

gunmaking recommended a barrel length twice the length of pull, which allowed the gunmaker to place the centre of balance on, or just in front of, the hinge pin. This position effectively places the weight between the hands and governs the individual gun's swing characteristics.

There are many mathematical theories on how to achieve this essential balance, however discovering the combination of balance and feel that works best for you is as uniquely individual as you are. An experienced shot recognizes this special feel and that it differs among guns depending on their purpose. They have learned which "feel" works best for them and can understand and distinguish the slight nuances in a gun's handling that will make it the best match to the quarry being shot. The beginner and intermediate shooters do not yet have this experience and need advice in their first gun choices.

Recoil

Newton's Third Law of Motion states: "For every action, there is an equal and opposite reaction." So in a shotgun, the rearwards thrust equals the velocity of what goes out the end of the barrel.

Recoil has a greater impact on our shooting than we are aware of, perhaps even as much as the impact of how the gun fits.

There are two types of recoil:

1. Conscious: where you feel it on every shot.
2. Subconscious: where you are unaware of its impact.

Subconscious recoil, even though you do not physically feel it, can affect your shooting by throwing off your timing, rhythm and swing.

Controlling Recoil

If we are suffering from conscious or "felt" recoil, we need to learn how to minimize it both physically and with alterations to the gun. The first issue to address is gun fit – your gun should fit not only your build and height, but also your strength and reaction capabilities.

A gun that fits well is the first step in controlling recoil, however, good gun fit needs to be complemented by a good gun mount for all elements to work properly. A poorly mounted gun negates fit and increases felt recoil.

Too light or too heavy a gun can result in similar reactions, neither good. Barrel length should always be taken into the equation – for example, often a light gun with long barrels can have worse recoil than a heavier gun with short barrels. A longer-barrelled gun of the correct weight will always control recoil better. The inertia of the longer, heavier barrels minimizes recoil and reduces muzzle flip.

There are several ballistic options that can also help, but some are impractical in a game gun, increasing weight, affecting balance and reducing ballistic efficiency.

Factors that can help control recoil:

1. A shotgun appropriate to the individual's physical strength and build
2. Solid fundamentals of stance and posture
3. Comfortable grip – holding the gun correctly
4. Well-fitted shotgun
5. Good gun mount
6. Well-balanced shotgun
7. Appropriate barrel length
8. Suitable gun weight
9. Forcing cones
10. Choke
11. Recoil pads

Factors 1–5: If a gun fits and is held and mounted correctly, a large percentage of the recoil will be absorbed through the hands and arms, which act like shock absorbers on a car. The remainder of the recoil is then dispersed through the shoulder pocket. When the butt of the stock truly matches the shoulder pocket, the impact of the recoil is further spread and diminished.

Factor 6: The point of balance on a shotgun should be between the hands on, or marginally in front of, the hinge pin.

Factors 7–8: Longer barrels in a balanced combination with overall weight, further reduce recoil and muzzle flip.

Factor 9: The forcing cone concentrates the shot from the oversized chamber into the smaller circumference of the barrel. In the modern over and under, the lengthening and polishing of the forcing cone smoothes the transition of the shot and improves both patterns and recoil.

Factor 10: At the muzzle, the long, smooth parallel section of the barrel leading into the choke restriction works in the same manner only in reverse, by smoothing the pellets' transition from the larger barrel into the smaller choke area. This combination also improves patterns and reduces recoil.

Note: Another barrel modification, both factory and after-market, is back-boring the barrels where the nominal boring is over-bored from .729 to .735 or more. This improves patterns and reduces recoil. However, more and more estates are choosing to use fibre-wadded cartridges which do not work very well in back-bored guns. I would never recommend back-boring or lengthening forcing cones for any older game guns. It is a process more suited to competition shotguns than traditional game guns.

Factor 11: Recoil pads are only as good as the materials from which they are made. Some pads are as hard as the wood they are replacing, while others are so soft and sticky that they hinder a smooth gun mount. I prefer to use a Pachmayr Sporting Pad covered in pigskin. This reduces recoil and is smooth to mount.

There are recoil reducers of various types – springs, air or hydraulic. Fitted into the stock, they are excellent and effectively reduce recoil. However, they average about 12 ounces in weight and are not a practical option for an upland bird gun.

Controlling recoil is a big part of shooting straight. So consider a combination of the recoil-reducing options, practise good form and Newton's Law will not affect your shooting.

Words of Advice

Gun selection can be confusing – take your time, make every attempt to "try before you buy". Ask friends if you can shoot their guns, look for gun dealers who have access to shooting grounds and ask them if you can try some of their guns. Look for events where different manufacturers offer the opportunity to examine and shoot their shotguns.

Avoid excesses! Too heavy a gun will cause fatigue; too light a gun will create excess recoil. Attempt to achieve a balance, not only in the gun's handling, but in its overall design, length, weight, fit and feel.

Consider your physical and mechanical requirements. I have known people to persevere for years with an unsuitable gun because they are in love with some aspect of its construction – the maker, the wood, the engraving or the configuration. "A bad workman blames his tools", but if he does not have the correct tool for the job, he cannot expect to do his best work.

What makes a straight-shooting gun is a combination of elements that creates a hard-to-define, but "you will know it when you shoot it" harmonious balance. Find the gun that achieves this balance and you will have a gun that works *with* you rather than *against* you and, whatever its design or configuration, it will enhance your ability to shoot birds cleanly.

Guns come in all shapes and sizes. (TERRY ALLEN)

Chapter 5
Choke and Cartridges

Many books have been written explaining the minutiae and mysteries of shotgun ballistics and they are packed with formulas, tables and charts. But the sum of their contents is that the effective range of a shotgun consists of two elements: Pellet Energy and Pattern Density and these are achieved by the correct combination of choke and cartridge.

Birds are far harder to kill cleanly than one would think. The pellets require sufficient down-range energy to penetrate through the bird's protective covering of feather, skin, fat and muscle to reach the vital organs of the brain, spinal cord, heart and lungs.

Pellet Energy

A pellet's energy is in direct proportion to its speed and size. Shotgun pellets are as ballistically inefficient as a house brick and the smaller the size, the greater the inefficiency.

Smaller pellet velocity drops off quicker than a larger pellet moving the same Feet per Second (FPS). The pellet with the most mass loses its speed at a slower rate and ballistics improve as the size of the pellet is increased.

Think of it this way: which could you throw farther, a golf ball or a cricket ball? If two objects are moving at the same velocity, but one object has twice the mass of the other, the object with the greater mass will also have twice the momentum. The bigger pellet, having more mass, retains more energy down-range, which results in better penetration.

Pattern Density

Pattern density is controlled by choke and pellet energy is determined by the down-range feet per second (FPS) and size of the pellets.

The optimum Pattern Density is 70% of the cartridge shot load placed in a 30 inch circle at the range at which the birds are to be shot. If we do not have sufficient density at the correct distance, the pellets will spread so far apart and the gaps between them will become so big (Blown Pattern), that the bird could be centred in the middle of the pattern and still be missed or not hit with enough pellets to kill it cleanly. An open pattern is unreliable – though an individual pellet could still have enough energy to penetrate (i.e., fluke shots will occasionally kill cleanly when a single pellet strikes a vital organ), it is far more likely for the game to be pricked (wounded) and fly off, unable to be retrieved.

When a shotgun is fired, immense pressure is

Pellet Energy and Pattern Density. (JEFF COATES)

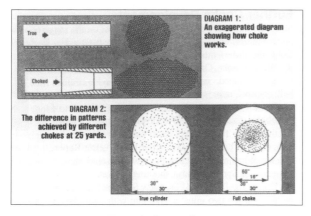

DIAGRAM 1:
An exaggerated diagram showing how choke works.

DIAGRAM 2:
The difference in patterns achieved by different chokes at 25 yards.

How choke works.

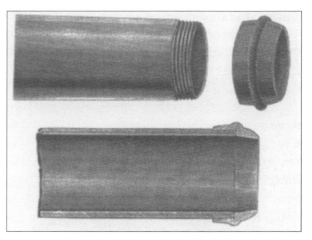

Roper's original multi-choke.

created, impacting the rear of the shot column, deforming and pushing the pellets into the layers in the front of the cartridge. Passage down the barrel causes further pellet deformation, by barrel scrub and the choke constriction. When the pellet cloud leaves the muzzle it is intact, but crashes into air resistance, (which is equal to the pellets' velocity) which expands the cloud laterally and longitudinally. Air resistance causes the deformed pellets to slow and "flyer pellets" to peel away from the core of the main column of shot, stringing out behind the main shot cloud, but choke delays the effects of air resistance.

Choke

Choke is a variable constriction at the muzzle of the shotgun. It "chokes" the shot column, constricting the shot cloud and effectively extending the range of the shotgun.

Increasing the amount of choke tightens the pattern and extends the range. Birds are shot at 20, 30, 40 and 50 yard ranges, so it is essential to determine the combination of choke and cartridge, controlling the shot stream's density and energy, to match the distances at which you will be shooting. The correct combination of choke and cartridge determines if a shot cripples or kills cleanly.

It is, simply, using the correct gauge of shotgun with the right combination of choke and cartridge to match the quarry's size and distance. You can read all of the data and charts you like, but only by "patterning" your shotgun (shooting at a pattern plate using various combinations of gauge, choke and cartridge at selected distances) will you know for certain what the right combination should be.

The important factors to consider are the barrel type, choke, alloy of pellets, pellet size and cup or wads. Making use of the right pellet alloy will prevent the shot from deforming due to extreme initial acceleration. Large pellets have the capability to retain their energy better at longer distances but create a low pellet cloud density. On the other hand, smaller pellets can lose energy much faster, but create higher pellet cloud density.

The Origin of Choke

The invention of choke in 1866 is generally credited to an English gentleman, Mr W. R. Pape. There is additional evidence that Sylvester Roper, an American gunsmith, patented the invention of choked barrels in April of 1866, several weeks before Mr Pape received his patent. All of this was contested by Mr Fred Kimble, another American, who claimed to have invented choke in 1867. Then W.W. Greener, another Englishman, researched and developed the concept further.

Whoever gets the ultimate credit, choke has done more to increase the effective range of the shotgun than any other invention. But the innovation to match the impact of choke itself was the Winchester

Company's introduction in 1970 of the first internal multi-choke, the "Winchoke". The interchangeable choke had been invented by Sylvester Roper who, in 1866, threaded the muzzle end of barrels to accept tubes of different constrictions.

Choke Technology Today

Jess Briley of Houston, Texas ultimately refined the development of the screw-in multi-choke. He created a system whereby any shotgun with sufficient wall thickness could have the barrels machined and threaded, and by screwing in matched tubes, the choke could be adjusted to suit the range of the birds being shot.

In the UK, Nigel Teague has further refined the multi-choke with his taper-choke technology. The introduction of choke increased the shotgun's range from 30 to 50 yards and subsequent refinements have extended the range even further. Cartridge innovations, such as the addition of antimony to the lead shot, added buffers and coatings, plus the invention of the plastic wad and the star crimp, have all been additional factors in increasing the shotgun's range.

How Choke Works

Choke means to constrict – to create a tightening effect – and that is exactly what choke does in the barrel of a shotgun. Choke works because of the difference in the diameter of the choke to the nominal boring of the barrel. The walls of the shotguns are parallel from the chamber to the muzzles. Before the invention of choke, all barrels were simply straight tubes, hence the designation "True Cylinder" (the most open choking, i.e., no choke at all).

Nigel Teague speciality after-maket multi-choke installation, considered by many to be the very best.

The addition of choke gradually increases the wall thickness of the barrels, so gradually decreases or constricts the inside diameter at the muzzles. The amount of this constriction is measured in thousandths of an inch as added to the nominal boring of the barrel, with the tightest, "Full Choke", measuring 40 thousandths of an inch.

Multi-chokes make one gun suitable for mulitple uses.

Terminology and Sizes

Different countries have differing terminology for the amount of choke present in a barrel. In the UK and US choke is measured in thousandths of an inch, in Europe in millimetres and the designations can be shown in letters, points and stars.

UK		Europe and America	Symbol
True Cylinder	0	True Cylinder	Cyl
Quarter	10	Improved Cylinder	****
Half	20	Modified	***
Three Quarter	30	Improved Modified	**
Full	40	Full	*

Terminology and sizes.

Name of choke	Marking	Nominal constriction
True cylinder	CL	0
¼ choke	*****	0.2–0.3 mm
½ choke	****	0.4–0.6 mm
¾ choke	***	0.7–0.8 mm
Full choke	*	0.9–1.0 mm

Note: There are specialized choke constrictions for Skeet and Trap. Manufacturers can differ on the amount, but Skeet is usually 5 to 8 thousandths of an inch and Trap has Light Modified, which is 15 thousandths of an inch. These intermediate choke restrictions offer additional flexibility in matching the various quarry ranges.

Choice of Shotgun Gauge

The gauge of a firearm is the diameter of its barrel. It is determined by the number of lead balls of equal size that would weigh one pound: 10 balls is a 10 gauge, 12 balls, a 12 gauge and so on, through 16, 20, 28. The one exception to the gauge measurement is the .410 shotgun, which is actually a bore diameter designation of .41 calibre or 67 gauge (if a pound of lead was used as the measurement).

Today, the most commonly encountered shotgun ammunition sizes are the 10, 12, 16, 20, 28 and .410. There is an incremental effectiveness in choke constriction as the gauges decrease, so in the smaller gauges, you require less choke to achieve the same pattern density at range. For example, full choke in a 28 gauge would be 0.026 thou.

Name of choke
Nominal constriction (inches)

True Cylinder
None

Improved Cylinder
0.010

Modified Choke
0.020

Improved Modified Choke
0.030

Full Choke
0.040

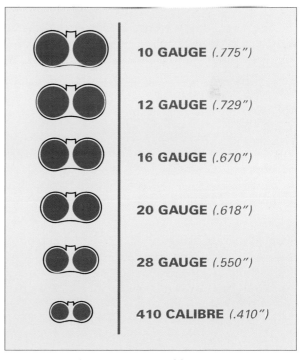

Gauges – nominal borings.

Range and Distance

The more choke that is present in the barrels, the greater the shotgun's effective range. The extended range is achieved by holding the shot column together longer, so that, as it leaves the barrel, it is narrower and more air resistant, reducing the amount of stringing or spread.

"Full Choke" will place 70% of the pellets inside a 30 inch circle at 40 yards. It was discovered that increasing the constriction did not increase the pellet percentage and so the 0.040 choke restriction became known as "Full".

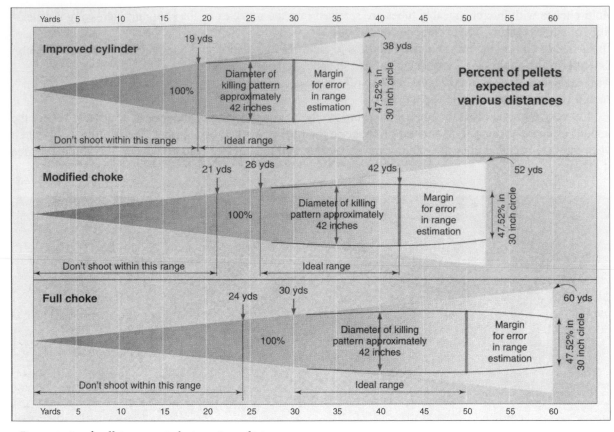

Percentage of pellets expected at various distances.

The accepted optimum range of different chokes is:

Full Choke	30" pattern at 40 yards
Improved Modified	30" pattern at 35 yards
Modified	30" pattern at 30 yards
Improved Cylinder	30" pattern at 25 yards
Cylinder	30" pattern at 20 yards

Note: Modern powders, wad innovation and choke improvements have extended the effective range of the shotgun. Modern cartridge case and shot wad combinations, with full choke, place 80% of the shot in a 30 inch circle at 40 yards, effectively increasing the range of the shotgun by 10 yards. This is yet another reason for patterning your gun and cartridge combination. I believe many of today's hunters are shooting with too much choke in their guns and are over-choked for the ranges at which they are shooting.

RIGHT: Ranges, chokes and shot sizes.

Centimetres	Range in metres					
Boring of Gun	*10*	*15*	*20*	*25*	*30*	*35*
True Cyl.	54	71	88	105	122	140
Imprvd. Cyl.	38	55	72	89	106	124
¼–Choke	34	49	64	80	97	115
½–Choke	31	44	58	73	90	108
¾–Choke	27	39	52	66	82	101
Full Choke	23	33	45	59	75	94

Inches	Range in yards						
Boring of Gun	*10*	*15*	*20*	*25*	*30*	*35*	*40*
True Cyl.	20	26	32	38	44	51	58
Imprvd. Cyl.	15	20	26	32	38	44	51
¼ Choke	13	18	23	29	35	41	48
½ Choke	12	16	21	26	32	38	45
¾ Choke	10	14	18	23	29	35	42
Full Choke	9	12	16	21	27	33	40

Target	Shot size	Target	Shot size
Geese	BB. 1 or 3	Grouse	6 or 7
Capercaillie	3, 4 or 5	Partridge	6 or 7
Bush fowl	4 or 5	Pigeon	6 or 7
Hare	4 or 5	Squirrel	6 or 7
Duck	4, 5 or 6	Teal	6 or 7
Crow	4, 5 or 6	Woodcock	6 or 7
Rabbit	5 or 6	Snipe	7 or 8
Pheasant	5 6 or 7		

Multi-Chokes

Multi-chokes allow increased flexibility in shotgun chokes and the most common chokes used in game guns are the flush-fitting type. It is very important that the multi-chokes match the nominal boring of the gun to accurately reflect the amount of choke present. The degree of choke is marked on the side of the tube. When the tube is installed, this marking is obscured, so chokes are grooved around their top edge to inform you of the degree of choke.

Note: The amount of choke present in a shotgun can only be confirmed by measuring the nominal boring of the barrel and the degree of choke at the muzzle. This requires a specialist tool called a barrel gauge. Regardless of whether your gun has fixed or multi-chokes, you need to confirm that the indicated choking is correct and not simply take it for granted, going by manufacturer's markings. You may find that those mystery misses could have a real, not a very mysterious reason – inaccurately marked chokes!

Multi-Choke Markings by Number of Grooves:

None: True Cylinder
One: Full
Two: Improved Modified
Three: Modified
Four: Improved Cylinder

Note: Extended multi-chokes are either colour-coded or the degree of constriction is written on the rim.

Choke Versus Air Resistance

The retort that you hear on firing a shotgun is not simply the cartridge exploding, but a mini-sonic boom as the shot column exits the muzzle, breaking the sound barrier. The shot stream meets a wall of air resistance, slowing it down and forcing the component pellets apart. The deformed pellets or "flyers", created by the pressure generated by passage through the barrel, peel away first. Then progressive erosion peels the outer layers of pellets, stretching them out, forming the shot string. It is this shot dispersion that gives the shotgun its margin for error and allows a moving target to be shot.

But the shot string needs to be balanced. If it is too stretched (long), there will be gaps big enough for the bird to pass through untouched. It is important to choose the appropriate choke for the distance at which the bird will be shot to produce a dense, short shot string, which is far more ballistically effective and has more knock-down power.

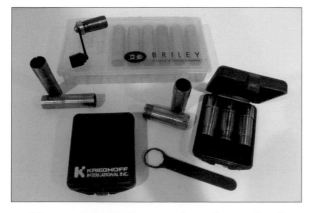

After market installation or being factory fitted, multi-chokes give greater flexibility.

Most common gauges 12, 16, 20, 28 and .410.

Cartridges

Choke and its effectiveness are very much affected by your choice of cartridge. It is very easy to be overwhelmed by the variety of cartridges available on the market today and each cartridge box promises better performance, more speed, denser patterns and harder shot. For the beginner and intermediate, it can appear that there is a cartridge solution that will be a short cut to improved performance and shooting success.

The reality is, all cartridges contain the same components – the difference is in the quality of the components and how they are made. The component parts are: the case, primer, powder, wad, shot pellets and crimp. The cartridge, when fired, acts like the piston in a bicycle pump. The primer is struck and ignites the powder, which creates combustion similar to fuel and air in a combustion engine when ignited by the spark plug.

This combustion, combined with the crimp or the way that the cartridge is closed, creates the pressure that propels the shot charge along the barrel. At this point, the wad performs a very valuable task, protecting the shot column from the heat of the powder combustion and acting as the piston and seal to ensure maximum efficiency from the pressure generated.

As the shot column travels down the barrel at great speed and under high pressure, it is inevitable that there will be some shot deformity. The more deformed pellets or "flyers", the poorer the pattern and the longer the string. Passage through both the forcing cone and choke creates many more deformed pellets. In fact, when choke was first used in shotguns, it actually resulted in worse or "blown" patterns.

The individual shot pellets need to be hard enough to resist deforming as they are pushed through the barrels at several hundred miles per hour. It was only with the introduction of antimony into the mixture of lead shot that it became hard enough to resist these forces and the damage they caused. Like most things in life, the best costs more and antimony is ten times the price of lead.

When you see a cartridge that has an antimony content of 5% or more, the antimony is the reason that cartridge is more expensive. High antimony cartridges are the premier products within every brand. If a manufacturer elects to use high antimony shot in a cartridge, they will use better quality components in the rest of the cartridge, resulting in an overall better performance.

Cheap cartridges have cheap components with the pellets containing little, if any, antimony. If you cut open a cheap cartridge, the shot will often be of irregular sizes and shapes which creates irregular patterns, long strings and low down-range energy – quality counts, especially at distance!

Components of a cartridge: case, primer, powder, wad and pellets.

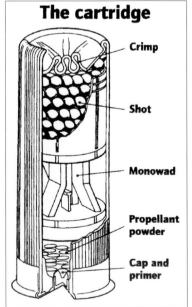

The cartridge

Crimp

Shot

Monowad

Propellant powder

Cap and primer

Inside of a cartridge.

Note: copper and nickel coatings have been applied to lead pellets to help avoid shot deformation and they work, however, the process requires that the coating is bonded to the pellet and is not just a copper wash, which does not improve pellet deformation at all.

Cartridge Components Impact Choice

When choosing a cartridge you should always consider:
1. Wad
2. Shot Size
3. Recoil

Taking them in order:

Wad

Wads are made from felt, fibre, or plastic. Many estates and plantations are insisting on the use of the bio-degradable felt and fibre wads for environmental reasons. However, from a ballistic point of view, the plastic wad is superior as its shot cup and petals has a wad with a built-in seal and shock absorbing piston to better protect the pellets on their journey down the barrel.

There have recently been many improvements in the felt and fibre wad cartridges – better materials, including a small orbitrator or seal that better seals and protects the shot column, so that their performance is only a small percentage short of the plastic wad.

Note: There are now cartridges with bio-degradable plastic wads. With the increasing use of clay competition over and unders, in an effort to match ballistics to the modern high pheasant, these shotguns can, and often do, have length-ened forcing cones. There are various opinions on the use of cartridges with felt wads in guns with lengthened forcing cones, indicating that the wads do not effectively seal the gasses, allowing "blow by" and poor patterns. The bio-degradable wad is the perfect solution to this debate.

Shot Size

First, it is important to understand that the number desig-nating pellet size is the opposite of the number designating gauge. In gauges, the bigger the number, the smaller the gauge – a 28 gauge shotgun is smaller than a 12 gauge. With shot sizes, the larger the number, the smaller the size of the individual pellet – number 9 shot is smaller than number 4 shot.

Proper shot size selection is essential to achieve clean kills. The shot size must achieve sufficient down-range energy to penetrate a vital organ. It can be a little confusing for the beginner and intermediate hunter, but for the more experienced sportsman, shot size becomes a matter of personal preference.

DETAILS OF SHOT SIZES (nominal)

Desig.	Diameter		Pellets	
	mm	in	per 10g	per oz
LG	9.1	.36	2	6
SG	8.4	.33	3	8
Spec. SG	7.6	.30	4	11
SSG	6.8	.27	5½	15
AAA	5.2	.20	12½	35
BB	4.1	.16	25	70
1	3.6	.14	36	100
3	3.3	.13	50	140
4	3.1	.12	60	170
5	2.8	.11	78	220
6	2.6	.10	95	270
7	2.4	.095	120	340
7½	2.3	.09	140	400
8	2.2	.085	160	450
9	2.0	.08	210	580

g = grams

SHOT SIZE EQUIVALENTS (nominal)						
English	Metric mm	American*	French	Belgian †	Italian	Spanish
LG	9.1	–	–	–	–	–
SG	8.4	00 Buck	–	9G	11/0	–
Spec.SG	7.6	1 Buck	C2	12G	9/0	–
SSG	6.8	3 Buck	C3	–	–	–
AAA	5.2	4 Buck	5/0	–	–	–
BB	4.1	Air rifle	1	00	00	1
1	3.6	2	3	–	1 or 2	3
3	3.3	4	4	–	3	4
4	3.1	5	5	–	4	5
5	2.8	6	6	5	5	6
6	2.6	–	–	6	6	–
7	2.4	7½	7	7	7½	7
7½	2.3	8	7½	7½	8	7½
8	2.2	–	8	8	–	8
9	2.0	9	9	9	9½	9

* also Swedish. † also Dutch.

NUMBER OF PELLETS IN SHOT LOAD									
Weight of shot		Size of shot							
g	oz	3	4	5	6	6.5	7	8	9
46	1⅝	228	276	356	439	492	552	726	944
42.5	1½	210	255	330	405	455	510	670	872
36	1¼	175	213	275	338	385	425	568	739
34	1³⁄₁₆	166	202	261	321	363	404	536	698
32	1⅛	157	191	248	304	342	383	504	657
30	1¹⁄₁₆	149	181	234	287	321	361	473	616
28.5	1	140	170	220	270	305	340	450	585
26.5	¹⁵⁄₁₆	131	159	206	253	284	319	418	544
25	⅞	122	149	193	236	268	298	395	513
24	²⁷⁄₃₂	118	143	185	227	257	286	379	492
23	¹³⁄₁₆	113	138	179	219	246	276	363	472
17.5	⅝	87	106	138	169	187	212	276	359
16	⁹⁄₁₆	78	96	124	152	171	191	252	328
12.5	⁷⁄₁₆	61	75	97	118	134	149	197	256
9	⁵⁄₁₆	44	53	69	84	96	106	142	185

Cartridge manufacturers often name a particular shell after the bird that they have designed it for or will print recommendations for the size and game combination on the box.

A simple formula is – small birds need small shot and big birds need big shot!

Recoil

Recoil is a big factor in cartridge choice. Recoil is not only unpleasant, but is the cause of flinches and second-barrel misses. Take two shells of equal Feet per Second performance – one can be smooth, with little felt recoil, while the other can be harsh and shoulder numbing. This disparity is directly proportional to the quality of the powders. In the first, lower recoil shell, the powder burns in a steady, progressive push; in the latter, the powder explodes violently.

The differences could be compared to the acceleration of a Rolls-Royce and a Hot Rod. Both will get you to your destination, but the journey is far smoother in the Rolls. Quality smooth-burning powders deliver speed at comfortable pressures, reducing felt recoil and delivering improved patterns.

Cartridge Speed's Effect on Lead

The speed of a cartridge has little impact on the forward allowance required to hit a bird passing at distance. A bird at forty yards, travelling at 40 mph, requires approximately 8 feet of lead. The difference in the lead required between cartridges of standard and high velocity is a few inches and the down-range velocity is practically the same.

Lead Cartridges

Magnum Loads

Shotgun cartridges containing more shot than a standard 12 gauge shell in a standard 2¾" cartridge require lower velocities to ensure safe chamber pressures. If higher velocities are required, cartridges are both longer and have increased pressure capabilities. Shotguns using high velocity cartridges need to be the correct chamber length (3" to 3½") and proofed to those chamber pressures. Magnum cartridges are primarily used for shooting dense patterns of large pellets at long distances.

High Brass versus Low Brass Loads

There was a time when a low brass cartridge meant a light load with small shot and lower velocity, while high brass implied a heavy load with bigger shot and higher velocity. However, today there is often very little difference in performance between the cartridges. In the past, high brass was required to support the paper and plastic cases from the pressures generated from higher velocity loads, but today's modern plastics are so strong that the high brass is no longer required and is more usually a marketing strategy.

Spreader Loads

Spreader or brush loads are cartridges that effectively spread or disperse the pattern quicker than a standard cartridge. They can be used to good effect when hunting grouse, woodcock and quail at close ranges or to effectively open the chokes of a fixed choke gun without the need to make any permanent alterations.

Non-Toxic Shot

It is illegal to shoot wildfowl with lead shot in the UK. Similar bans apply in the USA, Canada and many other countries worldwide. The ban required the introduction of non-toxic shot. The non-toxic shot options that are currently available are: steel, tin, bismuth, tungsten and Hevi-Shot™.

There are opinions for and against all five non-toxic cartridges:

Steel versus Lead

Steel is 70% lighter than lead. Take pellets of the same size, one of each metal, travelling at the same speed: at 40 yards down-range the lead pellet would retain twice the penetration potential of the steel pellet. A steel pellet, to retain the same energy, would have to be two sizes larger than the lead pellet.

However, steel shot is so hard it does not deform like lead shot, so steel shot has much shorter shot strings and tighter patterns. As a result, at distance there are more steel pellets in the pattern than lead. Lead shot deformity increases with velocity and 1,350 feet per second (FPS) is the optimum velocity for a dense pattern while steel shot can withstand velocities in excess of 1,500 (FPS) without deformity.

Note: When using steel shot, the general rule is to use a pellet size two times larger than lead; if you used number 4 lead shot, you would use number 2 steel shot.

Steel is the cheapest and most easily sourced non-toxic shot available. But be aware that it is not suitable for older guns (where the steel shot is harder than the barrels) or in guns with more than modified (half) choke. *It is essential, before using steel shot in any gun, to check that the gun has been proofed to be used with steel shot.*

Tin

Tin is very similar in density to steel. Tin also requires an increase in pellet size of 2: if you were using number 4 in lead shot, to have the same down-range velocity you would use number 2 tin shot.

Bismuth

Bismuth shot is high-performance and produces high-density patterns. It is marginally lighter than lead, but with similar properties, so it can be used in all shotguns.

Tungsten

Widely available, tungsten creates high-density patterns, is high-performance, and can be used in all shotguns. However, there are tungsten/iron mixtures which are *not* suitable for British-made guns.

Hevi-Shot ™

A combination of tungsten, nickel and iron, Hevi-Shot™ has a specific gravity of 12, making it heavier than lead. As a result of this density, Hevi-Shot ™ produces excellent patterns and has good penetration. The down side is, it is extremely hard. I would only recommend its use in guns proofed for steel shot. It is not suitable for vintage guns and guns with thinner walls.

Testing Choke and Cartridge Combinations

The only way to determine precisely how your choke and cartridge combination performs is to shoot the pattern plate. There you can determine if you have the correct mix of choke and cartridge to match the bird and distance with penetration and density.

If you have grooved a sound technique and your gun is correctly fitted, poor ballistics will result in clean misses and crippled birds. Consistent clean kills can only be achieved using the correct gauge of shotgun and the right combination of choke and cartridge to match the quarry's size and distance. You can read all of the data and charts you like, but only by patterning your shotgun will you know for certain what each combination should be.

Traditional Patterning at the Pattern Plate

Testing Pattern Density at the Pattern Plate

A typical pattern plate is a four foot square of ¼" thick steel, with the centre 8 feet above the ground. The plate is painted or greased and is fired upon to determine the number of pellets hitting the target within a 30 inch circle at specific ranges. Traditionally, the distance was 40 yards, but it is more useful to pattern at the yardages at which your quarry will be shot.

A 30 inch circle is drawn on the plate, and the centre marked. After you have fired at the plate, draw marks to divide the pellet pattern into quarters. Count the number of pellets in one quadrant and multiply by 4 to determine the number of pellets within the circle. This process should be repeated 5 times, painting the plate between shots.

If you own a digital camera, take a picture of the individual patterns, download the photos to your computer and you can do the pellet count at your leisure.

The next step is to cut open several of the cartridges and count the number of pellets in each – a tedious but necessary task. This will give you an accurate number of pellets in a particular brand and load. The number of pellets on the pattern plate is then subtracted from the number of pellets in the cartridge. This determines the pattern density and is expressed as a percentage. A percentage of 70 is considered an excellent density, but with

PATTERNS AT ALL RANGES

It is possible to calculate the number of pellets in a 75 cm (30 in) circle for any shot size and in any of the six borings of gun at the ranges stated (total pellets in the charge) and the following table:

Percentage of total pellets in 75 cm circle

Boring of Gun	Range in metres							
	20	25	30	35	40	45	50	55
True Cyl.	75	63	53	43	35	28	22	18
Imprvd. Cyl.	85	74	64	53	43	34	27	22
¼–Choke	90	80	70	58	48	39	31	25
½–Choke	97	86	76	64	54	43	34	27
¾–Choke	100	93	83	70	58	47	38	30
Full Choke	100	100	90	74	62	51	41	32

Percentage of total pellets in 30 in. circle

Boring of Gun	Range in yards								
	20	25	30	35	40	45	50	55	60
True Cyl.	80	69	60	49	40	33	27	22	18
Imprvd. Cyl.	92	82	72	60	50	41	33	27	22
¼–Choke	100	87	77	65	55	46	38	30	25
½–Choke	100	94	83	71	60	50	41	33	27
¾–Choke	100	100	91	77	65	55	46	37	30
Full Choke	100	100	100	84	70	59	49	40	32

Example: Charge 30 g (1¹⁄₁₆ oz) No. 6; find pattern at 40 yards for a ½–choke barrel. Total pellets: 287 multiplied by 60 (from the table above) and divided by 100. Answer 172.

OBSERVED VELOCITIES AND FORWARD ALLOWANCES

Eley standard game loads have a nominal observed velocity of 325 m sec (1070 ft sec). Eley high velocity loads have a nominal observed velocity of 340 m sec (1120 ft sec).

One might suppose that the change in velocity would make a noticeable difference to the forward allowance but, as will be seen from the table, the question is one of inches in a forward allowance measured in feet. The difference may for all practical purposes, be ignored.

COMPARISON OF CARTRIDGES

Forward Allowance

Birds crossing at 65 km ph (40 mph)   No. 6 shot

Range	30m	30yd	35m	35yd	40m	40yd	45m	45yd	50m	50yd
Standard Velocity	1.89m	5' 6"	2.26m	6' 8"	2.68m	8' 0"	3.29m	9' 6"	3.97m	11' 1"
High Velocity	1.81m	5' 3"	2.18m	6' 5"	2.58m	7' 8"	3.16m	9' 1"	3.02m	10' 8"

STRIKING VELOCITY (nominal)

Metres per second

Cartridge velocity level	Shot size	Range (metres)					
		20	25	30	35	40	45
Standard Game 325m/sec	BB	284	269	254	238	226	212
	3	272	253	236	219	203	188
	4	269	249	231	214	197	181
	5	265	244	224	205	188	171
	6	261	239	219	199	180	163
	7	257	234	212	191	172	154
	9	247	220	196	171	150	128
High Velocity 340m/sec	3	281	261	243	225	210	195
	4	277	257	238	220	203	187
	5	273	251	231	212	194	177
	6	269	247	225	206	187	169
	7	265	241	218	198	178	159

Feet per second

Cartridge velocity level	Shot size	Range (metres)					
		20	30	35	40	45	50
Standard Game 1070ft/sec	BB	942	860	815	770	729	688
	3	915	804	753	704	657	612
	4	905	788	735	683	635	587
	5	893	768	711	656	604	555
	6	883	752	691	634	579	528
	7	871	731	667	606	549	496
	9	840	680	608	537	475	412
High Velocity 1120ft/sec	3	948	827	772	722	677	632
	4	935	811	758	707	656	608
	5	922	792	733	678	626	574
	6	911	774	715	657	601	547
	7	897	755	689	628	570	514

modern cartridges, 80% is achievable. To complete the analysis, the pattern should be examined for distribution. A good pattern has an even spread with no gaps or tight concentrations.

Pellet Penetration

The process described establishes pattern density, but the only way to establish good pellet penetration is to take some old telephone directories, soak them in water and place them at the pattern board. Repeat the above shooting experiment, only this time, examine the depth to which the pellets have penetrated the phone directories.

Note: If patterning steel shot, do not shoot steel shot at a steel pattern plate because of the chance of ricochets! Use a 4 foot wooden sheet instead, but in either case always wear eye protection.

STRIKING ENERGY FOR INDIVIDUAL PELLETS

Metre kilograms | **Foot pounds**

Cartridge velocity level	Shot size	Range (metres)						Range (yards)					
		20	25	30	35	40	45	20	30	35	40	45	50
Standard Game (325m/sec) 1070ft sec	BB	1.65	1.48	1.34	1.17	1.04	0.93	12.4	10.3	9.24	8.25	7.38	6.56
	3	0.762	0.660	0.574	0.494	0.425	0.368	5.79	4.48	3.92	3.43	2.99	2.59
	4	0.614	0.526	0.453	0.389	0.330	0.278	4.68	3.54	3.08	2.66	2.30	1.97
	5	0.462	0.391	0.330	0.276	0.232	0.192	3.52	2.60	2.23	1.90	1.61	1.36
	6	0.365	0.306	0.257	0.212	0.173	0.142	2.80	2.03	1.71	1.44	1.20	1.01
	7	0.281	0.233	0.192	0.155	0.126	0.101	2.16	1.52	1.27	1.06	0.86	0.70
	9	0.152	0.119	0.096	0.075	0.055	0.040	1.18	0.77	0.62	0.48	0.38	0.28
High Velocity (340m/sec) 1120ft sec	3	0.814	0.702	0.608	0.522	0.455	0.392	6.22	4.73	4.13	3.61	3.17	2.77
	4	0.652	0.561	0.482	0.411	0.350	0.297	4.99	3.75	3.28	2.85	2.45	2.11
	5	0.490	0.414	0.351	0.295	0.248	0.205	3.76	2.77	2.37	2.03	1.73	1.46
	6	0.387	0.327	0.271	0.227	0.187	0.153	2.98	2.15	1.84	1.55	1.30	1.08
	7	0.299	0.248	0.202	0.167	0.135	0.108	2.30	1.63	1.36	1.14	0.93	0.76

A rough guide to the minimum requirements for a clean kill is: Small birds – 2 pellets each of 0.07 m kg (0.5 ft lb) striking energy; Medium birds – 3 pellets each of 0.12 m kg (0.85 ft lb) striking energy; Large birds – 4 pellets each of 0.21 m kg (1.5 ft lb) striking energy.

Testing Distances

Distances to the pattern plate typically used to check different aspects of shooting:

1. Point of Impact .... 25 yards
2. Choke and Cartridge.. 40 yards
3. Choke Regulation...... 40 yards
4. Barrel Regulation....... 40 yards
5. Gun Mount............... 32 yards
6. Gun Fit................... 16 yards

Analyzing the Results

From the information gleaned at the pattern plate you can determine the following:

1. How any given cartridge patterns in your shotgun; how the cartridge interacts with the fixed choke or different multi-chokes, to achieve the optimum 70–80% density of pellets evenly distributed over the 30 inch circle.

2. Exactly how the different degrees of choke correspond to the traditional percentages at any given range. These are: True Cylinder–40%, Improved Cylinder–50%, Modified–60%, Full–70%. This information will allow you to accurately determine the true performance of choke in your shotgun. If the pattern is producing 60% at 40 yards, it is a modified choke regardless of what degree is measured at the muzzle.

3. Once you know how the various cartridges and chokes pattern, you can regulate your shotgun by altering the amount of choke or the cartridge used until you achieve the desired distribution for a specific species and at the optimum range.

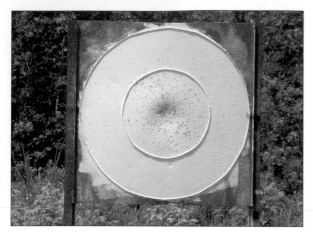

Testing at the pattern plate for pattern density at any given yardage.

PATTERN DENSITY

You can calculate the number of pellets in a 30 inch circle at a given range for any combination of shot, size and choke constriction by using the table below (total pellets in the charge) and the following table:

PERCENTAGE OF TOTAL PELLETS IN 30 INCH CIRCLE

American	CHOKE English	Constriction	20	25	30	35	40	45	50	55	60
True Cylinder	True Cylinder	.000"	80	69	60	49	40	33	27	72	18
Skeet-1	Improved Cylinder	.005"	92	82	72	60	50	41	33	27	22
Improved Cylinder	1/4	.010"	100	87	77	65	55	46	38	30	25
Modified	1/2	.020"	100	94	83	71	60	50	41	33	27
Improved Modified	3/4	.030"	100	100	91	77	65	55	46	37	30
Full	Full	.040"	100	100	100	84	70	59	49	40	32

Example: Say you'd like to find the pattern of a 1 oz. Charge of No. 6 shot at 40 yards for a modified barrel. First determine the number of pellets in the charge by using the table below. Answer: 225. Using the table above you can determine that the percentage of total pellets for a modified barrel at 40 yards is 60. Multiply the total number of pellets, 225, by 60 and divide by 100. Answer: 135 pellets in the 30" pattern at 40 yards.

PATTERN SPREAD

Diameter in inches covered by the bulk of the charge at various distances for different chokes.

DIAMETER IN INCHES

American	Choke English	Constriction	10	15	20	25	30	35	40
True Cylinder	True Cylinder	.000"	20	26	32	38	44	51	58
Skeet-1	Improved Cylinder	.005"	15	20	26	32	38	44	51
Improved Cylinder	1/4	.010"	13	18	23	29	35	41	48
Modified	1/2	.020"	12	16	21	26	32	38	45
Improved Modified	3/4	.030"	10	14	18	23	29	35	42
Full	Full	.040"	9	12	16	21	27	35	40

Example: The diameter of spread covered by the bulk of the charge for an improved cylinder or 1/4-choke at 30 yards is 35 inches.

APPROXIMATE NO. OF SHOT IN VARIOUS LOADS

Shot Size	Shot Diameter	2 oz.	1⅞ oz.	1⅝ oz.	1½ oz.	1⅜ oz.	1¼ oz.	1⅛ oz.	1 oz.	⅞ oz.	¾ oz.	½ oz.
#9	.08	1170	1097	951	877	804	731	658	585	512	439	292
#8	.09	820	769	667	615	564	513	462	410	359	308	205
#7½	.095	700	656	568	525	481	437	393	350	306	262	175
#6	.11	450	422	396	337	309	281	253	225	197	169	112
#5	.12	340	319	277	255	234	213	192	170	149	128	85
#4	.13	270	253	221	202	185	169	152	135	118	101	67
#2	.15	180	169	158	135	124	113	102	90	79	68	45

Misleading Information

There are several things that can negatively impact on your pattern testing and can result in misleading pellet counts and percentages. Be aware of the following:

1. Poor gun fit or inability to shoot straight.

2. Inaccurate pellet counts. Accurate pellet counts can only be achieved by cutting open the cartridges and physically counting the pellets.

3. Variation in cartridge performance. You should always shoot the pattern plate a minimum of 5 times per cartridge and choke combination.

4. Inaccurate pattern distances. Patterning is traditionally carried out at 40 yards, but patterns should be double checked at the ranges you actually shoot your quarry.

5. Inaccurate choke measurements. Choke can only be measured by comparing the nominal boring to the constriction present. The modern advances in choke taper technology and the lengthening of forcing cones can greatly increase the effectiveness of choke of any given constriction.

6. Cartridge variations. Cartridges of the same specifications from different manufacturers can vary greatly because of the different powders and components used.

Choke and Cartridge Combinations for Various Game Birds

Different birds have different flight characteristics and these impact upon the choke and cartridge combinations we need to match the species being hunted.

Note: Please refer to Eley Chart for Choice of Shot Size for Game and Wildfowl on page 68.

Walked-up and Upland Birds

Walked-up or upland birds are flushed from cover, so the majority of shots are at birds which are climbing and rising, straight or quartering away. These angles expose their most vulnerable areas, protected by only thin back muscles and a minimal layer of feathering. These birds are usually shot within 15 to 35 yards. Open chokes and smaller shot.

Passing and Crossing Birds

Where high-flying birds present passing or crossing shots, the wings and pectoral muscles are a shield between the pellets and the internal organs. These shots can be out past 40 yards. Tight chokes and larger shot.

Driven and Migratory Birds

Driven or migratory birds passing overhead have the breast bone, large pectoral muscles and heavier feathering which act like a Kevlar vest, protecting the vital organs. These shots can be well past 40 yards. Tight chokes and larger shot.

Decoyed Birds

Birds drawn to decoy patterns are shot within 20 to 35 yards, head-on or during flared landings which expose the most vulnerable and least protected areas of brain, spinal column and internal organs. Open chokes and smaller shot.

Note: Decoyed wildfowl will always require larger shot than pigeon or doves.

Shot Placement

The optimal place to ensure a clean kill is pellet penetration of the brain or spinal column. It is necessary to place a minimum of 120 pellets, centred on the target, to allow a minimum of 3 pellets to penetrate to have at least one strike a vital organ.

A clean kill is achieved by pattern density (amount of choke), penetration (mass and velocity of pellets) and, most important, the shooting skills to consistently centre the pattern on the target.

Decoyed pigeons in Paraguay.

Chapter 6
Equipment, Clothing and Accessories

As in any other sport, in wingshooting you need the correct equipment to consistently shoot well. You will need to invest in a potentially bewildering variety of clothing and accessories. It is essential that you make the right choices, as your equipment can have a considerable impact on your comfort and performance. So careful consideration should be given to the selection of the various items you will need to perform to the best of your ability.

Equipment can be broken down into two categories: **Essential and Recommended.**

Essential Equipment

Shooting Glasses

The first essential piece of equipment is a good pair of shooting glasses with polycarbonate lenses able to resist the impact of a pellet strike without shattering. I believe these should be compulsory when hunting, especially when hunting in cover. In addition to projectile protection, they should also provide UV/UVB protection from the sun's rays and, beyond safety, shooting glasses should enhance your vision; after all, the better you see it, the better you will hit it.

Shooting glasses need to perform three distinct functions:
1. Provide protection from the impact of a shotgun pellet. Even when the shot is in a safe direction, there is always the risk of being struck by a ricochet, an accidental discharge or an unsafe shot.

2. Wingshooting is an outdoor sport and protecting the eyes from the harmful effects of the sun's ultraviolet rays is vital, as in any outdoor activity.

3. We need to see the quarry as well as we possibly can. Shooting glasses should enhance definition and contrast, as different species of game birds have different-coloured plumage and are shot against a diverse range of backgrounds, in ever-changing light conditions. Shooting glasses with interchangeable lenses offer the distinct advantage of being able to select the correct lens tint to define and sharply contrast the various quarry in any light condition or background.

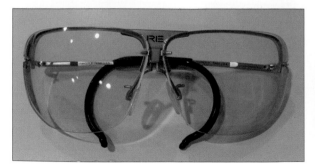

Shooting glasses offer three benefits: enhancing vision, protecting the eyes from errant pellets and from damaging UV rays.

RIGHT: The right choice in lens tint can enhance contrast, resulting in a sharper image.

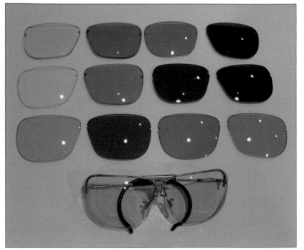

Selecting the right tint

In low light conditions, your pupils enlarge to allow more light into your eyes, resulting in softer focus. In bright light, your pupils shrink in size, constricting the amount of light, but allowing sharper focus. In differing light conditions, you need to find the right amount of tint that works best for you. The tint should allow as much light as possible to enter your eyes, without causing you to squint. For example, if you are shooting duck in the murky gloom of early dawn, then a clear or light lens would be a good choice, but for opening day of dove season, with bright egg-blue skies, a medium/dark lens would work better.

Fitting the Frame

The frame should sit high on your face, so that when your head is lowered to the correct shooting position, your eyes are looking through the centre of the lens. I prefer frameless shooting glasses so the frame does not restrict one's vision. The arms should have sprung temples and should be curled and cushioned so that they keep the glasses from slipping while shooting. An adjustable bridge not only allows the proper positioning of the glasses, but keeps them from touching the forehead, which allows airflow and prevents fogging.

Lenses

Lenses can have various coatings: "oleophobic" (resisting smudging), "hydrophobic" (rain runs off the lens), anti-glare, anti-reflective, and anti-fogging.

Note: If prescription lenses are required, they should be ordered in single vision, for distance only. Bifocal, trifocal or Varilux lenses create refraction similar to a straw in a glass of water and can cause problems in seeing the target. But if you cannot clearly see the primer of the cartridge in an open gun while loading, then you cannot see clearly if the "Safe" is on or off. A small bifocal at the bottom of the lens will allow you to see these and will not interfere with "hard focus" on the target.

Hearing Protection

The next essential piece of equipment is hearing protection, the piece of equipment that is all too often ignored by field shooters. I have heard many reasons and excuses – "I can hear better without them" is the most frequently repeated. Well, not for long, you won't! "I knock the stock against my muffs" is another reason. Well, learn to mount your gun correctly!

With the range and variety of modern hearing protection available, there are no excuses not to protect your hearing. With the recent advances in modern digital systems, they offer more than simple blockage of damaging noise. The report of a shotgun, though just a millisecond in duration, is louder than a jet plane at take off – 150 to 155 decibels.

Repeated exposure to sustained noise over 90–95 decibels will cause permanent hearing loss. You could compare this to a huge rock under a constant drip of water; it may take years but eventually the rock will be eroded away. Hearing damage is permanent and once sustained cannot be repaired.

Protection Options

The choices range from simple foam plugs to custom-fitted digital plugs that allow natural hearing, but clip and shut off sound at 90–95 decibels. Muffs, likewise, are available in a simple format of complete suppression to the same digital technology. Many consider that the muff offers better protection because some of the noise is transferred through vibration of the bone surrounding the ear and the muffs' cushions, fully enclosing the ear, suppress this. Many do not like muffs because they make wearing a hat with a full brim impossible.

I like the freedom that the custom (moulded to the ear canal) digital ear plugs allow. I can hear and converse normally with fellow shooters and have enhanced hearing in the field. I can hear the whistle signalling the end of a pheasant drive, the horn for "no more shooting in front" on the grouse moor and the whirr of wings as a bird flushes from cover, but still enjoy full protection. I also have a pair of digital muffs, because when you are sitting in a duck blind, in a whistling wind and freezing temperatures, they double as ear warmers!

Note: Anticipated recoil is greatly exacerbated by the noise generated at the discharge of a shotgun. Quality hearing protection, well-fitted, helps eliminate this and the tendency to flinch that it causes.

Basic Ear Protection

Disposable Foam Ear Plugs
Pro: Inexpensive, do not require custom fitting.
Con: Block all noise, often incorrectly inserted.

Rubber/Plastic Ear Plugs
Pro: Inexpensive, do not require custom fitting. Can be cleaned and re-used.
Con: Block all noise, often incorrectly inserted.

Passive Ear Muffs
Pro: Simple to use, inexpensive, keep ears warm in cold weather.
Con: Block all noise, can hinder gun mount, hot in warm weather.

There is a whole range of hearing protection; buy the best you can afford.

Custom Ear Protection

Custom Moulded Ear Plugs
Pro: Moulded to the individual's ear canals, improved fit giving improved protection.
Con: Block all noise.

Digital Electronic Ear Plugs
Pro: Moulded to the individual's ear canals, fitted with either analogue or digital electronic circuitry, allows normal range of sounds but can be adjusted to amplify. "Clips" (shuts off) at any noise over 90–95decibels; maximum protection.
Con: None for protection, but they are expensive: the digital is twice the price of the analogue.

Electronic Ear Muffs
Pro: More reasonably priced, but with the same benefits as the in-ear electronic plugs.
Con: Can hinder gun mount and can be susceptible to wind noise.

Head Protection

The hat is definitely an essential bit of kit. While a hat is basically a head covering, and can be made of a soft or stiff piece of cloth, a brimmed hat offers so many benefits you should never venture afield without one.

1. The extended brim covers the gap between forehead and glasses, offering essential protection from errant pellets that, falling between your shooting glasses and forehead, could enter the eye area.

2. In strong sunlight, the brim creates shade and looking from shade into light enhances visual clarity.

3. The brim keeps rain off your shooting glasses.

4. It protects you from harmful UV rays.

5. In cold weather a great deal of heat is lost through the top of your head. A hat reduces this loss, keeping you warmer in winter and, in warm weather, shades your head and keeps you cooler.

6. The brim creates a shadow over your face – essential when decoying pigeon and wildfowl.

There are an incredible number of hat styles, and the style you choose affects the amount of protection you get. If you choose a baseball cap or flat cap, it only shades your face, whereas a hat with a full brim shades your face, ears and neck.

The hat is an essential part of your shooting kit.

Note: In the USA, 144 square inches of hunter orange is required to be worn for upland bird hunting. A hunter orange baseball cap fulfils this requirement. If wearing a hunter orange vest, buy a hunter orange hat band that can be wrapped around any brimmed hat and fastened with Velcro.

Recommended Equipment

Gunslip
A gunslip can be made from either leather or canvas, with a fleece lining, with a top flap and buckle or full-length closure. Ensure that the fastenings are gun-friendly and will not scratch the stock or barrels. A good gunslip ensures that the gun is protected in transit and is safe to carry.

Cartridge Bag
For the wingshooter, a bag in the Payne-Galwey design is the most practical as its wide-open mouth and hinged flap allow quick access to your cartridges. The mouth of the bag should be large enough for you to reach into it, grip and remove cartridges without getting your hand trapped like the monkey's hand in the bottle. The outside should be canvas or leather, the inside lined with suede leather. The bag should be fitted with a wide, adjustable canvas shoulder strap, for ease of carrying. The bag should hang comfortably from the shoulder opposite the one off which you shoot. A simple flip back of the front flap will give you instant access to your cartridges, while allowing an unimpeded gun mount.

A cartridge bag is the most practical way to carry enough cartridges for a drive.

Cartridge Belt
The cartridge belt, in leather or canvas, with 25 pouches or clips, should hold a full box of cartridges. The advantage of a cartridge belt is that it places the weight on your hips, leaving your shoulders a free range of motion which is especially useful when rough shooting or pursuing upland bird hunting.

Shooting driven game, a cartridge belt is often worn as a backup for the times when a full bag of cartridges should prove inadequate – i.e., when one is in a real "hot spot". Take care that the stock doesn't get scratched against the cartridge rims in the belt.

Depending on the shooting you are participating in, various kit is required, from sunblock to a compass.

LEFT: A cartridge belt can make loading easy or act as a back-up magazine for those in the "hot spot".
(BETTWS HALL SPORTING)

Game Bag
The best game bag has a wide shoulder strap, is made of canvas with a waterproof inner lining for feathered game and an outside pocket of netting for placing rabbits.

Walking Stick
A sturdy walking stick is a real asset when walking up a steep grouse moor or fording a stream. The stick should be long enough so the depth of the water can be checked before putting "one's best foot forward" as well as being a steadying aid when walking on slippery surfaces. A good walking stick also makes a great coat and cartridge bag hanger when shooting on a peg.

Shooting Stick
A shooting stick with a leather folding seat also doubles as a walking stick.

Pocket Knife
A good pocket knife, especially one of the "Leatherman-type" multi-tools, can be indispensable for sorting the odd gremlin like an ejector overriding a cartridge or a loose forend screw – the list is endless.

Flask
Both thermos and hip flasks are handy for refreshment in the field.

Torch/Flashlight
Keep a good, bright light operational and to hand.

Priest
A priest is a weighted length of wood or horn used for the humane dispatching of wounded game.

Compass or Pocket GPS
For upland bird shooting or woodcock hunting in a dense wood, particularly in the USA, a compass and/or a pocket GPS unit can be very useful.

First Aid Kit
A small first aid kit with antiseptic, bandages and antibiotic ointment for you and your dog can save the day.

Insect Repellent

Spray or lotion insect repellent suitable for the region in which you are hunting is always advisable.

Sun Block

For bright sun or even on overcast days, protect yourself with a good 30 + UV/UVB sunscreen or sun block.

Boots and Socks

What price can you place on dry, warm feet? The right combination of boot and sock can make a world of difference to your shooting comfort. Shooting boots have to fulfil several criteria – first, the design and material must match the type of shooting in which you are taking part. Second, a good fit is as crucial to comfort and performance as the materials that make up the boot. Fortunately, today's modern hunting boots offers a combination of comfort, light weight, support, stability and traction that is essential to a bird shooter whatever his quarry.

Boots for Driven Shooting

There are different requirements of boots for grouse, pheasant and partridge shooting. The grouse moor has its own "climate zone" ranging from extremely hot in the summer, to rain, hail and snow in the fall and winter, with dry, wet or even frozen conditions where temperatures can range from 10°C to 30°C. These weather extremes, combined with steep and rough terrain, mean you will be walking great distances to the butts so it is important that your boots be worn-in and comfortable, have a good grip to prevent slipping and be of a material suited to the temperature. In warm weather, for example, waterproof hiking boots and gaiters are a much better option than the traditional "Wellington Boot".

When shooting driven pheasant and partridge, there is less walking as Guns are transported to a location close to the drive and walk a short distance to their pegs. The pegs are usually situated in pastures or arable fields which, in the fall, can be quite wet and muddy. The knee-height, waterproof "Wellington Boot" is the perfect choice for this situation.

Note: In 1827, The Duke of Wellington ordered a new pair of knee-height boots, requesting that they serve a dual role – he wanted to be able to wear them in battle then, in the evening, under long trousers in the mess.

The Russell Boot Co. makes a full range of hunting boots; a favourite of mine is the Art Carter Travelling Hunter. Smart enough for the plane, tough enough for the hunt.

The modern "Wellington Boots" are made of rubber or leather, lined with an insulating neoprene or leather, and have a full-length zipper to ease putting them on and taking them off. There are also leather boots of the same design, lined with "Gore-Tex".

Boots for Rough Shooting

With the exception of rough shooting for grouse, walked-up shooting over dogs in the UK does not involve walking great distances and the choice between "Wellington Boots" or boots and gaiters is a matter of personal preference.

Boots for Upland Bird Shooting

There are a great variety of game birds in the USA, hunted in very diverse habitat. The distances covered in a day's shooting can be considerable and good boots are as essential as a good gun and a good dog. According to terrain and temperature, boots can range from a strong, light boot with no insulation, made from leathers like Kangaroo, for hunting quail in the South, to a heavier, robust boot with extra insulation and waterproofing, for hunting chukar, pheasant and partridge in the North.

The amount of insulation in a boot is determined by the temperature, the amount of activity involved and the type of hunting. For really cold conditions and periods of inactivity, as in shooting from blinds and hides, 1,000 grams of Thinsulate works best. In temperate climates, 400 grams of Thinsulate is a good choice. In warmer climates, boots with 200 grams of Thinsulate, or no insulation at all will suffice. In very warm areas, proper Snake Boots should be considered an option as well.

Wader Boots for Decoyed Shooting and Wildfowling

Waders are waist-height waterproof boots, either unlined or neoprene lined, with fully sealed, taped seams, held up by shoulder straps, with an adjustable waist belt. These straps should always be fitted with quick release buckles and adjustable waist belt. The thickness of the neoprene lining, i.e., insulation, should be chosen to match the climate being hunted.

Socks

Even the best boots are worthless if worn without good socks. Avoid cheap socks made from acrylic, polyester or cotton materials. Look for good quality merino wool hiking or hunting socks or a wool blend with a mix of Lycra or nylon. Liner socks made of polypropylene worn under the heavier socks will wick perspiration away from your foot and transfer it to the outer sock. Keeping your feet dry is essential in preventing blisters. If shooting in really cold conditions, thicker socks and an insulating liner sock are a great combination.

Note: When shooting driven game in traditional attire, long socks are worn with breeks, but the liner sock is still recommended. Be sure that socks worn with breeks are of sufficient length to have a generous turnover.

Waders are as essential as a gun, dog and decoys when decoying wildfowl. (JOHN TAYLOR)

Shooting Gloves

There is no "Swiss Army Knife" glove. You will need several pairs of shooting gloves to fit the criteria of what (Quarry), what with (Shotgun type), where (Terrain) and when (Season). Shooting gloves should offer improved grip and control as well as protection from hot barrels.

Gloves should be thin, supple and should fit closely. If shooting in temperate weather, select a glove that gives good feel and a good grip, as this will give you better control. This glove is usually unlined and fits snugly, like a golf glove. If shooting in cold or wet weather, use insulated gloves and if it is extremely cold, the addition of a pair of thin liner gloves will keep your hands warm on the coldest of days. If decoyed shooting or waterfowling, a pair of waterproof mittens over your gloves will keep your hands warm and dry, but will need to be removed to shoot.

The new, close-fitting synthetic gloves are an excellent option. The "MacWet" glove keeps hands warm and waterproof; they give an excellent grip, even in wet conditions, and they allow a tactile feel that lets you pull the trigger without having to peel the index finger back as with traditional shooting gloves.

There can be no argument that the American-made "GripSwell Glove" is the glove for the job, both on the shooting ground and in the field, when shooting a side by side. Its layered protection is specifically designed to protect the barrel hand of the shooter, keeping fingers out of contact with hot barrels and giving maximum control.

The traditional shooting glove is made of "Pittards" leather, silk lined, with the trigger finger exposed on the trigger hand with a Velcro pull back. These gloves have knitted cuffs, are supple and warm but, unfortunately, not waterproof.

A collar and tie not only look good but will stop water creeping down your neck in a downpour.

Shooting Clothing

Clothing comes in two categories – Good Weather and Bad Weather. But whether shooting in the heat, the cold or the wet, coats and vests must be designed to allow good arm and shoulder articulation to enable a smooth gun mount, but not with so much slack as to impede it. Trousers or breeks (knickers) should be comfortable and not restrict one when walking, bending and crossing fences.

Good Weather Clothing: Driven Shooting

Traditional Tweeds
When looking for the very best clothing for Driven Shooting, you should look at what the professional guides and gamekeepers wear. It is no coincidence that all UK gamekeepers wear tweed breeks, vests and coats in combination with long socks, and for good reasons.

Tweed is a unique cloth – properly chosen, it will blend into the background and it does not go dark when wet like some materials. You do not want to become an inky blob against a lighter background, causing grouse, wildfowl and pigeon to flare away. Equally important, avoid bright, unnatural colours that would stand out rather than blend with the terrain.

Tweed does not chill when wet, and is robust enough to cope with hard use. I would always recommend that you purchase tweeds that are lined and waterproofed with "Gore-Tex", "Ventile" or a similar product. Early season days for grouse and partridge can be very warm but can also be very wet.

Clothing for grouse and partridge shooting should be lightweight and waterproof, so wearing your winter tweeds in the heat of summer will be uncomfortable. Far better to invest in a lighter-weight tweed and match it with a waterproof jacket and over-trousers. If it is too warm for a coat, then a sleeveless shooting vest or "Gilet" is an excellent option. Likewise, "Wellington Boots" are too hot for summer, so boots and gaiters are the better, more comfortable choice.

As the season progresses, medium or heavy weight tweeds are worn. As it becomes really cold, thin layers, starting with thermal underwear, trap heat and insulate better than a heavy and restricting coat.

Breeks, Ties and Cravats

Breeks should always be "plus twos" and many prefer "plus fours" as there are no cuffs to snag and muddy, and they are well-suited to be worn with "Wellington Boots" or boots and gaiters. The "plus twos", so called because they overhang the top of the boots by "plus two inches", act as an eave to stop water from getting into the boot.

A shirt and tie or cravat (Ascot) is traditionally worn and, putting style and tradition to one side, either one works very well at keeping rain from running down your neck, and keeping you warm in crisp winds. Even though many are now choosing not to wear a tie, an open collar can be considered too casual at a proper shoot.

Upland Bird Shooting

Brush Pants and Chaps

Brush pants, briar pants or chaps are designed specifically for the Upland Shooter. These come in a whole range of fabric weights and can be waterproof and snake proof. Your selection needs to match the terrain and protect you from the type of briars, brambles and branches in which you will be hunting. Choose the most comfortable weight and material for the weather and temperature you expect

Tough cover requires tough clothing.

to experience. If you are hunting in really heavy cover, "Turtle Skin" chaps or the Cabela's "Briar Guard", faced with "Turtle Skin", are lightweight and waterproof. For colder weather, Columbia "Briarshun" pants are my personal recommendation.

Hunting Shirts

Hunting shirts need to be protective, comfortable and, if decoying or wildfowling, conceal you from the quarry. The sleeves at the shoulders need to permit full articulation for free movement and reach, particularly overhead. Breathable fabrics with underarm vents ensure airflow for comfort and double-layer elbow patches provide briar and bramble protection.

Hunting Vests

Choose a vest that can protect you in the thickest of cover – a dry-wax finish or a waterproof lining will keep you dry on wet days. In warmer weather, mesh panels allow cooling ventilation. Whether you need Blaze Orange to stand out, or camouflage to blend in, choose a vest for overall comfort plus protection against briars, brambles and the elements.

The upland bird hunter needs to carry, on his person, everything he and his dogs may need during the day – cartridges, water, remote controls etc. – the list is long and the load is heavy. The majority of the equipment is strategically packed in and about a myriad pockets, hung on hooks and loops and added to, hopefully, by a limit of birds.

Storage pockets should be bellowed and hand-warmer pockets are a real boon in colder weather. A blood-proof game bag is useful with front and back access for easy storage of birds with a zip to open for emptying and cleaning. Try to find one with gun-friendly buttons, zips and buckles that will not scratch or mar woodwork or bluing; avoid loading cartridge loops and store cartridges and hang whistles, compasses, GPS and dog controller on the opposite side from the shoulder you shoot off for the same reasons.

Though hunting vests are well-designed for the stowage and even distribution of this load, they are not designed to enable a smooth gun mount. Nearly all vests stop at the waist, so all of the weight is borne on your shoulders. As your limit is harvested and birds are placed in the vest, you are pulled backwards by the combination of heavy gear and game. All of this weight impedes your gun mount; it restricts your freedom of movement from poorly-placed, overstuffed pockets which can get in the way. A careful choice of vest and the way you distribute the necessary equipment for a long day in the field can have a big impact on your gun "mount and move" to the bird.

Bad Weather Clothing

A good vest makes carrying all your cartridges and equipment easy work. (TERRY ALLEN)

Jackets and Sweaters

"Gore-Tex", the breathable and waterproof membrane invented by William Gore, revolutionized outdoor clothing. It is used like the jam in a sandwich, between the outer layer and the lining of jackets, coats, sweaters, breeks, trousers and boots.

Technical fabrics like "Ventile" use the properties of cotton fibres which swell when they become wet; the way the cloth is woven causes a uniform expansion and the fabric closes up, becoming water and windproof. "Ventile" fabric has the advantage of being used as a single layer, so "Ventile" coats are lighter. However, for the fabric to work, it needs to absorb a certain amount of water before becoming waterproof and this can cause the fabric colour to darken, which can be a disadvantage in certain hunting circumstances.

All overcoats must protect you from the elements, allow freedom of movement and permit a smooth gun mount. They should not have any fastenings that can mark a shotgun. With the exception of upland bird hunting where visibility is a legal requirement, your coat should blend in with the background in which you are shooting.

Whatever the manufacturer, you should look for the following criteria in a jacket: it should be made of 100% waterproof, breathable fabric, windproof with adequate insulation to match the weather conditions you will experience, give superb comfort (you cannot shoot to the best of your ability if you are uncomfortable or restricted) and have hand-warming pockets. A removable fleece lining is a bonus as are large, bellow-shaped cartridge pockets with waterproof lining, drainage holes and a strap to hold the pocket flap open when shooting. Other good additions include inside security pockets, storm cuffs (which should be adjustable), a detachable hood, and finally, a "poacher's pocket" that can be unsnapped and flapped down to use as a seat.

Unless the weather is exceptionally cold or wet, I prefer to shoot in a heavy sweater that is "Gore-Tex" lined, windproof and waterproof and, over the sweater, a sturdy shooting vest. This combination allows me the greatest freedom of movement when shooting.

The clothing you wear and the equipment you use when hunting are as important as the shotgun you shoot. Your choices impact on your comfort and performance, and good selections can allow you to participate to the best of your ability. When considering both quality and price, remember that while quality products may initially cost more, in the long run, you will be paid back with years of good service. As the saying goes, "There is no such thing as bad weather, only bad clothes."

A Barbour sweater and a Gilet make a perfect shooting combination,
allowing unrestricted movement.

Chapter 7

Eye Dominance

Starting Out

The first and essential test before learning to shoot is to establish which is your *dominant* or *Master Eye*. Your Master Eye determines the shoulder you will shoot off, the stance you will adopt, your clothing and equipment choices, and how you will have your gun fit.

It is simply amazing how many experienced shots come for lessons or a gun fitting and have eye dominance conflicts. Often they are totally unaware of any problems or convinced that they are dominant in the wrong eye. As they never had their eye dominance accurately diagnosed at the outset of their shooting career, they have spent years of frustration wondering why they cannot shoot better than they do.

It is your Master Eye that determines which shoulder you should shoot off, not whether you are right-handed or left-handed.

In a perfect world, we all would have begun our shooting careers with a first lesson which established our Master Eye and we would have started our learning curve shooting off the shoulder of our dominant eye. In reality, there are many older shooters who have never received instruction at all or they started taking lessons after they had been shooting off the wrong shoulder their whole shooting life.

What is Eye Dominance?

Eye dominance is the visual equivalent of being left-handed or right-handed. The human being is preprogrammed to see with two eyes. This binocular vision or seeing with both eyes open (stereoscopic–three dimensional vision) originates in the visual cortex of the brain and links the focusing mechanisms of the two eyes together.

The optic nerve is made up of a million individual nerve fibres. It travels from the retina to the brain's vision centre, carrying electrical data that the brain interprets into images. You may wonder why we have two eyes but see only one single picture. To achieve this, the two eyes have to work in tandem. They both look at an object, but one perceives it a nano-second before the other.

The images are overlaid, one on top of the other, in the brain. Their convergence creates our ability to place objects in space by size and distance, known as *stereopsis*, more commonly known as *depth perception* – an essential requirement for shooting a moving object.

The first registered image to arrive on the visual cortex is the one arriving from the *dominant* or *Master Eye*. If you shoot off the shoulder opposite to your dominant eye, the dominant eye looks across the gun and disrupts the process of binocular vision. The result is confusion in the eyes' focusing mechanisms, and a shot that is missed some four inches to four feet off-centre.

4" to 4' OFF TARGET

1⅞"

Too much drop at comb can cause cross dominance.

LEFT: Impact of cross dominance.

Binocular and Monocular Vision

It is widely and correctly believed that you can only shoot to your full potential with both eyes open (Binocular Vision). You have greater depth perception, increasing your ability to judge distance, an essential skill in wingshooting. Shooting with one eye closed (Monocular Vision) is a definite handicap. Yes, with practice, perceived distance can be learned. However, the loss of both peripheral and spatial awareness can create unexplained misses and frustration in the field.

There are the unfortunate few who suffer from central vision issues, where neither eye is dominant. This situation is further complicated by the fact that central vision can occur to a fluctuating and variable degree.

Eye dominance is not an equal opportunity affliction – 75% of women and 35% of men experience eye dominance conflicts that adversely impact their shooting consistency. From youth to middle age there can be subtle changes in eye dominance.

Robert Churchill wrote that many of his middle-aged clients were not so much cross dominant, but their eye dominance softened with age, resulting in almost central vision. His answer to their problem was to give extra cast to their guns. You will often find a Churchill shotgun with excessive cast or one that has been "swept at the face" to achieve the same effect.

But in the final analysis, it is a definite advantage to shoot with both eyes open (Binocular Vision). There can be no argument, YES it is! Acquisition of the bird is quicker, there are no blind spots to create unwanted head movement, and the bird will appear closer and slower.

Try this experiment: with your head erect and looking straight ahead, hold your left arm out to your side, so that your hand is just in your peripheral vision. Slowly move it backwards until it disappears. Now close your left eye and, keeping your head fixed and still, bring your left hand slowly forward until it appears again in your peripheral vision. It has a lot further to go before you can see it, doesn't it? *All that extra distance your arm travelled is out of sight with your left eye closed.*

I hope this experiment demonstrates one of the disadvantages of shooting with only one eye open (Monocular Vision). You would never drive a car or attempt to catch a ball with one eye closed! The eyes work in tandem and to close one is a handicap to both eye *and* hand co-ordination.

Left eye dominant.　　　*Right eye dominant.*

Diagnosing the Master Eye

There are many ways to determine your eye dominance. The simplest is, with both eyes open, pick out an object at distance. Raise your arm and point at it with your forefinger. Close first one eye then the other. You will find that your finger will remain firmly pointing at the object with one eye – that is your *Master Eye*. It will move off-line with the other, which is your *Non-Master Eye*.

If your finger moves an equal distance on either side of the object, this is referred to as *Central Vision*, where there is no dominant eye. Another self-test is to take a piece of cardboard with a hole pierced in it. Hold it at arm's length and look through the hole at a

Central vision.

Using a used kitchen roll tube allows a more accurate diagnosis.

Alternative eye dominance test.

distant object. Now bring the card back to your face. The eye that it naturally comes to is your *Master Eye*.

There are several variations on this theme, all of which are useful. I like to use a used kitchen or toilet roll or CD in place of the piece of cardboard; either one allows a more accurate diagnosis of the degree of dominance. Eye dominance is not cast in stone and is not affected by visual acuity. The Master Eye can often be the weakest eye when measured optically. Fluctuations in dominance can occur with fatigue and with the onset of middle age.

If you find that you miss birds at certain angles or directions or you inexplicably lose sight of the bird or stop the gun on certain shots, these can be the symptoms of dynamic or shifting dominance.

Gun Interference

Consider that at the critical moment of taking the shot you are placing a three-foot long, black stick directly between your eye and the point of focus (bird). This can create a number of Master Eye conundrums, and in the split-second of taking the shot, can often result in an inexplicable miss, though you could have sworn the bird was "in the bag".

You should never look directly at the gun, but your subconscious has to be aware of it in your peripheral vision to recognize where it is pointing. The various configurations of barrels, ribs and beads can influence this, drawing the Master Eye's point of focus away from the bird. This can explain why you can shoot well with one gun and poorly with another – this is especially true of side by sides and over and unders.

Remember that these eye dominance tests do not allow for the interference created by the gun, the barrels and their configurations. So any initial test needs to be re-checked with the unloaded gun correctly mounted in the shoulder.

The gun can impact on eye dominance, creating visual interference.

Definitions, Faults and Fixes

True Dominance

Your Master Eye is on the same side as the shoulder from which you naturally shoot. No fault, so no fix is needed.

True Cross Dominance

Your Master Eye is on the opposite side of the shoulder from which you are shooting. This is a common fault and there are several fixes.

A shotgun's barrels should be a subconscious awareness in your peripheral vision.

Fix Number One

For the many shooters who are diagnosed with true cross dominance, the solution is simple: learn to shoot off the same shoulder as your dominant eye. This is practical and easy if you are starting out in your shooting career, but it is not so easy for the large number of more experienced shooters who have always shot off the "wrong" shoulder.

They may not be able to change to the "correct" shoulder because of a vision handicap or they may lack the co-ordination to be able to shoot off the other shoulder. Often, the very experienced shot may be unable or unwilling to make the commitment to learn to shoot off the opposite shoulder and will have to either close the cross dominant eye or obscure it in some way.

If the decision is made to switch shoulders, you need to be willing to take the time to relearn the barrel–target relationship, and re-educate your brain on the differences in the pictures that have always worked for you in the past.

Changing your shooting shoulder will take great willpower and effort on your part. Your shooting could suffer, your scores will drop and your limits will be harder to come by until you have re-learned the pictures that make it all work. Over time you will begin to recognize the difference between seeing with one eye (Monocular Vision) and two eyes (Binocular Vision) in the bird/target-to-muzzle relationship.

Learning to shoot off the other shoulder can be very frustrating and many give up. However, with perseverance, you will learn that by shooting with both eyes open you can focus on the bird better and you can guide the gun in your peripheral vision, the same as you would when riding a bike or driving a car. You look where you are going or where you are pointing, and not at your vehicle or your gun.

If, for whatever reason, you cannot make the switch to the opposite shoulder, all is not lost. There are many cures for True Cross Dominance problems, some as old as shooting itself.
See Solutions: Obscuring the Master Eye, Cross-over Stocks, Fibre Optic Sights and Shooting Glasses.

Central Vision

There is no Master Eye. Each eye perceives the image equally and simultaneously. This is a more uncommon fault and there is only one fix.

One could be forgiven for thinking that this would be the perfect shooting scenario and people with central vision can usually shoot moderately well. Unfortunately, depending on the angle and direction of the bird's flight, one or the other eye will take over and, if it is the off-shoulder eye, a "mystery miss" is the result.

Fix for Central Vision

The unlucky few with central vision or fluctuating eye dominance have to take some measure to block or obscure the dominant eye, as shooting off the opposite shoulder is not an option. It may be that shooting with both eyes open might not be best or absolutely right for everyone.
See Solutions: Obscuring the Master Eye, Blinking, Cross-over Stocks, Gun Fit, and Shooting Glasses.

Partial Dominance

With the onset of middle age, someone who had true dominance all of their life can experience an increased interference from the non-dominant eye.

Fix for Partial Dominance
Changing shoulders would not be an option.
See Solutions: Obscuring the Master Eye, Blinking, Cross-over Stocks, Shooting Glasses.

Fluctuating or Shifting Dominance

These incidences of shifting or fluctuating eye dominance are difficult to detect. You generally shoot well, but have days where, with no explanation, you under-perform. This fault is caused by stress, tiredness or the inability or failure to maintain hard focus on the bird.

Fix for Fluctuating or Shifting Dominance
Switching shoulders is not an option.
See Solutions: Obscuring the Master Eye, Blinking, Gun Fit and Shooting Glasses.

Solutions

Obscuring the Master Eye
The easiest and most successful solution is to close or block the vision of the Master Eye which allows straight shooting off the opposite shoulder. The major drawback to this solution is it seriously disrupts the binocular vision (stereoscopic–three dimensional), so valuable to shooting a shotgun.

The traditional method was to place a smudge of Vaseline, a small, triangular piece of frosted Scotch Magic Tape or a Magic Dot on the lens of the shooting glasses over the centre of the dominant eye. Then, when the gun is correctly mounted, with the head on the stock, one of the corners of the triangle or the Magic Dot covers the centre of the Master Eye. Up until the shot is taken, the brain is receiving binocular signals in both central and peripheral fields of vision and can co-ordinate the target acquisition. Then, at the moment the shot is taken, the "patch" allows the non-dominant eye to take over and become the Master Eye.

Today there is a new and very effective method that can effectively change eye dominance – Fresnel Prism Lens Films. These are used in corrective ophthalmology and need to be carefully and professionally applied on the shooting glasses over the centre of the Master Eye.

Another new solution for this issue is called *Shotspot* – a product that takes the masking of the Master Eye to a new level of "correction without obstruction", utilizing a Swiss-made optical foil. The surface of the foil contains microscopic patterns which ensure that optical consistency is maintained. While the

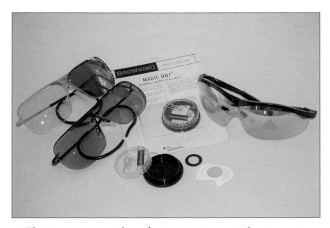

There are many ideas for correcting eye dominance.

LEFT: The best cure for cross dominance or central vision is the Shotspot.

foil "masks" by degrading the image and disrupting light transmission, it does so in a regular, controlled, optically correct manner. The *Shotspots* are positioned to ensure that the full advantage of binocular vision is maintained, at the same time eliminating the fluctuating eye dominance that disrupts the shooting process.

Blinking

If the eye dominance is central, partial or fluctuating, a technique can be learned where both eyes are kept open (Binocular Vision) during target acquisition and the initial move to the target. Then, on completion of the gun mount, as the shot is being taken, the non-shooting eye is blinked. This technique requires learning the correct timing of when to blink the eye and that the timing can be different on the various quarry presentations. (Be aware that closing an eye can result in aiming!)

Cross-over Stocks

It is possible to have a gun stock shaped so you can shoot off the shoulder opposite your Master Eye. The Cross-over Stock has such a considerable degree of cast or bend in the stock that it places the rib of the gun in line with your Master Eye. The degree of this cast or bend depends entirely on the degree of dominance. In cases of Partial Dominance, a little extra cast can work wonders. Central Vision would require a Semi-Cross-over Stock, and True Cross Dominance would need a Full Cross-over Stock.

(Note: excessive cast can create more "felt" recoil.)

Fibre Optic Sights

Fibre optic rods or sights channel light down a narrow tube along the sight plane of the shotgun. When the gun is correctly mounted, a bright, fluorescent dot appears at the end of the "tunnel" created by the tubing and can only be seen by the eye in line with the rib. This effect has been used to enable cross-dominant shooting.

Shooting Glasses

Experiments using different coloured lenses in the same shooting glasses have had great success. A grey lens is fitted over the Master Eye and a lighter-coloured lens is fitted over the non-dominant eye. This causes the non-dominant eye to become the Master Eye.

Some shooters who are near-sighted or far-sighted have prescription shooting glasses made with their far-sight or distance prescription in the eye that matches the shoulder from which they shoot.

Others who wear contact lenses or have corrective laser surgery, have their "distance eye" match their shooting shoulder. This eliminates the need for prescription shooting glasses as well.

Fibre optic sight, which can only be seen by the eye on the side of the shoulder being shot off, can often cure cross dominance.

Gun Fit

For the shooter with central vision and those middle-aged shooters where neither eye is dominant, corrections can be made with subtle stock alterations. A higher comb height can help with cross dominance. If hard focus is maintained on the target, the gun softens in the peripheral vision. This reduces the tendency to "cast a glance" back to the bead that so often occurs when a gun is set up with a lower comb. Experimentation at the pattern board and on targets is required to find the right combination of adjustments to "cure" the specific degree of eye dominance.

Often we try to improve our marksmanship by changing our shotgun, cartridge or choke, but the mystery misses are, in many cases, eye dominance conflicts that are, as you can see, simple to diagnose and simple to fix.

Chapter 8
The Fundamentals of Straight Shooting

Eighty percent of all misses are caused by bad habits or poor fundamentals; straight shooting requires mastery of these fundamentals. To hit a small moving target consistently, especially at distance, requires an enormous amount of skill. To develop this skill, you need the correct footwork, stance and posture, combined with a grooved gun mount. The purpose of the fundamentals is to ensure that the body is in the correct position throughout the swing and move to the target. Poor fundamentals lead to compensations and extra movements in the "swing and move" which result in misses.

You need to develop a repeatable and efficient "swing and move" to the target. The reason good shots are so consistent is, when they shoot, there is no wasted movement.

Set Up

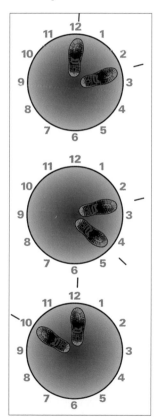

TOP: *Foot position for straight away or incoming bird.*

CENTRE: *Foot position for quartering bird to the right.*

BOTTOM: *Foot position for quartering bird to the left.*

Balance is essential to compete well in all sports and shooting is no exception. If you can start and finish a shot in balance, you'll hit more birds, it is as simple as that. Balance is created by the interaction of the skeletal and muscular systems. The skeletal structure is like the girders of a tall building – it is the core of your strength – and the core is the engine of your body. The muscles are the cladding connecting the components of the skeleton. When you use the skeleton correctly to provide strength, you need only a small amount of muscle-effort. Your movements become smoother and better co-ordinated and you are able to move efficiently in any direction.

Footwork

"The deadliest move a wingshooter can make is with his feet".

Foot position and footwork are other important parts of all sports. In boxing, for example, the correct positioning of the feet and the step create the power base for a solid punch. Similarly, in shooting, the feet create the power base for a controlled and efficient move to the target.

There are two classic shooting styles. One is "The Stanbury Style", which is a simple step into the line of flight, where lateral movement is achieved by the shooter stepping right or left into the line of flight.

The other is "The Churchill Style" – when birds are to be taken in front, you step into the line, moving your body weight fully forward. If the bird is high and incoming, it is taken off the back foot. Crossing targets are accommodated by lifting the heel of the foot opposite the target's direction, and the toes pushing and rotating the body into the line of flight.

I like a blend of the two. If you visualize yourself standing in the centre of a clock, your leading or left foot would be on the 2 of the 12 o'clock and your right

Stanbury style for crossing and quartering shots, a small step into the line of flight.

Churchill style for a high incoming bird; the heel of the front foot is raised in a smooth transfer of weight onto the back foot.

Churchill style for crossing and quartering birds, lifting the heel opposite the line of flight and the toes pushing and rotating the body into the line of flight.

foot would be pointing halfway between the 2 and 3 o'clock mark, with 6 to 8 inches between your heels. An imaginary line drawn from your right heel and passing though the big toe of the left foot would point directly at the target.

Note: This would be reversed for the left-handed shooter, with the right foot on the 1 of the 12 o'clock and the left foot halfway between the 9 and 10 o'clock mark.

This position places the gun at a 45 degree angle to the body and opens the shoulder pocket up nicely for an unimpeded gun mount. A narrow stance about 6 to 8 inches between the heels is far better than a stance that is too wide. A wide-spread stance causes the shoulder nearest the direction of rotation to drop, resulting in the windscreen-wiper effect of rolling off the target line. The only time a wide stance should be adopted is when shooting on a slope or hill. Then the stance should be opened and the knee of the leading leg flexed. In this manner you can establish a sound and square footing on the incline.

Your feet should be squarely underneath your body. This allows an uninhibited rotation, and a relaxed pivot around your body's central axis. The swing should be created with your legs, hips and torso, using your whole body to swing the gun, not just your arms. Try to start thinking about your body as a tank turret turning the gun, with your hands and arms lifting and pointing the gun to the target.

When the opportunity of a double presents itself, you will need to step from one bird to the other. This move should be practised in your gun mounting drills. Note that this step is a small movement of inches, not a lunge of feet; it is more about pivot and direction than an actual stride.

Note: For the upland bird shooter, hunting in heavy cover, briar and bramble can impede or make the step impossible. Similarly, hunting in second growth poplar or heavily wooded areas, the quarry is more of a fleeting image than sharp target. I consider this shot to be truly an "Instinctive or Reactive Shot" and, as I have not been able to work out the kinks in this shot for myself, I would not have the audacity to advise others how to do it!

When "quick is the step, then swift will be the action" then footwork is the anchor of the Instinctive Shot"!

Posture

Having your back in the correct position is critical for optimum performance in any sport. Correct posture relates directly to muscle control and functional strength, which are essential to any efficient and dynamic movement. Posture is not static; it is a momentary alignment of individual muscles, and their smooth movement is determined by a fluid transition from one posture to the next. If one muscle or link in this dynamic chain is out of sync, it will result in poor performance.

Posture is created by the combination of footwork and body shape that achieve the essential head stability and consistent gun mount required to consistently hit a moving target.

Head Position

Your head position and its stability throughout the shooting sequence have more impact on the successful outcome of a shot than any other factor. During the act of shooting, any unwanted or uncontrolled head movement negates gun fit and makes even the best-honed skills go awry. Great emphasis should be placed on the importance of the correct head position and the rigid maintenance of it throughout the process of taking a shot.

To emphasize this importance, I would ask you to carry out two short experiments which demonstrate the effect of (unconscious or conscious) unwanted head movement.

With your arms hanging comfortably at your sides, look across the room and pick out an object or mark. Using your leading arm (the one that grips the forend) swing your arm up, forefinger extended, and point at the object (in the same manner as a "quick draw").

"Right on the Button"! You can try it again and again, and you will always get the same result. Through the gift of hand and eye co-ordination, without conscious reference to your finger, you will always accurately point at the object you look at.

Now, repeat the exercise, but this time, as your finger comes on to the object, lower your head. You will find that you are pointing over the object! Now repeat this exercise, moving your head left and right as you come on to the point of aim. You will never be on the object.

To emphasize this effect, pick out the same object and this time simply point at it. Gently rotate your head in a slow circular motion. Your next discovery will be that your finger will match your head's movement and rotate around the object you are pointing to. The result will always be the same – off the mark in the opposite direction of the involuntary and unwanted head movement.

Correct posture is a combination of footwork and body shape that ensures essential head stability and a consistent gun mount.

The correct head position creates a consistent gun mount.

From these experiments you should plainly see how head movement impacts on your shooting. You will never shoot consistently if you move your head when taking a shot. Whatever the cause, poor gun fit, (dropping, lifting or rolling the head to fit yourself to the gun), incorrect gun mount or poor footwork and posture, you will never shoot consistently if you move your head.

There are subtle differences in the individual head position to allow for the differences in physique. I always observe greater head movement from clients with longer necks than the shorter-necked individuals. The head position needs to complement the build and physique of the individual when they are comfortably poised, head gently extended with the chin pointing down and turned slightly to the right (left for the left-handed). Once the eyes have locked on target; *"the head position must not be moved except by the body's rotation"*.

Imagine your body is a tripod and your head is a video camera. The tripod's smooth rotation ensures a clear, sharp picture. So how do we go about creating our "tripod"? Head position is achieved by the combination of footwork and stance that places the head in the correct position to minimize unwanted head movement and allows a consistent gun mount throughout the swing and move to the target.

This correct position always begins with your feet. Adopt the proper balanced stance, your upper torso slightly inclined at the waist, neutrally facing the anticipated flush or line of flight. Your head is slightly forward and to the right with your chin parallel to the ground. This body shape is similar to a boxer's defensive stance, preparing to throw a left jab, but protecting his chin. This position opens your shoulder pocket up nicely for an unimpaired gun mount. Your head is in the correct position to receive the comb and stock into the cheek without any head movement, keeping your head forward and in the gun while the shot is taken.

Components of Good Head Position

1. Adopt a good stance.
2. Check that your gun is well-fitted.
3. Practise and groove your gun mount.
4. Maintain proper weight distribution on the shots conducive to head-lifting.
5. Reinforce head position by creating an anchor under the cheek bone.
6. Create the trigger of the repeated promise "to stay in the gun" throughout the shot.

Ready position – butt of the stock touching the tendon which joins the biceps to the pectoral muscle.

Both hands work together, lifting the gun in a parallel motion.

The front hand lifts and points the gun; the rear hand hinges, following its direction.

The completion of the mount is to the cheek, not to the shoulder.

Gun mount

It is impossible to achieve an accurate gun fit without an accurate gun mount. A good gun fit requires the fundamentals of good shooting: proper stance, grip and a stylish technique of gun mounting. Robert Churchill stated: "A man with a good gun mount will always outshoot the bungler with the best tailored pair of game guns London can produce."

"Eighty percent of all misses are caused by a poor or incorrect gun mount". A shotgun is a dynamic tool of movement, and a good gun mount maximizes the effect of this motion. A ball-bearing-smooth gun mount is one synchronized movement of the body and gun to the bird with the feet, body, arms and head making a free-flowing, balanced swing.

Gun mount mechanics is the process of taking the gun from a relaxed ready position and bringing it to your cheek in alignment with your eye in a smooth and consistent manner.

The following is a step-by-step look at how to master the perfect gun mount. Instruction is described for the majority right-handed shooter. The one in ten "southpaw" (left-hander) should simply reverse the directions.

First, you need to set up your body to receive the gun into the cheek, with stance and posture; there should be a slight forward inclination of your body from the waist toward the target. Your head should be positioned forward and down, with your chin parallel to the ground. Rotate your head slightly to the right. Now you will have created the perfect body shape to allow an unimpeded gun mount without any unnecessary body or head movement.

Components of a Good Gun Mount

1. Foot Position
2. Stance
3. Posture
4. Head Position
5. Forend Hand Position
6. Hands Working Together
7. Start
8. End

Remember

The three "Rs" of good shooting are: "Rushing Ruins Rhythm"– also the cardinal rule to a good gun mount. Take your time – do not rush. Smooth and smoother is the secret to more consistent shooting and cleaner kills.

Ready Position

To repeat any act consistently, there must be an established constant beginning and end. At the beginning of the gun mount, the gun is held in the "ready position". The last inch of the butt stock should be held gently on the tendon between your pectoral muscle and the biceps of your right arm. This gentle pressure takes some of the weight of the gun and allows your arms to relax. The muzzles should be on and just under the anticipated flush or line of flight, with your eyes looking directly over the barrels. This is the "ready position" that ensures a smooth move to the target.

The Zygomatic Buttress is the anchor of the gun mount: place your forefinger where your teeth meet and lift it up, until you feel your cheek bone.

Your left hand pushes the gun toward the target, doing the majority of the lifting; your right hand hinges, mirroring its movement, and the gun is raised to the cheek (The Zygomatic Buttress), and the end or completion of the gun mount. The butt should never lose contact with your body. The "bayonet movement" to the target encourages the movement of the shoulder to the stock, eliminating the fault of pulling the stock back into the shoulder. By lifting the gun to your cheek, you prevent the fault of dropping your head to the gun. If the gun is correctly lifted to the cheek, it will always be correctly positioned in the shoulder.

The completion of the gun mount is achieved when the gun is firmly in your cheek. Take a second to reach up with your forefinger and place it along the part of your face where your teeth meet. Now lift your finger up. It should be right under your cheek bone. This is where the stock must always be to complete a solid and accurate gun mount. The smallest gun-mounting error at the face means your eye is out of alignment with the muzzles, and the smallest error there increases incrementally at 20, 30, 40 and 50 yards.

A clearly defined beginning and end to your gun mount creates consistency and straight shooting. You need to practise your gun mount until it is a subconscious act that can be made smoothly time and again, even under pressure and without conscious thought. If conscious thought is required during the gun mount, then you have lost focus on the bird, and 100-percent focus is the secret to cleaner kills.

Faults, Causes and Corrections

There are many causes of a poor gun mount: bad stance, poor posture and incorrect use of the hands, unnecessary head movement, or mounting the stock to the shoulder instead of the cheek. Any or all of these faults will cause the gun to "seesaw" or "rock and roll" during the mounting action and the muzzles will "rock and roll" over and under the target line.

If your gun mount starts with incorrect foot position, your body's restricted rotation will also cause the classic "rainbow", or "windshield wiping", where the muzzles roll off the target line. This uncontrolled muzzle oscillation on and off of the target line is the cause of more misses than any other element of the shooting action. The main reason this simple lifting action goes awry is your hands. The "seesaw" is created by your right hand overpowering your left and mounting the gun to your shoulder instead of to your cheek.

In addition, pulling the gun back into your shoulder pocket and stopping short of your cheek rather than pushing the gun to the target, causes your head to drop to the stock and negates even the best gun fit and shooting technique.

Incorrect gun mount; weight is on the back foot and the head is erect.

"Seesaw" gun mount; rear hand overpowering the front, causing the muzzles to dip, gun is mounted to the shoulder first, not the cheek.

If the gun is mounted to the shoulder first, the gun mount cannot be completed correctly.

An incompleted gun mount causes the head to drop to the stock to try to align the eye with the rib, causing a miss off-line.

Gun Mount Faults

1. Poor starting position – the gun is held too low or too far from the body.

2. Flying the elbow – when observed from behind, the elbows of a shooter with a well-mounted gun should be at a forty-five degree angle to the body. By flying or cocking the elbow of the trigger hand, you close the shoulder pocket to the butt of the gun, the cocked elbow rolls the deltoid muscle towards the face, blocking the area on the clavicle where the gun should be mounted. This causes the gun to be mounted on the rotator cuff or the arm and results in unwanted head movement. If you suffer from bruising on your face after shooting, you need to look at your gun's fit and your gun mount.

3. The "seesaw" mount – the gun barrels, while being lifted to the face, "rock and roll" above and below the target line.

4. The incomplete mount – the gun stops short of the cheek, causing the head to be lowered to the comb.

5. The pull-back mount – the gun is overpowered by the right hand and pulled back into the shoulder rather than moved to the cheek and on to the bird.

6. The "mount, then swing".

7. The rushed mount.

Hands and Arms

Your hands and arms have the biggest impact on your gun mount. Your hands mount and point the gun and your body swings it. However, your hands are independent tools – one on each arm – and are not designed to work together in sync. Consider the golf grip, which also requires the hands to work together as a single unit – the beginner always finds this a most awkward and uncomfortable position to assume.

The hands need to work as a single unit; they should gently stretch or pull the gun in the same manner as cutting pipe with a hacksaw.

This is equally true when mounting a shotgun. The best way to describe the proper use of the hands during the gun mount is to think of your hands' placement and movement like cutting a pipe with a hacksaw. One hand is on the back handle, the other is on the front of the saw. To cut a straight line, you create a small amount of resistance between your hands. This stretching action helps your hands work together. With the palms of your hands in the same plane, facing each other, both hands work as a single unit to achieve a straight cut. If your front hand overpowers the rear, the line is straight but the cut weak and ineffective; if your rear hand overpowers the front, an inaccurate and jagged cut is made.

The gun mount is no different. The left hand points the gun to the target, effectively driving the gun. The right hand mimics this action and pulls the trigger. If both hands are working in unison, the resulting gun mount will be smooth and correct.

Grip

Your hands have to work as a single unit to mount the gun consistently and effectively. The easiest description of your rear hand's position is to take hold of the grip of the stock as if you were shaking hands with the gun. Your thumb should be wrapped over the grip. The thumb is the key part of the grip and gives you control during the shooting action.

Try this: hold the unloaded gun with your thumb firmly wrapped around the grip. Now move your thumb to the safety – the muzzles drop an inch. (I have seen many people push off the safety and leave their thumb resting on it. Believe me, you will need the toplever to catch your thumb only once to learn a very painful lesson about where not to place your thumb.) The pad of your forefinger should be correctly placed on the trigger.

The position of your leading hand is the next consideration. The target that requires the most gun movement is the high driven or passing bird. Adopt correct footwork and stance; now mount the unloaded gun into your shoulder replicating the movement of making the high overhead shot. The placement of your left hand should be on the forend so that the angle created between your wrist and the forend/barrels is approximately 45 degrees. Your hand, regardless of the gun configuration (over/under or side by side) should have the forefinger extended.

On a side by side, your forefinger should extend along the forend and barrels on the underside of the rib, forward of the forend catch. Your grip is achieved by the thumb and fingertips and extended forefinger. On an over/under, your forefinger should extend along the forend and onto the side rib. This positioning of your forefinger harnesses your natural ability to point at and maintain contact with a moving object.

Correct grip on over and under. Both hands are on the same plane.	*The extended finger of the leading hand on the over and under, again harnessing our natural ability to point.*	*Correct grip on the side by side. Note: the thumb is wrapped over grip, not left resting on the saftey. The fingers' and thumb's position on the barrels does not block the eye-muzzle relationship.*	*The finger of the leading hand is extended along the barrels of the side by side, harnessing our natural ability to point.*

Now, imagine that the action of the gun is made of rubber. Gently attempt to stretch it apart. Don't stretch so hard that you create too much tension and you become muscle bound. You want just enough "stretch" that your hands are aware of each other's actions. This slight pressure between the hands creates an awareness of each hand's actions and goes a long way in eradicating the dreaded "rock and roll".

The gun will be balanced between your hands, ensuring a horizontal mount and creating a controlled, smooth movement. In addition, your arms will act like a car's shock absorbers, soaking up a good amount of recoil, resulting in more comfortable shooting and more consistency with second-barrel shots.

Moment of Inertia

It is crucial to match the muzzles' speed to the target's speed. Certain shooting situations will require you to swing the gun at different speeds. By moving your leading hand forward or back (like playing a trombone), you can move the moment of inertia (MOI) or how a gun's weight is distributed between your hands, to accelerate or decelerate the muzzles.

Try this experiment. If you move your leading hand closer to the breech, the gun will swing quicker. Extend it a little farther toward the muzzles and the gun will swing slower. You need to experiment to find how much movement gives you the maximum benefit and, depending on the type of shooting, when to use what position.

A good gun mount starts with a step into the line of flight.

The big muscles of the body turn the gun like a tank turret.

The hands and arms lift and point the gun.

The completed gun mount into the cheek and the shot taken without pause or check.

The Left Hand Leads

The left hand should lift and point the gun at the bird, in effect driving the gun, and the right hand should mimic that action and pull the trigger. This way, both hands work in unison and the resulting gun mount will be smooth. Practice, Practice, Practice. You have to put in lots of practice to perfect your gun mount.

The place to practise is in your home or garage, not on the shooting grounds. Find a place where you can safely and comfortably mount the gun. Always double check that the gun is unloaded and safe. Adopt a good stance, good posture, and good hand and ready positions. Wear your usual shooting attire, including gloves. All gun-mounting exercises should be performed slowly and smoothly; the brain learns muscle memory far better when the action is performed in this manner. Consider the martial artist who learns by performing slow, controlled "kata" or drills to perfect the punch that allows him to break a board at full power. You need to learn the gun mount in the same manner.

The Mirror Exercise

Stand facing a mirror – create the correct stance and posture. Keep the gun level in the ready position, with the proper grip and, looking at your eye, mount the gun smoothly and slowly to your cheek. Look for any "seesaw" muzzle dipping caused by your right hand overpowering your left. Make sure that the mount is correctly to the cheek, not the shoulder first.

Using an unloaded gun, position yourself in front of a mirror. Adopt a proper posture and head position.

Pause for a count of one thousand and one when the gun is perfectly in your cheek and your eye is looking directly back at you along the rib of the shotgun. It is important to lower the gun in the same controlled manner.

The gun mount is grooved equally on the way down as it is on the way up. Repeat these slow mounting exercises daily until you are able to mount the gun perfectly to your cheek without conscious thought.

The Slip Knot Exercise

Take a piece of string and hang it from a beam or door frame at shoulder height and tie a slip knot at the free end. Place the muzzles of your shotgun in the loop and secure with the knot. Now, practise the gun mount you have perfected in the mirror, keeping the string taut. This will make you use a "bayonet" movement in your gun mount where you need to move your shoulder to take up the fraction

Tie a slip knot in a length of string. Secure the loose end to a beam or door frame. Using an unloaded gun, place the barrels in the slip knot.

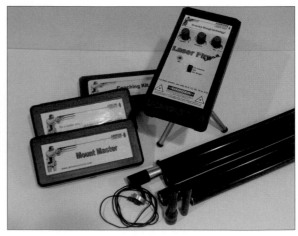

The Arrow Laser Shot or a Maglite placed in an unloaded gun, gives instant feedback when practising your gun mount using the lines of walls and ceilings to practise the complete moving gun mount.

of an inch created between the butt and shoulder pocket. It will create a natural and essential move to the target.

Flash Lights and Laser Shots

When you have mastered the initial gun-mounting movement, you need to progress to a moving mount, combining the mount with a full body swing. Place a small Maglite or Arrow Laser Shot in the end of your barrels; mount the gun, turning the gun with your body and lifting and pointing with your arms and hands to trace a light path along the joint of the walls and ceiling. You instantly will be able to see just how smooth your mount and swing are. Is the light smoothly online or is it fluctuating above and below the chosen line?

As you develop these new motor skills, you can introduce snap caps to the exercise and dry-fire the gun on completion of your gun mount. Use markers on the wall to replicate visual pick-up, insertion and break-points so you can set up and execute each practice correctly.

Shooting Grounds

When you have grooved the gun mount in dry-fire practice, it is time to visit the shooting grounds and practise and perfect these new skills on clay targets before using them in the field.

Practice, Practice, Practice

"Perfect practice makes perfect", but it is quality practice that will improve your shooting. Practising the wrong techniques will ingrain poor fundamentals and cause you to develop bad habits. Learning to shoot straight requires patience and practice and, if it is your goal to improve, you have to understand that there are no shortcuts to perfecting the correct fundamentals.

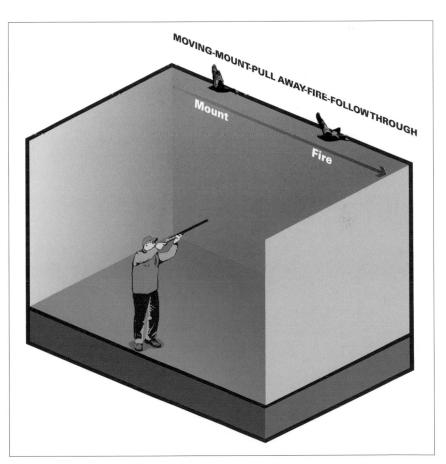

Gun mount and snap cap drills.

Chapter 9
Gun Fit: Truth, Fact and Myth

Y ou cannot and will not get a good and accurate gun fit without a good and accurate gun mount. Beginner or winner, you need to bring the sound fundamentals of stance, posture and gun mount to the pattern plate.

In the Beginning

When it comes to gun fit, starting out, near enough is good enough – you can get along quite well with a gun's original factory dimensions. (The exceptions are ladies and youths, or if you are extremely tall or short.) However, as you improve, there is no doubt that a well-fitted gun can make a dramatic improvement to your performance.

It Has to Fit to Hit

The act of shooting requires hand and eye co-ordination and total focus on the bird throughout the shot. To hit the target, the gun needs to point where the eye is focused. If you have to adapt yourself to the gun to achieve the proper eye–rib relationship, you break your connection with the bird, ruining your natural rhythm and timing and causing a miss.

In wingshooting, it is very important for the gun to fit the shooter's build, style and technique, because when it comes time to take a shot, there just isn't time to adjust to the wrong dimensions. Wingshooting is so instinctual that any distraction which breaks the visual connection with the bird will result in a miss and a poorly fitted gun can cause this.

Individual Characteristics

That we are all built differently is a given. Consider your first actions getting into a new or strange car. When you first enter, you need to make alterations to make the seat and controls fit you in order to

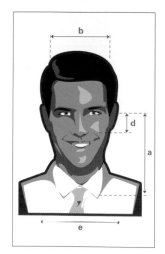
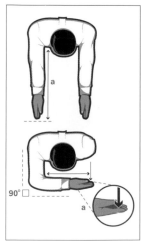

The length of neck, face and eye placement all impact on cast and drop.

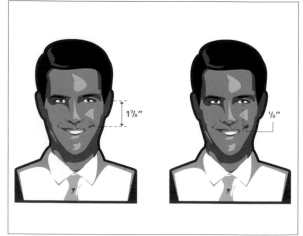

Drop and cast achieve the the correct eye-rib alignment.

operate the vehicle safely. You make adjustments for height, length of both legs and arms, and the mirrors are adjusted to suit your natural eye alignment.

All of these personal adjustments enable us to drive the car both comfortably and safely, while we give our full attention to the road and surroundings without conscious thought to the car and its operation. This experience can be compared to a gun fit; a properly-fitted gun allows us to concentrate on the bird without any of the distractions brought about by a poor eye-to-rib alignment.

Factory Fitting

An accurate gun fit cannot be achieved in the shop, no matter the experience of the fitter. The correct dimensions can only be determined by watching the person actually shooting. The reason is simple: the way the gun is dry-mounted in the shop can be very different from the way a person would mount when live-firing at a moving bird. Likewise, fitting a gun by measuring only forearm length, chest and shoulder width is inaccurate and can have little bearing on where the gun actually shoots (barrel flip and impact), nor does a "shop fit" take into account a shooter's personal style and shooting technique.

There are two ways to achieve a well-fitted gun:

1. Self-fitting by trial and error
2. Custom fitting by a professional gun fitter

Every gun fitting should begin with the diagnosis of eye dominance and the determination of the Master Eye, with any necessary corrections made for central vision, partial or cross dominance.

Gun fit has seven separate but inter-related dimensions:

The Gunfitter's Measurements

1. **Length of Pull**: This first measurement is taken from the trigger (the front trigger on a double-triggered gun) to the end of the stock at heel, middle and toe. Allowance needs to be made for the impact of the individual's shooting stance and style. The correct length should be that, when the gun is correctly mounted, there is a space of between one and a quarter and one and three-quarters of an inch between the trigger hand and the nose. This should place the eye two to three inches from the comb/nose or two-thirds up the stock from the butt.

Length of pull is the only variable in gun fit. The British have traditionally favoured a longer length of pull than the Americans. A longer length has the advantage of increased recoil control, both perceived and mechanical.

It is crucial to find the correct length; too long a stock is difficult to mount and will often check halfway up the shoulder or, more painfully, be mounted on to the biceps or upper arm. A low mount causes the head to drop and the gun to shoot high and, if the mount finishes on the arm instead of the shoulder, to shoot to the side (left for the right-handed and vice versa for the left-handed).

Too short a stock creates an inconsistent gun mount caused by the incorrect extension of the

TOP: *Length of pull at heel, middle and toe –*
CENTRE: *Drop at comb, face and heel –*
BOTTOM: *Degree of pitch.*

arms and dramatically increases felt recoil. Other symptoms of a too-short stock are bruising of the second finger of the trigger hand and the collision of the trigger hand and nose.

2. **Drop at Comb**: The measurement is made from a parallel line taken from the rib of the gun to the stock at the comb, face and heel and determines the height at which the gun will place its pattern. Too little drop and the gun will shoot high, too much drop and the gun will shoot low, causing head lifting, or worse, cross dominance. Of the two options, the higher relationship of the eye to the rib is preferable. As in any gun fit measurement, a good gun mount is imperative.

3. **Cast**: A vertical line through the centre of the heel of the stock is measured against a straight edge from the rib, at the heel and toe. (A specialist tool called a banjo is usually used for this important measurement). The correct cast ensures the proper alignment of the eye, directly along the rib, and is achieved by the shaping or bending of the stock to accommodate left- or right-handed shots.

4. **Pitch:** This is the angle created by the butt of the stock and the rib of the gun. Pitch affects the standout of the gun or how high or low it shoots. Pitch is often a neglected measurement and the amount of standout needs to be balanced against the need to place the maximum amount of the sole of the butt in contact with the shoulder pocket, which is essential to dispersing felt recoil.

Cast Off (Right)

Cast On (Left)

Cast Off – Right-handed – Cast On – Left-handed.

5. **Grip**: The shape of the stock, grip and trigger placement is another often-neglected aspect of gun fit. Straight, semi-pistol and full pistol grips will all have a different length of pull and the radius, depth and thickness of the grip, combined with the position of the nose at the comb, can often transform the performance of a gun. These measurements should be carefully compared to the size and length of the hand.

6. **Comb Thickness**: The thickness of the comb at the face is the last essential measurement to consider. For example, if you were measured using a thick-combed 12 gauge trap gun, an inch and a half thick at the face and requiring a quarter inch of cast, then you were to purchase a 20 gauge field gun with a comb one inch thick at the face, you would only require a reduction in the amount of cast to compensate for the difference in stock thickness.

7. **At Face–Zygomatic Buttress**: The most essential measurement is the distance at the "face". This is the place on the stock where, when the gun is correctly mounted, the cheek should be spot-welded on every shot. This is where the height and width between the eye and the rib "at face" are measured and the correct dimension ensures that the gun shoots "to point of aim". This position in the face is known as the "Zygomatic Buttress". The measurement "at face" is achieved by the combination of the drop at comb and heel. You can have several combinations that

The Zygomatic Buttress is the anchor of the gun mount: place your forefinger where your teeth meet and lift it up, until you feel your cheek bone.

all give the same measurement at the face. The comb should be of a shape that presents a parallel and level surface for an inch or more at the face.

This is so that when the gun moves back under the force of recoil, it does not rise up into the cheek bone. Also, this parallel area makes allowance for the different head positions when taking the various shots called for when shooting different quarry. When taking lower shots, your head will creep forward; when taking an overhead or passing shot, your head will creep back and when shooting at eye level, your face will take the middle position. So having a parallel measurement "at face" creates a single sight picture on every shot made.

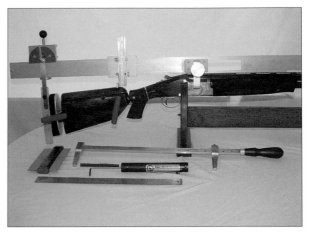

Over and Under Try Gun.

Barrel Flip and Impact

Before any alteration, the gun to be altered should be checked for its point of impact, the relativity of the barrels' placements, and, particularly in the case of small bores, barrel flip.

The Try Gun

The try gun, invented by W.P. Jones in the 19th century, is a gun with a fully-articulated stock, which can be adjusted for length, cast, drop and pitch. When used in conjunction with the pattern plate, it enables the fitter to make alterations to achieve a perfect fit.

It is essential, during the fitting process, to fire the gun. This allows the gunfitter to make allowance for the effects of recoil which have a large input on gun fit, especially in comfort and second-barrel target acquisition. Once the fit is obtained at the pattern plate, it can be proved on moving targets, where comfort and accuracy can be double checked.

A Dry Fit

Using the try gun, the gunfitter will set up an initial fit, referred to as a "Dry Fit". During this part of the fitting session, the fundamentals of straight shooting and consistent gun mounting are checked. If you are unable to consistently mount the gun correctly, it is difficult, if not impossible, to ensure an accurate gun fitting.

Starting with length of pull, followed by alterations to drop, cast and pitch, the fitter works to achieve a gun that is smooth to mount and where the eye–rib relationship is correct and suitable for the discipline that will be shot. I like to use a laser device at this stage to confirm my initial fitting and to double check both the fit and impact tests. After the initial dry fit, the measurements need to be confirmed with live firing on the pattern plate and shooting at clay targets. This is where the fit is really proven to be correct, for when live-firing there are many movements, both muscular and mechanical, that are not apparent during the fitting and at the pattern board.

Pattern Plate

The pattern plate's role in gun fitting is to check the point of impact of the pattern by firing at the plate from sixteen or thirty-two yards. The eye is, on average, three feet or one yard from the end of the barrel. If the plate is shot from the sixteen yard marker, the mathematics of three feet into sixteen yards equates to a sixteen to one ratio, so two inches on the plate is an eighth of an inch adjustment on the gun.

If you are a right-hander shooting four inches to the left of the aiming mark, then you would require a quarter inch of cast off to align the gun to the eye. This formula applies equally at thirty-two yards but there four inches equals an eighth of an inch on the try gun.

Four to six groups of shots are usually made at the same mark. This repetition allows for the inevitable flinch or bad gun mount that can occur when shooting a static target – both noise and recoil are greater than when shooting a moving target. The shot placement on the pattern plate gives the accurate reading to the gunfitter who can make the necessary adjustments, dialling-in the try gun to shoot point of aim and achieve a perfect fit.

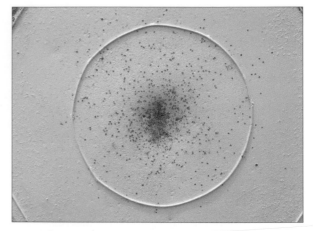

Gun fit is tested and regulated at the pattern plate.

Measurements

Using the gunfitter's specialized tools, the accurate measurements are taken from the try gun and transcribed on the fitting sheet. This "prescription" can then be used to achieve your correct stock dimensions when purchasing your new gun. It can also be given to a competent gunsmith who, by the use of heat and oil, can bend the gun's stock up, down or sideways to the "prescribed" shape. Adjustment to the length of pull is done by removing wood and/or adding a pad to the butt.

Do-It-Yourself or Trial and Error Fitting

While all of the above is applicable and sound advice, even without a professional gunfitter, a try gun (hard to find) and experience (even harder), you can achieve a pretty good fit by personal trial and error.

If possible, enlist the help of an experienced friend. Most people shooting straight at Skeet and Trap and in the mid-eighties and higher at Sporting Clays have a good understanding of gun fit and can help you get a good fit.

Use your club's pattern plate or make a temporary pattern plate out of cardboard or plywood.

If your gun is too long and too high, try to use a shotgun that is too short and has a good deal of drop and neutral (straight) cast. Then using extension pads, comb raisers, "Blu-tack" and mole skin you can add to and subtract from the dimensions. Work until you are happy with the fit and

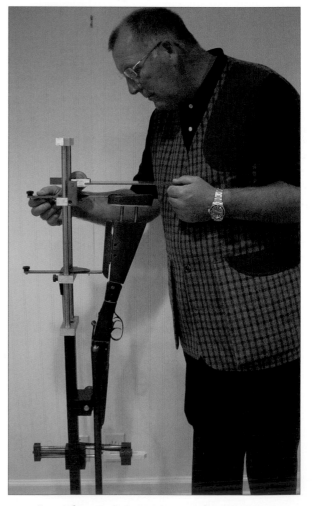

Specialist equipment ensures that accurate measurements are taken from the try gun.

the gun feels comfortable, then check the point of aim at the pattern plate.

The cast requirement needs to be analyzed from the shot pattern placement and, using the sixteen-to-one ratio, you can work out the amount of cast you need.

Next, you should shoot a few targets. This is where your experienced friend's input is invaluable. He will be able to recognize, when you miss, if it is gun fit or operator error.

Once your dimensions are proven at the pattern plate and by shooting targets, measure your gun using a straight edge, a protractor and a piece of string to determine the length of pull, the drop, the cast and (if comfortable) the pitch. Using

DIY Fitting Kit.

these measurements you can select your new gun, have your gun altered to them or just shoot it for a while. This way you can see if it needs a tweak or two before settling on the final dimensions (this is often the choice of the top shots). The nice thing is, if the gun is bent, lengthened or shortened, it can always be redone if you did not get it 100% right the first time. The carpenter's advice is always worth repeating: "Measure twice and cut once".

Eye Alignment

When the fitted gun is correctly mounted, observed from the front of the muzzle, the pupil of the eye should be sitting on the rib like a rising sun. This is the optimum position for successful shooting.

Much is made of the relationship of the eye to the rib for the different types of shooting and the guns used to shoot them, but the typical standards are only a guide and make no allowance for impact, barrel regulation and pattern placement.

Furthermore, there is no taking into account the refraction caused by bifocal, trifocal or "Varilux" lenses, which can dramatically alter a shooter's sight pictures. Plus, an individual's cache of sight pictures, built over many years of shooting with a gun that might not fit, is a factor as well. They may have physically adapted themselves to the ill-fitting gun, perhaps shooting several inches under and to one side of the target to hit it. Given

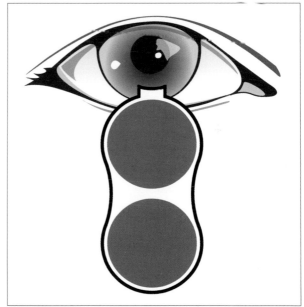

The ideal eye-rib alignment for wingshooting is 60%–40%.

a gun that fits and shoots to point of aim, they will need to relearn all of their sight pictures.

Wingshooting requires a gun that shoots 60-40, where 60% of the pellets are distributed above the horizontal of the rib. This setup allows the bird to be kept in view throughout the shot by floating it on the rib. If it is set up for 50-50, the rib will obscure the bird and cause head-lifting.

A gun that fits and shoots where you look is one of "The Trinity of The Instinctive Shot": Fundamentals–Gun fit–Technique. Remember, "It Has to Fit to Hit"!

Chapter 10
The Mechanics of an Instinctive Shot

What is an Instinctive Shot?

The "Instinctive Shot" is a grooved (unconscious) chain reaction of body movements which swing the shotgun and successfully direct the shot at the intended quarry. As with any chain reaction, a successful end cannot be achieved without a successful beginning. The purpose of the fundamentals of stance, posture and gun mount is to get the shooter into the balanced body position that will facilitate a consistent smooth and synchronized movement towards the target.

Overlearning

Repeating a technique or skill until the action becomes an automatic reaction, is known in shooting and other sports as "overlearning". The process requires learning the proper sequence and timing of muscle movements and, by repetition, grooving them into "muscle memory" where the learned action can be repeated without conscious thought.

For example, in a martial art like karate, to become a black belt (one of the highest ranks) requires hundreds of hours of practice, much of which is in the form of "katas" or drills. To become an "Instinctive Shot" requires the same dedicated practice and repetition of drills for the action of taking a shot to become automatic and unconscious.

The level of your ability to shoot "*instinctively*" is directionally proportional to your mastery of the fundamentals. This mastery requires dedicated practice – and the more you practise, the better you will get.

Doubting Thomas

There are cynics of this "instinctive technique" – they believe it is impossible to "instinctively" know the various leads and swing-speeds for birds shot flying in different directions, at different distances and different angles. Further, they don't think it is possible to achieve the required forward allowance (lead) by swing-speed alone.

I am in complete agreement with this aspect of their analysis: with the exception of a bird flying straight away, lead is required to place the pattern on the target and the amount of lead required increases with speed and distance. However, shooting at a clay target you have the luxury of time to analyze the target's speed and trajectory to calculate the lead required. Clay target shooters can quickly learn to mechanically lead the predictable target.

With the infinitely variable and unpredictable flight lines of feathered targets, the wingshooter does not have the luxury of time to mentally calculate the angle, speed and distance of a flying target fast enough to hit it. They need to harness their natural eye and hand co-ordination and their "instinctive" reaction to be able to do so.

An "instinctive" action originates in the subconscious mind which is hardwired to the nervous system. The process of training the subconscious is referred to as NLP (Neuro Linguistic Programming). Used in many types of sports, NLP has proved to develop faster reactions and improve eye-hand co-ordination. The method and technique of "instinctively" applying lead is learned by grooving and programming the conscious mind, but the actual application of lead during the act of shooting is made by the subconscious mind.

The "Instinctive Shot" is "See Bird Shoot Bird"

Time Management

The individual bird's speed of flight dictates the time you have to shoot it. Upland birds, like grouse and woodcock, present fleeting chances requiring a swift move to the target resulting in a snap shot. When driven and pass shooting, the birds are in view for a long time before they are within shot range so these require a more controlled, smooth move to the target. It is essential to take full advantage of the time given; training and controlling anticipation will hone your reaction time.

Reaction time is the interval between the stimulus of seeing the bird and the muscular response to that stimulus. This response is greatly affected by the number of stimuli present. In a covey rise, each bird competes to require a reaction and this causes a distraction!

Because one bird needs to be selected to be shot, (choice reaction time), it takes longer to determine which response to carry out. If there is only one bird, it takes a shorter time to react, as there is only one stimulus (simple reaction time). We all have different "reaction times", but "response times" can be improved with practise.

The Autonomic Shot

You cannot shoot birds consistently if you are thinking of the mechanics. The fundamentals must be practised to the point where they become automatic and the movement to and in front of the target can be made without conscious thought. To shoot your best, you need to concentrate totally on a single object: the bird. The more intense your concentration, the better your outcome will be. With total "autonomic

Timing is everything, your muzzle speed must match the bird's speed.

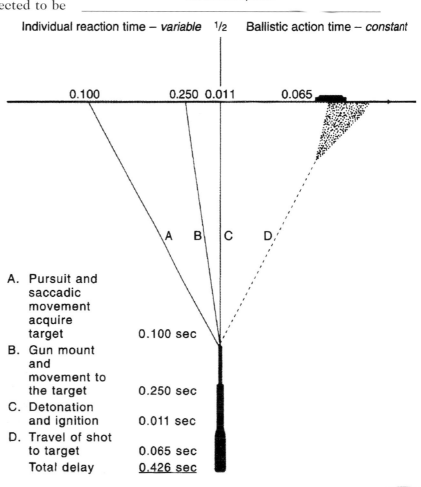

Individual reaction time – *variable*   ½   Ballistic action time – *constant*

0.100   0.250 0.011   0.065

A   B   C   D

A. Pursuit and saccadic movement acquire target   0.100 sec
B. Gun mount and movement to the target   0.250 sec
C. Detonation and ignition   0.011 sec
D. Travel of shot to target   0.065 sec
    Total delay   <u>0.426 sec</u>

RIGHT: The need to "lead" a target is because of the lag in pulling the trigger and ballistics of the shotgun.

concentration" and focus on the target, you avoid destructive thoughts of mechanics or measured lead intruding into your consciousness.

But you need to do more than just look at the whole target. You must single out the bird's head. Intense concentration on this small part of the bird blocks out unwanted thoughts and, effectively, causes the bird to appear larger and slower.

Every learning curve has three stages:

1. Unconsciously Incompetent – At this stage you depend entirely on your instructor – you are shown an exercise and then have to replicate it. You really have to think about every move before it is made.

2. Consciously Competent – At this point, the exercise has been repeated until it has become "muscle memory". The "on-board computer" in your brain is recognizably programmed.

3. Unconsciously Competent – Now you have grooved the mechanics to the point that you can make the moves as subconsciously as riding a bicycle... if you thought about how to ride it, you would lose balance and fall off.

You cannot hit birds consistently if you are thinking about the mechanics. Instinctive shooters are "unconsciously competent". Their conscious mind is free to lock onto only one thing – the bird.

Focus

Blur that Barrel

The majority of birds are missed behind – is this due to lack of lead, poor mechanics or an ineffective choke or load? In the early stages (1. and 2.) of the Learning Curve, it could be any one or a combination of these factors. But after a shooter has achieved some experience, the problem is often caused by not looking at the target, instead, by *looking at the gun*.

It is important to see both the bird and the gun, but how they should be seen in relation to each other is rarely explained. The ability to perceive two objects in two different fields of vision is what marries together the mechanics and the mind and allows us to shoot a moving object.

We have two eyes but only one receiver, our brain, which joins these two individual pictures seamlessly together, allowing us to see one clear, sharp image. But this clear single image can only be seen in one field of vision at a time, either up close or at a distance. So the field of vision other than our point of focus (our peripheral vision), will always be made up of two blurred or double images.

When we are shooting, if we hard focus on the bird, the gun will be seen in our peripheral

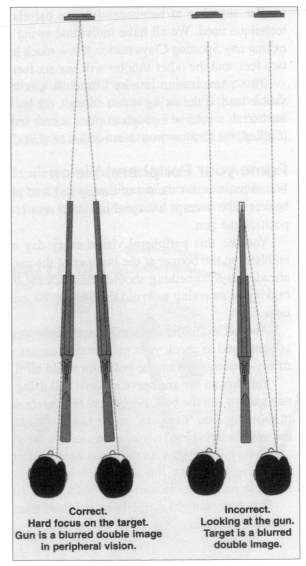

Correct.
Hard focus on the target.
Gun is a blurred double image in peripheral vision.

Incorrect.
Looking at the gun.
Target is a blurred double image.

vision as a double, blurred image of two gun barrels. If we attempt to place the bead at the end of the muzzle on the target, we are now looking at the gun, and the bird is a blurred double image of two indistinct birds. Which one do we shoot? Neither! This visual hiccup results in the gun slowing, stuttering or stopping altogether.

To consistently shoot well, we must learn to maintain hard focus on the bird throughout the shot. The more forward allowance or lead required, the more important it is to keep our vision firmly locked on the bird.

If at any time we quit the target and look back to the barrel of the gun, the target will double and blur and we will stop or slow our swing and miss behind. This is literally using a scattergun approach. We have all, at some point, experienced the following:

1. Inability to know where a bird is missed.

2. A stop-start stuttering swing.

3. Your instructor or loader is forever saying "You missed behind", when you could have sworn you had plenty of daylight between the barrel and the bird when you pulled the trigger.

Learn to recognize these symptoms and apply the cure: *re-establish hard focus on the bird*!

Barrel Awareness

Any shooter must, of course, be *aware* of the gun and the gap between the muzzle and the bird. But as individuals, we all see things differently. This is well demonstrated by the fact that one person sees inches of lead at the barrels, while another sees feet at the bird. *Individual Lead* is the lead we see between the barrels and the bird when we pull the trigger. This is less than the *True Lead* at the target. True Lead is actually greater; because of the delay in pulling the trigger.

For any shot to be successful, the barrels must be moving faster than the bird. We all have individual swing speeds and reaction times. If you asked several Guns at the end of a drive "How much lead did you give them?" one might tell you he gave two feet, and another would say ten feet.

Robert Churchill insisted that you could shoot directly at a target without visible lead. He taught that if the swing was fast enough, the lag between the time the trigger was pulled and the time the shot left the barrel, the overthrow would be enough to place the barrel and the shot string several feet in front of the target. But if asked, the shooter would insist that he had shot directly at the target. Churchill's theory does work on certain shots such as upland bird shooting, but when shooting the modern high pheasant, the gun would have to be swung at the speed of light to get the 9 to 12 feet of lead needed to hit a bird.

Prime Your Peripheral Vision

One of the big differences between the average shot and the good shot is, the good shot learns to shoot using peripheral vision to position the gun.

You use this peripheral vision every day of your life. When you drive your car, you do not aim the emblem on your hood at the car in front of you. You drive looking 10 or 20 car lengths ahead. But how do you keep it between the white lines and a safe distance from the cars in front of you? And if something should unexpectedly happen to the car directly in front of you, you react instantly, braking or swerving to avoid the danger. *We are gifted with peripheral vision so we can see in two places at once.*

Another example: say you are serving in a tennis match – you toss the ball up to serve. If you then looked at your hand, the result would be a fluffed serve. Yet if you keep your eye firmly concentrated on the ball, you will hit it in the "sweet spot" and serve an ace!

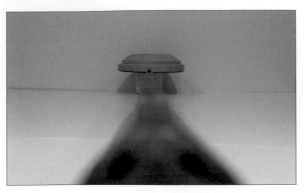

There are two things that you need to see but cannot look at, the bead and the lead: they should be an awareness in your peripheral vision and the bird pin-feather sharp in your central vision.

You drive a car and serve a tennis ball using both central and peripheral vision, *central* to look ahead and navigate or see the ball, *peripheral* to operate and control the car or see your racquet. It is exactly the same in shooting: you "navigate" on the bird with "*central vision*" and "operate" the gun with "*peripheral*". If you can see your barrels clearly, you have stopped the gun and missed behind.

You need to learn to swing the gun with your peripheral vision, while remaining locked on the target with your central vision. You must develop "*Awareness of the Rib*" (faint image in peripheral vision) along with "*Hard Focus on the Target*" (leading edge in central vision).

Forward Allowance

From the earliest attempts to shoot birds on the wing, it was quickly discovered that to hit a moving target it was necessary to place the gun in front of its path so that the shot string intercepted the bird along its line of flight. After all, **"They don't fly backwards"**! I consider the hardest-learned piece of the shooting jigsaw is to educate the brain that you have **"To miss it, to hit it"**.

In life, being punctual and accurate are attributes that are highly regarded. We are often encouraged **"To Hit the Nail on the Head"**. Well, to do so when bird shooting is to ensure a miss behind. As an instructor, I witness many clients who struggle to apply forward allowance. Their conscious mind understands the concept, but their subconscious will not allow them to apply it. When shooting, they consistently miss behind.

I refer to this conflict between the conscious and subconscious minds as "*Separation Anxiety*" where the struggle between the two concepts causes the brain to vacillate between action and paralysis. Experience plays a big part in solving this problem and the brain is capable of storing the equivalent of a photo album of mental forward allowance pictures based on previous trial and error.

The top shot with a wealth of experience has control over his subconscious mind and can override its command to "pull the trigger" until the barrel–bird relationship is right. By insight, understanding and repeated successful practice, these dedicated shotgunners train their subconscious to "Miss it to hit it".

The Need for Lead

Why is it necessary to shoot in front of the target to connect with it? After all, modern cartridges produce muzzle velocities in excess of 1,350 feet per second, or more than 740 miles per hour. This is faster than "Mach One" – indeed the bulk of the report heard on firing the gun is the shot cloud breaking the Sound Barrier as it exits the muzzles.

So we are firing a supersonic cloud of shot averaging 1,350 feet per second at a bird that is flying about 40 miles per hour or 70 feet per second. Surely, with this incredible speed advantage, we should be able to shoot directly at the target and hit it. If the bird is flying straight away from you, the shot cloud will quickly close the gap and hit the bird. But if the bird is presented at an angle to you, you need forward allowance or lead. Why is this? After all, the shot velocity and bird speeds have remained constant.

The answer for the most part, is your reaction time – the lag between deciding to pull the trigger and actually doing it. When shooting, we use our hand and eye co-ordination, the same as in many ball games. Only with shooting, there are more variables involved in "bringing the bat to the ball".

When we swing to the target, there is a judgement of timing as to when to pull the trigger. We are, in fact, absorbing visual information in the form of light through the eye. This light passes through the iris to the macula and from there to the frontal lobes, which, in turn stimulates it to travel down the middle of the cerebral corollas. These impulses produce the neuro-messages that make the muscles contract and react to co-ordinate our movements to the target, which finish with pulling the trigger.

But after the trigger is pulled, still more time passes. The hammer falls, detonating the cartridge (lock time) and the shot is propelled towards the target (ignition and powder burn, barrel and flight times). In all, this combined action takes an average of one tenth of a second. Hardly worth considering when we are talking about the shot cloud travelling at more than 740 miles per hour, right?

Well, in that one tenth of second, a bird travelling at about 40 miles per hour (70 feet per second) moves approximately three feet. The farther the shot travels, the more it slows down. And the greater the distance, the greater the lead required. At forty yards, you need to place the shot 9 to 12 feet in front of a crossing bird to intercept it!

Timing is Everything

Time is the past, present and future regarded as a continuous whole. When attempting to shoot a moving target, we are, in fact, working against time in an effort to complete the shot in a limited period. It naturally follows that the core skill in our shooting is our timing – our ability to judge when to pull the trigger. The same applies to hitting a ball or playing an instrument in an orchestra.

Lead is very personal to the individual shooter and you need to learn the different pictures for yourself. As your experience expands, so will your ability to judge distance, angle and speed. Once you have programmed in the correct information, you will have the confidence to let the "on-board computer" in your brain do the rest.

The Math of Gap Analysis

If we applied math to the question of lead, the formula would rely on the angle, distance and speed of the target, combined with the shooting technique used and the speed of the swing. But there are secondary factors that also affect lead, such as the velocity of the cartridge, the effect of choke on the pattern's width and density and the shooter's reaction time.

Such a formula could indicate the lead needed for a target that maintains a constant vertical or horizontal line. But game birds are of different sizes, they are migratory or upland, they are shot over dogs, decoyed or driven overhead. Further, they all have different flight characteristics which are affected by the wind and air currents and are often in transition, adding still another dimension to the equation of lead in two directions.

What the wingshooter needs to be is a *magician, not a mathematician*. The latter would do his maths and work out the precise lead required on any particular presentation, then attempt to apply it with slide rule precision. And he would fail. But if we apply a little mental magic and *trust* our programmed "on board computer", we will always put the gun in the right place, in front of the bird.

Speed and Line of Flight

Judging the speed and line of flight of a bird is a vital skill in wingshooting! Keeping your muzzles on the bird throughout the shooting action establishes both speed and line of flight, regardless of size and species. And you can miss 360 degrees around a bird; above, below, in front or behind. Staying on the line cuts your chances of missing in half by reducing chance of missing to a *"miss behind or a miss in front"*. By matching the bird's speed and staying on the line, it is much easier to recognize the fault, analyze the cause and implement the correction when a miss occurs.

Sweet Spot

The default setting for the eye is peripheral (panoramic), but any movement sends a visual signal that triggers the pursuit (centred) movement which allows the eyes to follow a moving object. When a bird flushes or comes into range, the eyes pursue it and lock on to it. This action is continuously modified by the ongoing visual feedback from the bird in motion. At a certain point along the line of flight the bird will, for an instant, appear sharper and slower. As in other sports this point is referred to as the "sweet spot" and is the optimum place to take the shot. Experience will help you recognize this point; the hinge pin around which every successful shot is made.

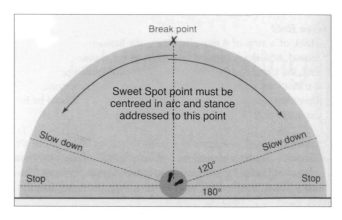

Addressing the Sweet Spot

In Driven, Pass and Decoyed shooting, you have an indication of the direction of the quarry's flight. When hunting over dogs, you have no idea of where a bird will rise, and you are also in motion. It is footwork that will rotate your body smoothly to the sweet spot, correctly making the eye – muzzle – bird alignment that is essential to straight shooting.

Alignment can best be pictured this way: imagine a set of railway tracks leading from the station to the bird. Your pivot and step should point your gun along that track, placing the bird in *"the centre of your swing"*. Again, the fundamentals of good footwork, stance, and posture create the correct head position, ensuring that the muzzles stay on the bird and line throughout the shot.

Visual Pursuit + Speed and Line + Footwork = Sweet Spot

This is the complete and correct sequence in which to make a successful shot.

1. As the bird flushes or comes into range, you begin your move to it in one continuous, smooth movement. It should all be a seamless flow.

2. Your eyes see and lock onto the bird and guide your hands to it, setting up a chain reaction of timing and tempo.

3. Once you get the big muscles in your body turning, your gun mount is smooth and unhurried. Everything turns together, the muzzles move with and lock onto the bird.

4. As the stock comes into your cheek, your shoulder rolls forward to complete the mount, the safety is pushed off and your finger moves to the trigger.

5. Forward allowance (lead) is perceived in your peripheral vision and the trigger is pulled smoothly without conscious thought.

Tailoring Your Technique

We are all distinctly individual. Just glance up and look around you at the difference in people's height, size, and weight. These differences also exist in the hidden internal workings of our personal co-ordination, reaction time and visual acuity.

The game of golf is, in many ways, comparable to the different types of wingshooting. Using golf as an analogy, an individual is required to negotiate a golf course in the least number of shots. The competitor is allowed 14 clubs in his bag. This lets him choose the best club to tackle the variety of shots he will encounter during the game. No golfer would dream of starting a competition without a full complement of clubs. He will also have practised with and be able to use each and every one of them.

In the same manner, to shoot well the wingshooter needs a "bag of clubs" or a variety of shooting techniques: Swing Through, Pull Away, Maintained Lead, Instinctive and Spot Shooting. All these techniques need to deliver three things: Line, Speed of Flight and Gun Momentum. The wingshooter must practise using this "bag of techniques" and learn to choose the best technique for the type of shots he encounters in the field.

Your "Bag of Clubs"

The sole purpose of a technique is to be able to *get the muzzles in front of and on the target line consistently*. Technique will allow you to harness instinct and co-ordination into a sequence of pre-planned movements *to* and *in front* of the target.

There are three mainstream shooting techniques: Swing Through, Pull Away and Maintained Lead. All achieve the essential requirement of placing the shot stream in front of the target. However, some achieve this more easily and consistently than others and some are more easily learned and applied, particularly by beginners.

But each technique has an advantage on a particular target presentation. Just like the golfer has a favourite club, we all will have a favourite method, but you should be able to shoot using all of them. The following will explain the technique, its origins, advantages, disadvantages and the quarry to which it is best applied.

Making the Shot

The gun's insertion point is the main difference in each method. The constants are: Gun Mount – Insertion Point – Forward Allowance.

Swing-Through or Follow-Through

History:
This is one of the oldest shooting techniques. Gunmaker Charles Lancaster wrote on the subject in the 1800s and it was taught by the legendary coach and champion shot, Percy Stanbury. Swing-Through is still taught today at the West London Shooting School.

Method:
The muzzles are inserted on the line of flight; not yards behind, but on the tip of the tail of the bird being shot. The gun is then consciously accelerated through and past the target before pulling the trigger.

Advantages:
The best use of the Swing-Through method is when upland bird shooting. With the unpredictability of a bird's flight

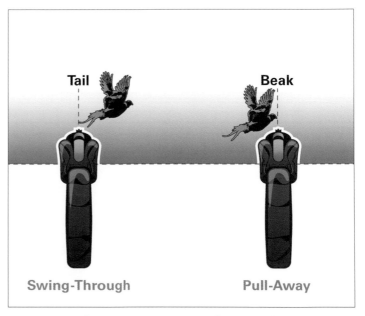

Muzzle insertion point according to technique.

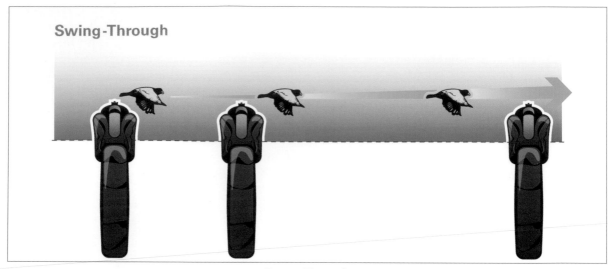

Swing Through.

where there can be no prior preparation for line, speed or lead, moving to the bird and "swinging-through" is, by far, the most popular and successful upland bird shooting technique.

Disadvantages:

Achieving forward allowance by muzzle speed alone creates its own pitfalls. If the swing is too fast you will miss in front, too slow and you will miss behind. And that is presuming you are on the bird's line and speed of flight. If the speed is misjudged, you need to rush to catch up and rushing results in a loss of control. A swing too far in front will make you stop and attempt to ambush the target. Too slow a swing and you are unable to establish sufficient forward allowance.

Pull-Away

History:

Clarrie Wilson of the British Clay Pigeon Shooting Association pioneered the Pull-Away technique in

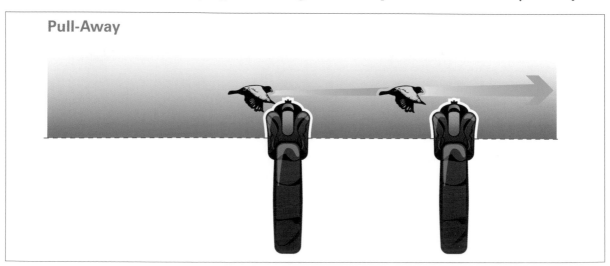

Pull-Away.

the 1960s. It is still the technique of choice for this organization and the British Association of Shooting and Conservation.

Method:
The muzzles are held on the line of flight and the bird is never allowed to pass the muzzles. The gun is pointed at the head of the bird then, with the muzzles on the line of flight and on the head of the bird, they accelerate *away* from the bird and the trigger is pulled as the gun reaches the cheek. This technique falls halfway between Swing-Through and Maintained Lead.

Advantages:
Pull-Away gives both speed and line of flight and no other technique does this. It is a great technique for beginners and I would compare it to the golf pro's use of the 7 iron to establish a smooth swing and groove sound fundamentals.

Disadvantages:
The most common faults in Pull-Away are: letting the bird past the muzzles and reverting to Swing-Through, or looking at the gun and "measuring" to try to establish the forward allowance which results in stopping the gun.

Maintained Lead

History:
Maintained Lead was developed during the era of match and flintlock guns. The slow percussion of black powder required a technique that kept the gun in front of and on the flight line of the bird while the combustion took place, after the trigger was pulled.

Method:
The muzzles are held on the line of flight, then inserted in *front* of the bird. They stay in front of the bird, maintaining the amount of forward allowance perceived to be correct, as the gun is mounted and reaches the cheek. When the gun is fully mounted, the muzzles should still maintain the same lead as the trigger is pulled.

Advantages:
The gun is in front of the bird throughout the shot, moving at the same speed as the bird, which, psychologically, makes you feel in control and a smoother movement results.

Disadvantages:
It is a technique dependent on very good hand and eye co-ordination to establish both line of flight and speed of the bird. Too far in front or constantly checking the forward allowance will stop or slow the swing and result in a miss behind.

Churchill Instinctive Technique

History:
Invented and pioneered by Robert Churchill, this technique, combined with his XXV short-barrelled shotgun, created a revolution in British game shooting in the 1930s. His controversial theory that there was no need to see daylight in front of a bird to hit it is still being argued today.

Method:
Robert Churchill's method requires that the muzzles be held on the line of flight. By hard-focusing on the bird and moving the hands and body with it, the gun progresses to the cheek. When the mount is completed, the trigger is pulled. With the muzzles always pointed directly at the bird, forward allowance is achieved by the speed of the swing.

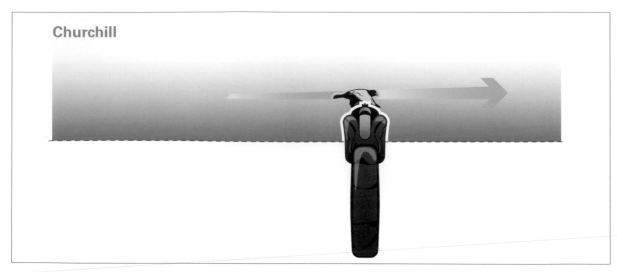

Churchill Instinctive Technique.

The movement of the hands and eyes, co-ordinated by the speed of the bird, automatically arrive in the correct position. The lapse between the time the trigger is pulled and the time that the shot leaves the barrel ensures that the muzzles are in front (overthrow) of the bird when the shot leaves the barrel, though, if asked, the shooter would swear he shot directly at the bird.

Advantages:
This is the one technique where you will definitely *not* check your swing or stop the gun. After all, you are shooting directly *at* the bird, exactly where your subconscious wants you to shoot. It is a good technique for upland bird shooters and traditional driven pheasant and partridge shooting, but will never create enough forward allowance for modern high-driven pheasant shooting.

Disadvantages:
The Churchill technique depends entirely on gun speed, consistent and accurate gun mount and complete trust in your hands and eyes. There are no mental pictures based on previous trial and error for the brain to store where instinct can be molded by previous successes. So each and every shot at each and every bird is a new challenge to your reactions.

Spot or Ambush Technique

History:
The technique of early wingshooters, this is a combination of "rifle shooting" and sustained lead.

Method: It *is* possible to spot-shoot a bird. This technique requires you to anticipate speed and line of flight, estimate the bird's arrival at a specific point, insert the gun and precisely time the shot and "spot-shoot" or "ambush" the target at that point.

Advantages:
Spot shooting is often used as a last ditch effort, where the bird is a fleeting opportunity or the Gun is taken by surprise. If visual contact was lost, as when a bird passes in front of the sun or behind obstacles, or it is the second shot of a double and there is no time to apply a more controlled technique.

Disadvantages:
This is a technique that is used very little. The ultimate test of hand and eye co-ordination, spot-shooting might better be called the "poke and hope" method.

Modified Churchill or Moving Spot Technique

The "Moving Spot Technique" is a hybrid of Pull-Away, Sustained Lead and The Churchill Instinctive technique. This method combines the strengths of "establishing the line and flight" from Churchill, "target control" from Maintained Lead and the "gun speed" from Pull-Away. In the "Moving Spot", you insert the gun a few inches in front of the bird, open the gap until your subconscious tells you the lead picture is right, then you pull the trigger. If the bird is close, you insert on the head of the bird; at thirty yards, insert two feet in front and at forty yards, four feet in front.

One Man's Lead...

It is possible to work out the theoretical forward allowance for birds at various ranges, but it is nearly impossible to apply these distances in practice. After all, one man's three feet is another man's five. While it may be impossible to judge a particular number of feet in front of the target mathematically, by practice, trial and error you can learn the "gap" that works for you on any bird at any given yardage.

This ability can be compared to the golfer who, after learning to hit the ball straight, learns to fade and drift the ball according to the obstacles on the course. He does not "measure", but he has learned how much to open or close the face of the club and how much swing-speed he needs to put the ball where he wants it.

Reactive Shooting

I believe that each and every one of us uses a variety of techniques while wingshooting. We are often unaware of doing so and it is an unconscious decision as to which one we use, bird to bird.

It is a simple synapse in the brain where the information about the bird, gathered by the eyes, guides and controls the body's movement to the bird. The technique we use is entirely dependent on the bird and what it is doing and our individual reactions to its actions. This automatic response is what I consider "Reactive Shooting", the unconscious adjustment of technique, bird to bird.

Shooting different species and types of wingshooting and practising different techniques will help you achieve two things. First, you will discover which technique best suits your individual style and timing for each bird. Second, you will pre-programme your subconscious with muscle memory so when making a shot, you can do so with no conscious reference to method or technique.

During this practice you will discover there is little difference in the techniques, simply differences in the gun insertion points. If you insert the muzzles behind the bird you will shoot Swing Though, insert on it, Pull-Away, in front, Sustained Lead – but the fundamentals remain constants.

Practical Application

I consider the single most important part of the shooting equation to be the *line*. Misses can occur 360 degrees around the bird. You can miss above or below, in front or behind. But if you can keep the muzzles on the line throughout the shot, you limit your misses to in front or behind.

You instantly achieve a 50% reduction in missing! You also gain a significant second benefit – if you miss, you need to know the fault or the cause and understand the correction. If you can stay on the line, it becomes easier to recognize the fault. You miss either in front or behind the target. Now you, your instructor or your loader can analyze the cause and apply the correction.

You can improve the odds even more. You can make sure that if you *do* miss, it is in front of the target. Consider this: if you miss behind, even by a nano-second, you can never hit the bird because it is flying away from the shot column. If you miss in front, even by a mile, there is always a *chance* that the target and shot string will connect as the target flies towards and through the pattern.

So, how can you attempt to be on line and in front on the majority of shots? Establish the line and speed of flight of the bird and your "on-board computer" can make the computation required to ensure bird and shot column collide.

On Line and On Time

The core requirement of any shooting technique is to establish speed and line of flight. However, this cannot be achieved just by the application of the technique itself. Its success is dependent on several factors.

The angle created by the intersection of the shotgun into the bird's line is the best indicator of the forward allowance the target will require; the smaller the angle, the smaller the lead; the larger the angle, the larger the lead.

The bird's speed and distance will add to the amount of forward allowance or lead it needs.

Judging distance is a skill that is easily learned. When you are next outside, whether walking the dog or just in town, pick out an object and guess its yardage. Now count the number of paces it takes to reach that object, with one stride counting as one yard. Soon you will be able to gauge distances accurately. Computing the distance with the speed and angle of a target will help the subconscious apply the correct forward allowance.

Elements of The Instinctive Shot

Hard Focus

Beginning with your eyes, you need to capture and maintain hard focus on the bird from the beginning to the end of the shot. To achieve this, open your eyes wide to allow the maximum amount of light in.

Soft focus into the place you think the birds will appear. The muscles in your eyes are more efficient at *coming down and in* to an object than *up and out*. This soft focal point allows a faster and better acquisition of the bird. Then maintain hard focus throughout the shot. Quitting the bird is one of the major causes of the gun stopping and missing. After all, we shoot them with our eyes.

Muzzle Insertion Point

The gun insertion point on the bird determines the technique applied. Insert behind and you will Swing-Through; on it and you will Pull-Away; in front and you will Maintain the Lead.

The biggest mistake that I see is the complete lack of connection between the gun and bird at this crucial "make or break" point in the shooting technique. The gun is often mounted and then swung in two separate movements, so all relationship to the bird is lost for a moment. The result is a chase to re-establish contact with the bird and the technique used becomes a lottery.

The swing and the mount should be one smooth motion…to wax lyrical, it should be "a synergy of muscle, steel and walnut" linked and directed by the eyes to the bird. The muzzles should always be inserted on the head (Pull-Away) or tail (Swing Through) of the bird. When you insert the gun it must be on, or close to, the bird to establish and maintain those essential requirements of speed and line of flight.

Swing Speed

To ensure that forward allowance is maintained, the gun needs to be moving only one mile an hour faster than the bird when the trigger is pulled. If it is not, then in the momentary lag after detonation, the bird will close the established gap and a miss behind will result. Speed is, indeed, lead and lead is speed.

Chapter 11
Driven Shooting

In traditional driven shooting, game birds are flushed ("driven") from natural and strategically planted cover crops by a team of beaters. The birds fly over a waiting line of Guns (usually 8) spaced 40 yards apart. How high the birds fly is determined by the topography of the land. Deep valleys, such has those of the West Country in Britain, can present birds soaring in excess of 60 yards over the line. In flatter areas, the birds will not fly so high and a 40 yard bird would be considered a high bird. This difference in presentation has created two types of driven shooting, the traditional 30 to 40 yard high birds and the exceptional "High Driven Pheasant and Partridge", which fly in excess of 50 and 60 yards above the Guns.

The red grouse, whose habitat is the Northern moors, are the opposite type of game birds. They fly low, skimming the heather as they are driven towards the line. But what they lack in height, they more than make up for in speed, which makes them the match of any game bird as a test of shooting skills.

Safety

Shot can travel over 200 yards before it is spent so you must always be aware of the position of the flankers, beaters, pickers-up and the other Guns in addition to your safe quadrants of fire.

When shooting *behind* the line, the shotgun must be held vertically and a smart about-turn made before shooting the flying-away bird. When shooting high pheasant and partridge, shooting over the line is allowed, but the barrels should never be lower than 50 degrees.

Traditional Driven Partridge

In the UK, the partridge species are the native grey partridge and the red leg partridge introduced from France in the 1600s. The difference in flight characteristics between the two is due to covey discipline. The red legs have little covey discipline, breaking rank at the first sound of beaters or guns. The undisciplined red legs are more dispersed, with the birds passing over the line in dribs and drabs of well-spaced twos and threes. The grey or common partridge will hold together in a covey until driven from cover, flushing over the line in one adrenalin-pumping starburst.

In the classic partridge drive, the birds are driven over hedgerows and tree lines to the waiting line of Guns. The positioning of the shooting line needs careful consideration – too close and the Guns are not given sufficient time for a controlled shot at these fast birds. If the line is too far away, the birds can break out of the drive, flaring and turning back when they see the Guns.

Once in the properly placed

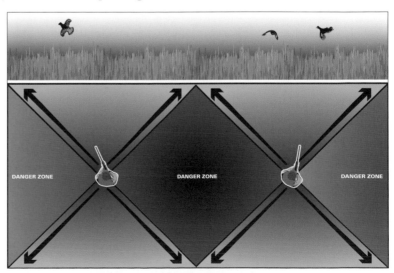

Safe arcs of fire for driven shooting.

line, the Guns should be tense but ready, poised for action like runners in the blocks. The butt of the stock should be touching the tendon that joins the pectoral to the biceps muscle, eyes looking out over the muzzles into the "blue" above the hedgerow. The keeper will blow his whistle – a short "peep" for a single or a long blast for a covey.

As the covey appears, do not be distracted by the blur of birds. Single out and focus on one bird – this will give you the best chance of a clean kill. The classic partridge presentation has been referred to as lowland grouse, and needs to be shot with the same authority and application of controlled aggression.

Your weight well forward on the front foot, attack the covey, picking out the lead bird at 50 yards, shooting it without hesitation before selecting your second bird. If your timing is right, you will drop both birds well in front of the line. Though I encourage taking the first shot early, please be sure that the birds are well clear of cover and are framed in sky.

Driven Grouse

Once you are positioned in the grouse butt, the first thing you need to do is establish your safe "arcs of fire". Pick out rocks or patches of heather to define the lines of the arcs. Position the safety sticks to limit your angles of fire and stop you from swinging through another butt. On steep moors, the next butt may be higher than the protection the sticks allow, so make a mental note that you cannot shoot in that direction.

If there are no safety sticks in your butt, place your cartridge bag and gunslip on the edge of the butt to catch your eye and remind you of the safe arc of fire. When you are in an end butt, be sure to mark the position of flankers.

Grouse shooting, take your first bird at 40 to 50 yards. (PAUL FIEVEZ)

Note: Your clothing should match and blend in with the colours of the moor. Avoid light colours that will make you stand out and be sure to wear a brimmed cap to shade your face.

Keep your gun flat to the horizon, cartridges laid out in pairs along the edge of the butt, readily to hand. Keep alert, concentrate on sighting the first birds of the drive as early as possible. Stay still and low in the butt – this requires a relaxed concentration.

I have seen many a first drive missed by a Gun who decided there was time to visit the "Casa de Pee Pee", have a cigarette, or who nodded off while waiting for the beaters to bring the birds to the line. Then he is shocked awake by the "rat-a-tat-tat" of the first shots and fumbles for his gun! What a waste! And it is not very fair to the beaters who have put so much hard work into the drive.

The grouse is a truly wild bird so you need to keep low and still until the moment you take your shot. If you so much as fidget, they will see the movement and flare and jink like pigeons coming into a pattern, often changing their direction entirely over another butt, making an already tough bird to shoot an even more difficult target.

Grouse fly low, hugging the contours of the heather; their speed can be deceptive. In reality, a grouse can fly the length of a cricket pitch (22 yards) in one second and, on the wind, even faster! This unanticipated speed of flight often catches the inexperienced shot out.

To better deal with the grouse's speed, pick out a rock or tuft of heather at 40 yards – when the grouse crosses that point, you will take your first shot. To do this, you need to look out past this mark to 50 yards, then lock on the lead bird and begin your gun mount when the bird is at the 50 yard mark.

Your gun mount should be minimal – a bayonet movement with your weight well forward on your front foot – controlled aggression is what is needed. As soon as the gun is in your cheek and shoulder, point out the bird's crop (to avoid missing high) and fire without hesitation!

Be sure to complete your mount, lifting the gun fully into the cheek and not the shoulder first. An incomplete gun mount will cause you to drop your head to the stock – another cause of shooting high. The bird's speed of flight and the shot cloud will connect around the 40 yard mark, giving you time to get a second shot off in front.

As the covey passes the line, good footwork is essential. With muzzles up and pointing skywards, execute a smart "about face" and then with muzzles flat to the horizon, shoot as if attempting to "knock their spats off"!

All shooting in front of the butts must cease at the sound of the horn which announces that the beaters are coming into range. Turn and, looking back over your shoulder, watch the coveys approach. Determine their anticipated line of flight, so you can attack them with minimum movement as they slip and slide away downhill.

Weight on the front foot, mount the gun smoothly with a bayonet movement to the grouse. Take the shot without pause or check as the muzzles align with the bird and the gun reaches the cheek.

Note: If a large number of grouse are in the drive, concentrate on shooting them in front of the line.

High Driven Pheasant and Partridge

The height of a bird's flight is directly proportional to the launch height. Spinneys, coppices and cover crops are planted in locations higher than the line of Guns so the pheasants driven over the cover will present higher and more sporting shots. The higher the point from which the birds are driven, the

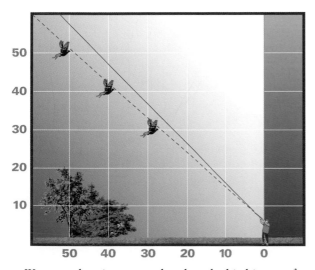

Wrong – shooting too early when the bird is out of range.

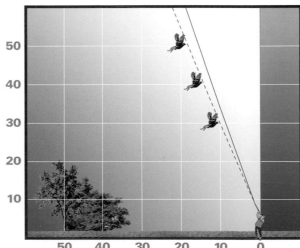

Correct – letting the bird come into range. The higher the bird the closer to the perpendicular it should be shot.

higher the pheasant will fly. Until the 1970s, a pheasant passing over the line at a height of 25 to 40 yards was considered a high bird. Today, birds soaring in excess of 50 and 60 yards are the new "*high*".

With the demand for higher, more testing birds, partridge are being presented in the same manner as pheasants. Where cover and terrain will allow, Guns are positioned in the bottom of the valleys and dales. These changes in height require changes in the technique to tackle the birds. Unlike the grouse and traditional partridge, these driven birds can be taken well out in front, where, if you shoot the first barrel at 50 yards, the bird and shot will hopefully collide at 40 yards.

The same shot 50 yards in front taken at a bird 50 yards high, will be out of range. High birds need to be shot just short of the perpendicular overhead.

The observed progress of a game bird is created by the beat of its wings and its passage against the background. The closer the bird is to the background, the quicker it looks. This fact, combined with the short window of shooting opportunity of the classic presentation, makes the driven bird appear to the subconscious like a winged rocket.

The same bird coming off high cover, travelling much farther and higher, offers a bigger shooting window – you have considerably more time in which to take a shot. The high partridge should be tackled in exactly the same manner as high pheasant with one caveat – the partridge is slower than the pheasant and does not require the same forward allowance as its bigger colleague.

To connect consistently with high pheasant or partridge, any bird flying in excess of 50 yards high, requires that everything has to be right. Any error in the fundamentals – gun mount, gun fit, choke–cartridge choice and technique – is magnified. What you can get away with at 30 yards, you will not be able to at 50. If you *start* right, you will *finish right*.

Range

Judging the accurate distance of an object is essential to determine if a bird is within range or not. But a high bird against the sky will always appear farther away than those which are the same distance away, but against a background.

You can practise judging distance in your everyday life. When you are walking the dog, pick out an

Silhouettes of life-sized pheasant at 30, 40 and 50 yards.

Right: To help judge range.

object: tree, postbox or streetlight, guess the distance, and walk towards it, mentally counting your paces. Compare the total against your estimate. Within a short period of time, you will become proficient at judging distance accurately. However, remember that an object against the background is more easily judged than a bird seen against a clear sky.

Judgement of the height of a high bird against a clear sky can be practised in the city by looking at high-rise buildings and monuments. The average floor height of a high-rise building is 13 feet so the 5th, 7th, 9th and 12th floors would correspond to 20, 30, 40 and 50 yards. In the field, a mature oak tree is about 20 yards high, a fully-grown beech, approximately 40 yards.

The best and most accurate way to judge a pheasant's range is to take a dead pheasant, spread it as if it were in flight and, placing it on a piece of hard cardboard, trace its outline. Cut four of these silhouettes and place them on posts at 20, 30, 40 and 50 yards. You can now accurately learn to recognize and learn the size of a pheasant at those yardages from the silhouettes.

Lines of Flight

Birds of the same species are not all the same. Differences in age, maturity, weight and amount of feathering means they fly at different speeds and heights and are affected by the wind. No bird is ever flying exactly the same speed and line of flight – they can be drifting, curling and sliding. Climbing or falling, accelerating or decelerating and flying at different altitudes, each bird presents a unique one-off shot.

When you are on your peg or in the butts, consider the wind – its direction and strength will give you a good idea of the bird's line of flight. In deep valleys, the wind is constantly gusting in different directions. Just watch the autumn leaves as they float down from the trees, observe how they swirl and change direction on the wind. The birds are constantly trimming their wings to match these air currents, minutely but continuously changing their trajectory, tacking and weaving in the same manner as the falling leaves.

Failure to step into the line of flight will result in running out of swing, with the involuntary dipping or rolling of the shoulder causing the muzzles to "rainbow" off the target line.

If the bird is obviously curling or drifting, you have two options: one, take your line off the wing on the inside of the curl or drift, the amount of which determines how far along the wing you insert the gun to compensate for the curl. Two, you can take the bird as a high crosser. At 150 feet up, the wind can push a bird off line and, if you are to be consistent, there is a real need to *lock on and stay on the line, on every shot*.

Timing

Essential in all forms of game shooting, timing is even more important when shooting high birds. You must be patient as well – high birds can be seen from a long way out and can take several seconds to reach the line; the most common mistake is to commence the gun mount or address the bird too early, when it is still out of range. This results in tracking the bird, using up available body movement, so that as the bird comes into range, you're running out of movement. Your swing slows and stalls, resulting in an almost certain miss behind.

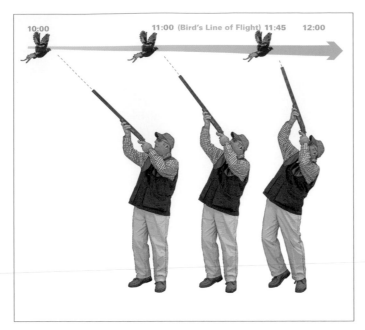

10:00   11:00 (Bird's Line of Flight) 11:45   12:00

LEFT: With very high birds, let them come well in, commence your gun mount when the bird is at 10 o'clock completing it at 11 o'clock and swing in front in one smooth move taking the shot at 11.45.

Your eyes can only hold hard focus for a short period of time – half a second or less. Staring at the bird too early in its flight results in a loss of hard focus when it is most needed, when the bird comes into range and the shot is taken. Your eyes guide your hands, so the point at which the move to the bird commences needs to be timed so your eyes acquire the bird first with a soft focus. This focus should increase incrementally, so as your gun mount is complete, total hard focus is established on the bird – at the correct time and place to take the shot.

Choke

Birds at longer distances will obviously require an increase in choke. Though most traditional game guns were choked Improved Cylinder and Modified, with the higher and higher bird presentations, Improved Modified and Full are more often the degree of choke chosen.

Footwork

The "Stanbury Method" for shooting driven birds requires you to step into the line of flight, maintaining your weight on your front foot throughout the shot. The "Churchill Method" requires you to lift your heel that is opposite to the flight line, transferring the weight from one foot to the other.

On a straight driven bird, Stanbury would have you continue to maintain your weight on the front foot, pushing your hip towards the bird. Churchill would have you transfer your weight onto your back foot. Whichever method you use, to ensure a smooth, accurate swing through the completion of the shot, the heel of one foot or the other needs to be raised from the ground.

You can demonstrate this to yourself by standing and, adopting a stance for shooting a driven bird, keeping both feet firmly planted on the floor. As you attempt to swing over the perpendicular, you'll find you can make only a limited amount of movement before the latissimus dorsi muscle connecting the shoulder to the hip runs out of its range of motion. This checks your body and your arm driving the gun, effectively checking your swing.

Churchill – taking a high incomer off the back foot.

Stanbury – off the front foot.

Now make the same move lifting the heel of your front foot off the ground and you will see that, by transferring your weight to your back foot (Churchill), you have a greater range of motion. Lift the heel of your back foot, placing your weight on your front foot (Stanbury) and you will feel the same benefit of an extended range of motion.

You have to experiment to see whether the Stanbury or the Churchill method works better for you. Stanbury was a tall bean-pole of a man, whereas Churchill was short and squat. I, personally, think their physical characteristics had a great bearing on their individual approach to the same problem.

The correct footwork is essential – it allows you to keep your muzzles accurately on the bird's line and, ensuring a smooth rotation of your body, keeps you from checking your swing and rolling or coming off the line.

For any bird that is not going to pass directly overhead, you need to step into the line of flight to the area where you intend to take the shot. This is crucial to avoid one of the most common causes of misses at this target – rolling off the bird's line of flight. You must move your feet!

If you do not step into the area where you intend to take your shot, your upper body rotation will be checked by the fixed position of your lower body, causing an unconscious transfer of weight from one foot to the other. You will run out of swing, causing an involuntary and unconscious rolling of the shoulder, resulting in rainbowing or windscreen-wiping the gun over and under the line of flight.

Dropping the Shoulder

If the bird quarters to the left or right of centre, you will need to deliberately drop your shoulder *opposite* the line of flight, placing the barrels flat on the line to match the target's angle, to avoid shooting low and behind. This action should not be confused with the involuntary fault of rolling the shoulder.

Step into line dropping the shoulder opposite the line of flight. This will place the muzzles perpendicular to the target's line of flight. The blackboard and shoulder alignment will help you visualize this tchnique.

Birds that quarter left or right of the peg require you to step into the line (Stanbury) or lift the heel opposite the line of flight (Churchill).

As you move your muzzles to the bird, begin to drop the shoulder opposite the line of flight.

This will keep the muzzles on line; this is essential to avoid a miss off line and particularly important when shooting a side by side.

Note: To perform this technique correctly, the gun is placed perpendicular to the flight line with the shoulders parallel to the line of flight. Simply canting the gun is inefficient and causes the shotgun to place its pattern low.

It all depends on the style you prefer – with Stanbury you move your front foot, with Churchill, you lift the heel of your foot opposite the line of flight. The requirement to drop the shoulder opposite the line of flight is important because when swinging on a high quartering bird, most misses are low and behind.

Grip

Remember the role of your left hand – it must always lead the mount and swing. Be assertive, extending your left hand on and through the bird.

The incorrect position of your hand on the forend can cause you to pull off the target line. Practise mounting and swinging an empty gun, tracing a direct line across the ceiling. You will quickly see the importance of the leading hand to holding a straight line.

There is a tendency to drift off the line to the left (for the right-handed, right for the left-handed). To counter this, hold the muzzles on the *right* wing of the bird at the point where it joins the body. This hold-point will result in a better move to the target and counters the tendency to drift off the line on high overhead shots.

Lead

The requirement for forward allowance increases with distance, but inches at the muzzle is feet at the bird. There are two things that you need to see but cannot look at, that is the bead and the lead.

Only experience will teach you what amount of lead you need to see for a successful shot at the different species. However, I have a simple formula to estimate that amount of lead: for closer birds – *some* – for middle distance birds – *more* and for far-away birds – *a lot*!

One-Eyed Shots

The one-eyed shooter experiences the most difficulty with the straight-on driven target, losing the target behind the barrel, causing the gun to stop and miss. If the target is sufficiently high, it should allow enough time for the "one-eyed jack" to turn into the line and shoot it as a crosser. They should be sure to turn into the line so the gun is being *pulled into* the face, not *pushed away* (right to left for a right-hander and vice-versa for the left-hander).

Some one-eyed shooters enjoy great success by swinging alongside the target, applying the lead before gently swerving onto the line as the shot is taken, in the same manner as overtaking a car on the motorway. Others learn to keep the gun moving even when the barrel has blocked the target from sight, and can achieve great success once the timing is learned. One of the great strengths of the Swing-Through technique is that the target is always in view until the application of lead is made.

Note: The two-eyed shooter can keep the bird in his peripheral vision with the non-dominant eye while guiding the shotgun with the dominant eye. This method is referred to as *looking through the shotgun*. The bird is kept in sight as is the awareness of forward allowance, creating more consistency than just swinging through the bird, trusting you can "*hit what you cannot see*".

Best Techniques for Driven Shooting

Pull-Away or Swing-Through are by far the best techniques, as both of these methods establish the line on every shot. There is no place for Maintained Lead on high driven pheasant or partridge.

Swing-Through

A word of caution on the Swing-Through technique: many people have the misconception that you insert your muzzles well behind the bird and then "swing through". This is incorrect and leads to an inconsistent swing speed. The muzzles should be inserted on the tail of the bird, followed by a firm acceleration of the gun, brushing *through and along the target line* to establish forward allowance. This action gives you more accuracy and control.

Pull-Away

You insert the muzzles on the bird's head, then follow with a firm acceleration to establish forward allowance.

Note: You will discover for yourself which technique works best for you, but you will often use a combination of both during a drive. When presented with a brace of birds, the first of a pair should be taken well out in front with a bayonet-like "pull-away" move. This will give you ample time to locate, lock on and shoot the second bird, coming from behind with "swing through".

Muzzle Speed

Picture your hand on the forend reaching up and catching the bird, as if you were catching a ball. Think of cricket or baseball, where you never have time to think about trajectory and speed, but just catch the ball. Well, that is the way to take care of the problem of differing elevations in shooting high pheasant.

Visualize reaching up and catching them with the shot cloud. This method eliminates the attempt to measure your lead, thereby slowing your swing. It also ensures a smoothly *"accelerating muzzle speed"* and *"follow through"* at the exact moment you need it.

Faults

Driven targets create a tendency to lift your head to keep eye contact with the bird, especially if it gets obscured by the barrels. Moving your head and leaving the gun causes a miss behind! Keep your head firmly "spot-welded" to the stock on incomers and always take the straight bird first, never the curler or quartering bird. Taking the curler first will cause inconsistency on the second bird of a pair.

Failure to lift the heel of either the front or back foot will result in a checked or stopped swing. With the Churchill style, the timing of the transfer of weight is critical and requires practise. If you prefer the Stanbury style, be careful you do not fall into the habit of simply bending backward from the waist, not pushing your hip forward. This fault is certain to check or stop your swing.

Keep your muzzles at 50 degrees while waiting for the birds to appear. Failure to keep your muzzles at the correct insertion point means wasted motion and an inconsistent gun mount.

Because driven birds are approaching and getting larger, they appear to be going slower than their true speed. It is very easy to fall into the trap of aiming or measuring the lead which will result in a certain miss behind.

Though this is the style favoured by the Prince of Wales, too straight a front hand impedes the swing, causing it to slow or stop. You will need to experiment to find the optimum front hand position given your build and length of pull.

The timing of the shot is critical. If you insert on the bird too soon, you will run out of swing and may fall into the trap of aiming. Keep your head glued to the stock! Do not fall into the habit of raising it too quickly to see the bird fall – this will cause a miss over the top.

Rushing

How many times have you cleanly killed a late-seen bird without any conscious thought, just a last second reaction? This is referred to as an "Instinctive Shot", but without the timing that allows the eyes to guide the hands to the bird, it will never be consistent.

The most common fault I see is rushing. The best shots know that consistency is only achieved by correct time management; they match their move and swing to the bird's speed, making a smooth and controlled shot. It takes years of practice and experience, but they know that the time gained from a smooth move allows them to shoot the target positively and deceptively quickly.

Creating time allows you to move your feet, if a pair requires it. More time allows better muzzle management – the time to shoot the first bird in the best place and to leave the muzzles in the optimum position to pick up the second bird.

The inexperienced shooter thinks that taking the bird with such authority is achieved by the application of speed and this is where it all goes horribly and confusingly wrong. To improve your consistency and hence, your kills, you need to go back to the equivalent of shooting school and learn the three "Rs" – "*Rushing Ruins Rhythm*".

Once you have learned to match muzzle speed to target speed, you will have, in effect, slowed the bird down and achieved more time in which to make a smooth move. With practice and consistent application, you will be making cleaner kills.

Practice and Lead

My recipe for taking really high pheasant and partridge is gun speed management – you need to start "*smoothly*" and finish "*swiftly*". It is essential that, when practising for these birds on clay targets off the high tower, the shooting station is properly placed so the target is under power and at similar speed to a pheasant or partridge at the point where you plan to shoot it. This will help you to regulate your timing and swing speed.

While this is the only viable practice available, if the target speed or station placement are incorrect, it actually teaches the wrong swing speed, as the high pheasant or partridge is accelerating or maintaining its speed and the clay target is decelerating. This fact complicates the perception of lead.

There are two types of perceived lead – lead by distance and lead by speed. The slowing clay pigeon needs lead by distance. This lead is applied with a slow swing that matches the target speed. So the *perceived* lead needed to break a clay target is greater than the lead perceived when shooting a high pheasant.

The reason is, the high pheasant or partridge is passing over the gun at "terminal velocity". Having been beaten out of a high cover crop, it powers into the air and looks for the cover (and safety) which has been strategically positioned to ensure it will fly to it. The high pheasant sets its wings and accelerates; just like a child riding a bicycle down a hill the pheasant "takes its feet off the pedals" as gravity speeds its descent.

The pheasant passes over the waiting guns at much greater speed than the inanimate clay target, requiring the application of *lead by speed*. This lead is *perceived* as much less than the lead required to hit the high clay target that is used in practice, if it is not presented correctly.

The difference in the perceived lead and gun speed between shooting clay targets and shooting high pheasant can be very frustrating on the first few drives. As the pheasant glides towards you, it is getting bigger. This impression, plus the lack of wing movement, creates the optical illusion that the bird is moving more slowly than it is. You match the muzzle speed to the bird's speed, and then swing slowly out in front of the beak to see the large lead picture you have been practising on the tower.

But the pheasant is actually hurtling toward you at a speed that can reach 50 miles per hour in a stiff wind. This is the total opposite of the slowing falling clay target. The deceptively high speed of the pheasant's flight eats up the lead and, accelerating past the slow-moving barrels, the result is a miss behind.

Your loader tells you to double your lead. But this accomplishes nothing, as the gun speed does not match the pheasant's speed. When the increased lead does not work, the frustration can be excruciating, as the last thing observed before the trigger was pulled was… a huge lead!

The solution to this frustrating situation is to make a smooth move to the pheasant, matching muzzle speed to the bird's speed, and on completion of the gun mount into the cheek, accelerate the gun smoothly in front, pulling the trigger without check or hesitation.

The ultimate place to take the bird is to pick the bird out at 10 o'clock, complete your gun mount and fire your first barrel at 11 o'clock and, if needed, the second barrel, perpendicular, at 12 o'clock.

The bird is at its most vulnerable at 75 to 90 degrees where the head and majority of the vital organs are exposed to the gun. It is also at its closest when overhead, making this the optimum point at which to take the shot.

If your first shot is a miss or wounds the bird, maintain hard focus, stay in the gun and give it the second barrel. A first barrel miss often sharpens the focus on the second shot and results in a clean kill.

Self-Loading

Loading a shotgun when under pressure is a little like shooting – remember *"Rushing Ruins Rhythm"* – so you need to create more time for yourself.

Let's begin with your equipment. Nearly as important as its accuracy, a shotgun should be able to cleanly eject spent cartridges a good distance. Weak or poorly-timed ejectors can ruin a drive, causing fumbling, dropped cartridges or that "Titanic" of loading disasters, where the ejector (extractor) overrides the rim of the shell, effectively ending the drive for you.

Avoid that simplest of mistakes of all, failing to take sufficient cartridges for a drive, which has you running to a neighbour's peg only to find out he does not shoot a 16 gauge!

So, a gun that ejects as well as it shoots and more than sufficient cartridges are required. This is the first hurdle.

A cartridge bag needs to be able to carry sufficient cartridges for the biggest of drives. It needs a Payne-Gallwey hinged flap that folds completely out of the way. The mouth must be big enough for you to get your hand in and out while holding a handful of cartridges. You should never load from the cartridge bag, but use it as the reservoir to fill your pockets and cartridge belt.

Good ejectors are essential when driven shooting.
(BETTWS HALL SPORTING)

Cartridges can be carried in many ways: bags, belts, pouches and speed loaders.

Pockets should be of the bellows-type, with flaps that can be secured open, and a cartridge belt can be leather looped or have plastic clips.

Give pockets and bags a good shake and the cartridges will "stand to attention", rims up, so you can pick them out the right way up, simply feeding them into the chambers.

Ease the cartridges in belt loops before the start of a drive for faster access and loading. The clip belts are swifter, but not so secure as the looped belts, and with the clips you can easily lose shells.

There are various speed loaders, but they have limited capacity and take time to fill. They also empty quickly and you have to fall back on loading from your pockets anyway.

The side by side will always have the edge in loading over the over and under because of its shallow gape.

There is a myth that loading the top barrel of an over and under is quicker, but to cock the hammers, the gun has to be hinged fully regardless. But to shoot the top barrel first is a bonus if only one shell is fired, and I do it simply because of this.

The Two Gun Tango – Shooting with a Pair of Guns and a Loader

Safety

The shotguns are always exchanged with the safety "*ON*". There are no exceptions, whether the gun is loaded, one shot fired or unloaded.

Position

The loader stands close behind the shoulder being shot off; this ensures safe exchanging of the shotguns.

Exchanging the Guns

After firing, the shooter remains facing the drive, looking for the next shooting opportunity. His first action is to put on the safety and hold the empty gun in his right hand, in a vertical position close to his body. Then with his left hand open and extended across the body, he is ready to receive the loaded gun.

The loader places the loaded gun, also in an upright position, into the shooter's left hand (preventing a potential barrel clash by firmly pushing/slapping the forend into the palm of the shooter's left hand) while simultaneously taking the fired gun by the forend from the shooter's right hand.

Note: The guns must always be exchanged on the right-hand side even if taking a shot behind the line, to avoid both a dangerous situation and damage to the guns. The sides are reversed for the left-handed shooter.

The loader stands behind the shoulder being shot off.

The safety must be placed ON and the shotgun held vertically against the body.

The loader should bend and turn away to allow a safe arc of fire.

The shooter's free hand must be extended to receive the second shotgun to avoid damage to the barrels.

Loader

The loader turns to his right, using his left-handed grip on the gun, he turns and lifts the butt up, gripping it between the forearm and body. With his right hand, he pushes the top lever and opens the gun. He then reloads and closes it and the gun is gripped and lifted vertically, ready for the next exchange.

The loader needs to be aware of the shooter's position and movements at all times and mimic them, while being as unobtrusive as possible, so as not to interfere in the shooting.

Shooting with one or two guns, pick your birds and attempt to shoot to a rhythm and timing that allows a steady flow of fire, not two or four shots, long pause and fumble, followed by a rushed poke and hope.

Chapter 12
Walked-up and Upland Bird Shooting over Dogs

In Europe, walked-up bird or ground game shooting is referred to as *"Rough Shooting"*, in America it is called *"Upland Bird Shooting"*. Habitats, terrain and cover are incredibly diverse, ranging from grassy flat lands, to rolling plains covered in scrub, to hills dotted with trees and hedges to forest and dense woods.

In all rough shooting, a good dog is almost as necessary as a gun. Depending on the quarry and the terrain, some type of pointers, spaniels or flushing dogs are the breeds of choice.

Dogs

Pointers usually work in pairs to hunt covey birds such as quail and grouse. When a bird or a covey is scented, the dog will go on point, the second dog "honouring" the first dog's point. The dogs will remain stationary, allowing the hunters to get into position to shoot.

The guide or a flushing dog will step in to flush the covey, and the hunters will shoot. Depending on the dogs and the customs of the area, either the flushing dog or the pointers will retrieve the fallen birds. If the flushing dog is used to retrieve, the pointing dogs should remain on point until ordered to break point and continue hunting.

Flushing dogs are also used on birds that run hard such as pheasants or blue quail. These dogs are trained to work close, quartering out and back within shooting distance as, when they flush the bird, there is little or no opportunity for the hunter to get into position.

Hunt-Flush Retrieve. (TERRY ALLEN)

Be Ready

When doing walked-up and upland bird hunting, you walk a lot and shoot a little. It is very easy to "switch off" and become lethargic, especially if the dogs are hunting for a while and not finding any birds. You need to develop a relaxed readiness so you are actively hunting, not just walking the dog. Otherwise, when the fleeting opportunity presents itself, you may not see the bird well and make a hurried, sloppy gun mount.

Focus

When the bird does flush, hard focus on the bird! It is not enough just to see the pheasant, you should be able to "sex" it as well. Focus on the head as it flushes – a pheasant is 30 inches long and if you shoot at the body, you will likely miss behind or wound the bird. Remember, the body has to go where the head leads, so if you focus on the head, you will hit the bird in the vital organs.

Shooting Quadrants

When hunting with more than one hunter or with a guide, dividing the field and your position into shooting quadrants is the safest way to allow for the most effective and efficient swing.

Double-barrelled Shotguns

Remember that the double-barrelled shotgun is simply two guns – two barrels, two locks and sometimes two triggers – on one piece of wood. If you should wound a bird, the second barrel is there to finish the job and kill it cleanly. If more than one shot presents itself, be sure to see the first bird fold and fall before moving to the second.

Safe arc of fire when shooting over dogs.

Chokes

Most upland birds are shot between 20 and 30 yards, so Cylinder and Improved Modified are a good combination.

Quartering Shots

The most common shots taken by the upland bird hunter are straight away or quartering, within 20 to 30 yards of the bird. The term "quartering" is used to describe a wide variety of lines of flight, both away from and towards the hunter. The variety of speed, angle and curl of the flight make these very difficult shots. For example, as Hungarian partridge make their escape on the slopes of steep hills, their flight lifts and curls into the wind, using it to accelerate away – usually quartering downhill.

Quartering birds are tricky as they require the shooter to match changes in the perceived lead to make the shot. For example, a true quartering bird requires more lead than a bird at a more acute (narrow) angle to the shooter.

Minimizing Gun Movement

Quartering targets do not require a great deal of gun movement. The most successful action is more of an insertion "to and through" the bird, rather than the swing one would use on a long passing shot. A precise gun movement is required as there is very little margin for error. A good shot begins with a step into the line of flight and an excellent, well-practised gun mount. The good quartering shot involves a full body swing, the body turning the gun like a tank turret, the arms lifting and pointing the gun to the bird. Using arm movement alone creates an uncontrolled fast swing resulting in inconsistency.

The majority of upland bird shots are quartering away. The speed, angle and distance are constantly changing, hence the lead required is changing as well.

The deadliest move a bird shooter can make is with his feet.

The step into the line is a small step and pivot, not a stride forward.

Footwork

You hear the whirr of wing beats or catch sight of the flushed bird. If you are walking, stop, and "harness" both the sight and the sound of the flush. By harnessing sight and sound, you will see the bird better, more clearly, before moving to shoot. Consider the bird's distance and direction of flight. Is it straight away or quartering? "The deadliest move a bird shooter can make is with his feet!"

Stepping with your leading foot into the line of flight, begin your gun mount, overcoming the inertia of the gun and starting it in the bird's direction. Make sure that you have stepped into your quadrant and will be in balance when the shot is taken. The step is essential to allow a smooth, full-body rotation throughout the firing point quadrant. If you don't move your feet and body into the direction of flight, you will run out of rotation at the firing point, which will slow or stop your swing and cause a miss behind. Or, if you are in the wrong position, you realize you are behind and attempt to throw the gun in front of the target, usually missing in front.

Ready Position

From your "walking gun carry", you need to adopt the ready position with the stock well up under the arm, between your biceps and pectoral muscles. With your eyes looking out over the muzzles, let the bird rise and gain sufficient distance (so you will not crush it and ruin it with too tight a pattern), step into the line while simultaneously pointing the leading hand and muzzles at the bird. As the stock is fully mounted into your cheek and shoulder pocket, fire the gun. *It is important that your head be kept still throughout the shot.* Pointing the muzzles at the bird throughout the shot effectively establishes its speed and line of flight, allowing the shot to be taken without pause or check.

It is important that you do not "ride the bird", but take the shot when instinct dictates. The more obtuse the angle created by the visualized interception point of the shot string with the target flight line and the distance of the bird, the greater the lead required. A straight-away or acute angle shot requires little, if any, forward allowance.

Hard focus on the bird.   *Let your eyes guide your hands to the bird.*   *Stay locked on the bird, complete your mount and shoot without pause or check.*

Anticipation

As a wingshooter, you cannot anticipate a bird's line of flight. Moving your hands to the target, i.e., pointing at the bird with your gun, is the only way you can react to the bird's speed and direction. If you can practise shooting the fast quartering targets on the Skeet field, you can fine-tune your reaction and move to the bird in the field. You see the bird, step into the line, smoothly move and mount the gun with eye and muzzle firmly on the bird, and gently brush through the line: *butt . . . belly . . . beak and bang*!

Techniques

I personally consider *Swing-Through* and *Pull-Away* to be the best techniques for the upland bird hunter. Using Swing-Through, insert the muzzles right on the tail of the bird, not feet behind. If the muzzles are too far behind, you are forced into a rushed, "catch-up" swing, bursting past the target, reactively stopping the gun and missing behind.

With Pull-Away, you insert the muzzles on the head of the bird and a deliberate, controlled acceleration of the gun establishes the lead. Your gun has to move only marginally quicker than the bird to make the shot. An aggressive, uncontrolled swing will cause a miss in front. I would caution against using the Sustained Lead method, as the often erratic flight of flushing birds makes it difficult to maintain the line. I recommend sticking with Pull-Away or Swing-Through for upland and rough shooting.

Lead

The correct amount of lead is learned by practice, to the point that making a shot becomes an "instinctive awareness" of where the target is when the trigger is pulled. Soon you will be able to apply the required lead without looking at it, or more important, thinking about it.

The first step towards developing this awareness is to control your gun speed. Because of its line of flight in relation to your shooting position, the quartering bird appears much faster than it really is.

When practising these shots on the Skeet field, look at two targets the same size, thrown at the same speed – low house 6 quartering-away, and low house 4 crossing. The going-away (quartering) target will always appear the faster of the two.

To the beginner and intermediate shot, this perceived speed is addressed with an equally fast gun swing to the bird. The greater gun speed causes the gun to overtake the bird and is the reason most quartering targets are missed high or in front. Using a light field gun can compound the problem, as a very light gun is quick to start, but equally quick to stop, causing misses behind from over-correction.

Complex Lead

A bird flying (quartering) towards you will require twice the lead of an outgoing bird on the same line. Also, the earlier you take a quartering bird in its flight, the more lead it requires. If you can wait a bit to allow the bird to settle into its flight, it will require less lead.

Another feather for his hat. (TERRY ALLEN)

Flushing roosters.
(TERRY ALLEN)

The complete triangle; gun, bird and dog.
(TERRY ALLEN)

Just like an aeroplane, any bird will try to turn into the wind to achieve lift. Observing the wind's direction will give you an indication of the direction of flight. Even if the bird flushes downwind, it will bank back. To do this, it will dip a wing. If it is the right wing, it will turn to the right and you need to shoot the right wing rather than the body; this allows for the continuous changes in direction that happen as the bird tries to escape.

A bird's curling-dropping-sliding moves in flight are exploiting nature's tricks of survival and require cunning and practice on the shooter's part to make the kill. Once again, practise on the Skeet field can "groove the move" to the bird in the field. These shots require *complex lead* – a combination of lead both *in front of* and *under or above* the target.

Complex lead allows for the time lag between the pull of the trigger and the shot cloud's arrival to the bird. Visualizing where to place the shot pattern requires you to educate your back brain or sub-conscious. This can only be achieved with repetitive practice on quartering targets on the Skeet field.

Every bird will have its own nuanced and subtle flight differences, demanding a matching expertise to consistently read the line, direction and drift, slide or curl. The practice that develops intuitive clay shooting also develops instinctive wingshooting – you can count on it when it really matters. Put in the practice time on a variety of quartering targets on the Skeet field – learn to recognize the curls, drops and slides – and you will see improved success in the field immediately!

Chapter 13
Decoyed and Pass Shooting

History

All forms of wingshooting are inextricably linked to the evolution of the shotgun, but no more so than decoying migratory birds. As early as the 17th century, wildfowl were being harvested using live birds as decoys.

With over 19 species of migratory quarry world-wide, from ducks and geese to pigeons and doves, decoyed and pass shooting have more participants than any form of wingshooting today.

Decoying

Migratory birds like pigeon, dove, ducks and geese are gregarious flock birds. They feed and roost together in large numbers and this behaviour pattern makes them very susceptible to decoying. If passing birds spot large numbers of their species apparently eating, their feeding instinct is triggered and they fly in to join the flock.

However, it is not enough to randomly place a large decoy pattern and expect the birds to start pouring in. The decoy set up has to be built in the right place and that can only be determined by reconnaissance in the actual field.

Flight Lines

Migratory birds are creatures of habit and use the same roosting areas and flight lines year after year. It is essential that you spend the time learning where their roosts are in your area and locate the established flight lines to and from the favoured feeding areas; these flight lines are the equivalent of motorways running to and from roosts to feeding spots.

Birds enter and exit the fields or water on these flight lines, so it is essential that you build your blind, hide or pit

Wind Direction

Incoming Ducks

15–20 Yards

HIDE

RIGHT: Simple duck decoy pattern.

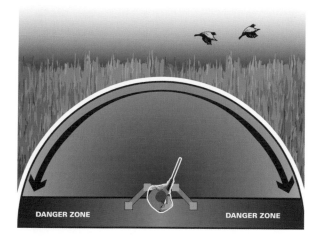

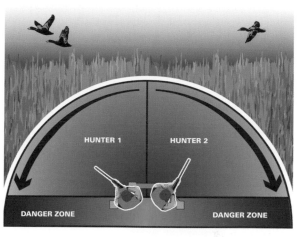

TOP LEFT:
Safe arcs of fire
when shooting
from a blind.

TOP RIGHT:
Safe arcs of fire
when sharing a
blind.

LEFT:
Safe arcs of fire
when two or
more blinds are
in a row.

on or under the flight line. It is extremely difficult, if not impossible, to draw the birds to a blind off the flight line.

Of course, the feeding areas will vary with the time of year and the available feeding opportunities. That is why successful pattern placement and decoying is totally dependent on successful scouting.

Hides, Blinds and Pits

Your cover, be it a hide, a blind or a pit, needs to look natural and blend in with the indigenous topography, foliage and vegetation of the area. Natural materials onsite can be used, but the better option is a hide that can be changed to match the background and season. Camouflaged netting with a set of hide poles makes an excellent hide, plus it is lightweight and portable so that you can build your hide in the optimum position on the flight line.

The hide, blind or pit should provide enough cover to conceal you from the quarry yet allow sufficient room for you to rise up from your seat and smoothly mount and swing a gun. It should also be large enough to comfortably accommodate your most essential piece of hunting equipment, your dog.

Clothing

When decoying, fidgeting, in fact any movement, is easily detected by the birds' wary eyes. The ability to be still and quiet is the first essential component of success, the second is camouflage clothing that blends with the background of your hide – this combination will markedly increase your success in drawing birds into range.

Modern camouflage clothing is remarkable in its concealment qualities. So many patterns are now available for so many diverse backgrounds – from snow and sand to trees, leaves and fields. A wide-brimmed hat will help conceal your face and many hunters choose to wear a face veil. Sitting and shooting against a solid background of the same pattern and colour as your clothing makes it very difficult for the birds to see you.

Decoys

To set up decoys that show birds eating in a safe and abundant food source, you need to spend time observing the species you intend to hunt. You will find their actual feeding pattern is full of movement, with birds constantly changing positions as they feed, while other birds are constantly entering and leaving the feeding group.

Shooting decoyed pigeons from a blind in the United Kingdom. (FIELDSPORTS MAGAZINE)

Putting out a decoy pattern for ducks. (JOHN TAYLOR)

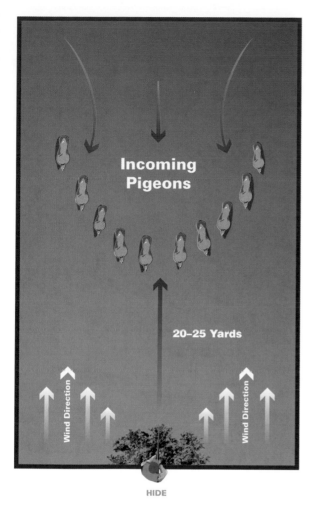

Incoming
Pigeons

20–25 Yards

Wind Direction

Wind Direction

HIDE

Simple pigeon decoying pattern.

You need a variety of decoys in different poses to replicate this appearance. Then you need to create movement with feeding, floating and flying devices like the pigeon magnet and roto-duck. There is a vast array of decoys to choose from, mostly plastic. But there are just one or two things to consider – first, weight. You have to be on the flight line and this could mean carrying all of your kit, hide, seat, gun, cartridges and decoys a good distance to your set-up point.

Buy the lightest and most realistic (life-like) decoys you can afford. As decoys rub against each other when being carried, they can quickly become shiny, so you need to inspect your decoys periodically. If they start to gleam or lose their colours, repaint or replace those decoys.

Patterns

Birds land and take off into the wind. Even if they take off *with* the wind, they will bank and turn into it as soon as possible because, like an aeroplane, they need the airflow for lift. When it is cold and windy, or when they are eating or roosting, they will have their heads into the wind as it helps to retain body heat. If their tails are facing into the wind, it will ruffle their feathers and chill them.

However, on a warm, windless day, birds will land, take off, feed and roost every-which-way. So the weather temperature and the strength of the wind is your first consideration when arranging your pattern.

Landing Zone

You need to create a landing zone in your pattern. Flock birds require room and a "runway" to land. If there is no clear runway or landing zone, they will fly on or land out of range beyond the pattern. The runway is what guides the birds into the pattern and into shooting range. It needs to be of a particular shape to do this and there are various options around a common theme. Common pigeon patterns are U, V, and W shapes, and the legs and the gap between the legs should be about 20 yards long.

Setting Up

First set up your hide. Place the point decoys twenty yards in front of the hide, next, pace out the legs, placing a decoy every 3 strides in random directions. Don't put the decoys with all the birds aligned in the same direction – this does not represent a natural feeding pattern. Floaters, feeders and pigeon magnets are set up to simulate birds entering and leaving the pattern and to create movement.

Wildfowl patterns are a little different. Ducks, for example, still require a runway to encourage and guide the birds into range. Create the runway by spreading the decoys in random clusters of three or four. The best pattern should contain a mix of duck species and sexes – this is essential to accurately replicate the scene of ducks feeding.

Be sure to place the dominant species in the middle of the pattern and the lesser species at the fringes. If you look at ducks feeding, there is no rhyme or reason to their movement or grouping. The better you duplicate this random effect in your pattern, the bigger draw it will be to passing ducks. Most decoyed birds are shot within 20 to 40 yards. When decoying, let the birds come well in, shoot one and then take the second as they turn and attempt to escape.

Technique

Shooting from a blind requires timing. If you move too soon, the bird will flare and fly out of range. The secret is to be patient and allow the birds to commit to landing. Then, you can shoot from your seated position or rise and shoot in one smooth movement. The bird will see you move and it will take evasive action, so if the shot is not made in one continuous move, mount, shoot action, you will be shooting at a retreating, jinking and twisting bird, hard to hit and often missed.

When sharing a blind, *only one person should shoot at a time*! You take turns, with the non-shooter acting as a spotter. The danger when both are shooting is that while focusing on the decoyed bird, it is all too easy to swing through your fellow Gun, especially if you have remained seated and he has stood up to shoot. If you choose to shoot two in a blind then I would urge you to agree to safe quadrants and for both to shoot seated or both to shoot standing.

Note: I always advise that only one person shoot in a blind at one time.

Pass Shooting

There are times when you cannot set up where the birds want to feed, whether from lack of

Shooting decoyed geese from a pit. (JOHN TAYLOR)

access or lack of permission to use the area. But all is not lost! The birds have to fly from their roost to feed and then fly back. Fieldcraft plus observation and knowledge of the location of the roosts, waters and the fields the birds prefer to use will establish their flight lines and the optimum position from which to pass shoot them.

The choices for pass shooting locations are tree lines, rivers, water holes or fields, and these spots need to be within shotgun range to ensure clean kills. You need to be as close to the flight line as possible, which may require a hide or blind and camouflage clothing.

Though the birds will not decoy to feed in your location, the use of decoys, rotary machines or lofted decoys in trees can help bring them within range. Most pass shooting is between 25 and 45 yards from the quarry.

Once you are set up, the long crossing shots you will be taking are among the most challenging and satisfying forms of shooting. It is also one of the most difficult, and you will need to practise to consistently hit those high, testing birds.

The biggest cause of misses at distance is not keeping the gun on the line. This is often caused by not using your feet and swinging the gun using

Shooting decoyed geese from a pit surrounded by water. (JOHN TAYLOR)

only your arms. This causes your body to run out of rotation, so you subconsciously bend at the waist to keep the gun moving, which causes your shoulders to roll, making the gun arc off the line. If you step into the line of flight and use your body to turn the gun, and use your hands and arms to lift and point the gun to the bird, you will rotate on-line throughout the shot.

Your success at decoyed and pass shooting is equal to the time spent on reconnaissance and field-craft. Do your homework, build a well-concealed blind or hide and create a realistic decoy pattern. There is nothing quite as satisfying in wingshooting as having truly wild birds see the pattern and instantly commit to flying in to land. It really is "homemade" shooting!

Labrador retrieving a duck in Zululand, South Africa.

Chapter 14
How to Practise Using the Inanimate Target
(Grooving the Instinctive Shot)

As in any sport, you cannot improve without practising! Wingshooting is no different – repeated practise grooves the shooting action so that it can be repeated effectively and consistently.

The Natural

It is impossible to be born with "natural" shooting talents. I can guarantee you that any of the Best Shots have spent hundreds of hours perfecting their timing and swing. It is exactly the same in other sports, such as golf – anyone who wants to shoot better needs to practise in exactly the same manner as a golfer, and the shooting grounds are the equivalent of the golfer's driving range.

Live Quarry versus Clay Targets

Clay targets can replicate any live quarry from a high pheasant to a bolting rabbit, but it is important to understand the difference between shooting a clay target and a live bird. The clay is decelerating, while the bird is accelerating or sustaining its flight speed. This difference requires different swing timing.

The clay target is launched at a speed of between 60 and 90 mph. However, without an on-board propulsion system, it is constantly slowing and falling and, whatever the target presentation, its flight pattern is in the shape of a parabolic arc.

A clay target crossing at 40 yards requires, mathematically, about 9 feet of lead. But, because the target is slowing and the gun speed should match the target's speed, the apparent lead, seen between gun and target, is more than it would be if shooting a passing dove at the same distance. Shooting the dove, you match its speed of flight with the equivalent gun speed. The slowing clay target requires lead by distance, whereas the live bird requires lead by speed.

Promatic Clay Trap.

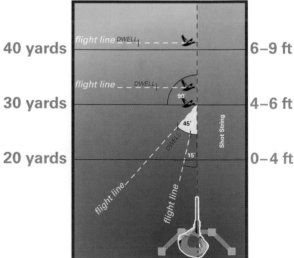

The visualized angle created by the shot string and the bird's line of flight, combined with its distance, determines the lead required.

A Skeet field; the perfect place to practise for upland bird hunting, pass shooting and decoyed shooting.

The high tower at Holland & Holland.

Shooting Grounds

Gunmakers of the 19th century opened shooting grounds offering gunfitting, instruction and practise shooting inanimate targets that simulated shooting in the field. At first, they shot at glass balls then, in the mid-1880s clay pigeons became the target of choice.

The best practice is done at shooting grounds focused on wingshooting instruction and practice for shooting in the field. They will have high towers, grouse butts and walked-up scenarios that realistically replicate the different species, especially their speed and line of flight. If this most effective practice is not possible, any of the clay target disciplines, Trap, Skeet or Sporting Clays offer useful practice opportunities.

Fundamentals of Practice

To be able to shoot with the Instinctive Style consistently, the fundamentals need to be learned, practised and grooved so that the shooting action can be performed without conscious thought. This skill, combined with a gun that fits, will allow one hundred percent concentration on the target, in the same manner as the outfielder concentrates solely on the ball.

In Chapter 8 I described the fundamental building blocks that are essential to straight shooting. But these need to be combined with an understanding of lead and how to correctly apply it – how to drive the gun in your peripheral vision while maintaining hard focus on the bird with your primary vision.

If the muzzles and the bird are in close proximity to each other, it is possible the bird can be hit. If the muzzles are close enough to the bird to maintain the bird in view throughout the shot, it can be shot consistently because of a combination of the narrow angle target presentation and the margin for error created by the shotgun's pattern/column.

But the "wheels fall off" when the target is at a greater angle and distance, requiring greater lead. The mathematical shooter, looking at the larger lead, loses sight of the bird in his peripheral vision and his gun stops completely, with a miss behind. Or, his swing stutters along as his eyes repeatedly lose and find the bird in his peripheral vision and the bird is hit or missed with a "poke and hope" shot.

The good shot maintains hard focus on the bird throughout the shot, receiving a continuous flow of information of speed, angle and distance. With his peripheral vision, he accurately places the muzzles in the correct place on the line of flight to be able to break the target or kill the bird.

Movement and Focus

Your eyes are drawn to movement and they will shift focus to look at the fastest moving object. With the clay target, it is its passage against a background that creates the vision of movement. With the bird, its flapping wings create the sense of movement.

If you concentrate on the leading edge of the target or the head of the bird, your focus narrows to a single point rather than seeing the whole bird, or clay target. This hard focus will reduce the gun to a blur in your peripheral vision. The more gun you are aware of, the less target you can see, whereas the harder the target focus, the less gun you will see!

Shooting the bird's head will create the correct forward allowance (lead) necessary to hit this moving target, putting the full pattern on the most vulnerable part of the bird – the head and internal organs.

Concentrate on the target, with your body being driven by your eyes' reaction to the bird's movements and over time, you will acquire a cache of lead pictures applicable to the different wingshooting presentations.

Learning to maintain hard focus is far from easy and requires repeated practice. The clay target sports are the way to get it.

Lead is Exponential

It is helpful to physically demonstrate this concept: I place a piece of pipe three feet long on blocks at 20 yards, a pipe six feet long at 30 yards and a pipe nine feet long at 40 yards. Look downrange and holding your fist out in front of you, palm down, extend your forefinger and your little finger and place them on each of the markers. You will find that they all look pretty much the same! The lead increases exponentially with the increase in distance.

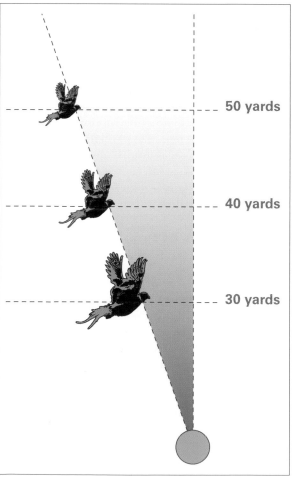

50 yards

40 yards

30 yards

Lead is exponential.

Lead is exponential; white poles 3 feet, at twenty yards, 6 feet at 30 yards and 9 feet at 40 yards; they look very much the same from the Gun's point of view.

The ability to judge a target's distance is a valuable one and well worth the trouble of acquiring. But the judgement of distance does not take into account the speed of the target. For example, the lead for a slow, long crosser at 40 yards will appear to be the same as for a fast crosser at 30 yards.

Trying to calculate lead in feet and inches induces measuring and looking at the lead instead of the target. It is far better to visualize the amount of lead as an object, say the length of a flat of cartridges. Depending on your picture bank, a fast quartering target might need half a flat of lead, but a true 50 yard crosser might need 6 full flats of lead! And yes, there are targets out there that need to be led by the length of a school bus!

Mathematical Lead

There are two types of lead: mathematical and perceived. Mathematical lead is the sum of the component parts consisting of individual reaction time, hammer-fall, barrel length and flight time of the shot column, combined with the target's speed and distance and, for the purists, the speed of the cartridge.

The correct mathematical calculation will give a definitive amount of forward allowance for each and every target shot. However, mathematical lead is applied with the conscious mind and the conscious mind can only process one thought at a time. In the application of the required amount of lead, this means that the focus is on the lead rather than on the target.

Perceived Lead

Perceived lead is applied with the subconscious, and the subconscious mind can juggle a whole myriad of inputs at the same time. This phenomenon allows the subconscious to apply the correct forward allowance or lead, with total focus on the target, making an "Instinctive Shot"! When the shot is taken there is an awareness of the lead, but the mind's total concentration is on the head of the bird.

Trigonometry

The biggest impact to perceived lead is found in trigonometry. When making a shot at a bird on the wing, we are, in fact, completing a triangle. The lines of the triangle are invisible but essential parts of the equation used to judge forward allowance. The three sides of the triangle are: the line from the shooter to the inception point of the bird's flight, the bird's line of flight, and the line to the anticipated interception point of the shot on the bird's line of flight. The angle created between the line of flight and the shot interception point, gives the best visual indicator of the necessary lead required to successfully hit the bird.

To make this easier to understand, consider a Skeet field – all the targets are flying the same distance and speed. If you shoot a target from the Low House on Station 3, the angle created between the line of flight and shot string is approximately 90 degrees, and requires 4 feet of lead. Yet the same target from Low House, Station 7 requires no lead! But it is the same target travelling at the same speed, distance and height. Mathematically, the leads are the same. However, at each station you see different angles and hence different lead pictures, proving my point that lead is more a question of perception of angles than mathematics.

Now moving on to the practical application of trigonometry: in sporting clays, when you are waiting your turn to shoot, consider the station and its relationship to the trap – imagine a straight line between the two. This is the baseline of your triangle. Next, visualize the target's flight line by pointing your index finger at the target, as if shooting it. This is the second leg of your triangle. Last, visualize the interception point of the shot column on that target line – the point where you intend to break the target. This completes your lead-finding triangle. The latter can be best achieved by visualizing where your muzzles will be when you intend to pull the trigger.

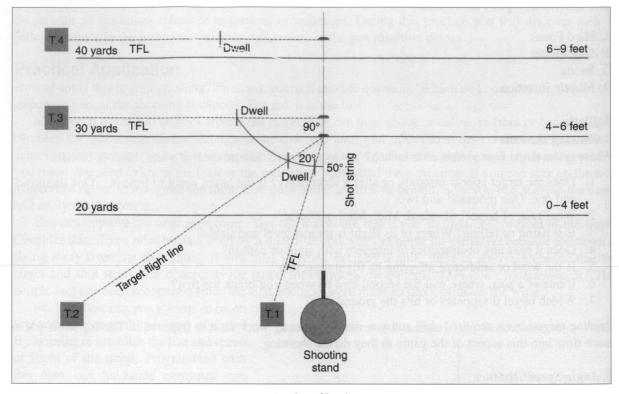

Angles of lead.

The angle created at this point is the key to the amount of lead each individual presentation requires. If the target is a straight-away, it requires no lead, you shoot straight at it. But as the angle between the target's flight line and the shot column increases, so does the amount of lead required.

The Angle of Dangle

The simple formula is: the smaller (more acute) the angle, the less the lead, the larger (more obtuse) the angle, the more lead is required. A good example is the long quartering incomer. Because it is coming towards you and the target is getting bigger and easier to see, the brain perceives it as slowing, and more of these targets are missed behind than anywhere else.

In reality, on an incoming target, or bird, the angle created between the flight line and shot string is very large – more than 90 degrees – and requires much more lead than you would think to give it. This is why so many birds landing into a decoy pattern are missed.

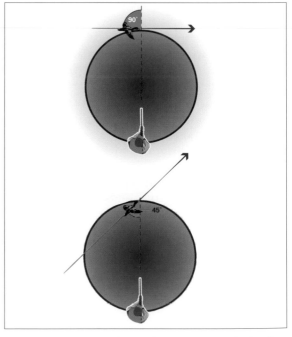

The more obtuse the angle, the greater the lead required.

However, this angle is constantly in transition. Consider Station 5 on the Skeet field: if you shoot the Low House target past the centre peg, it requires less and less lead, the farther it travels past the centre. Because the angle is changing from obtuse to acute, hard focus on the target allows you to make the miniscule adjustments to speed, distance and angle so essential in second barrel shots in the field.

OBSERVED VELOCITIES AND FORWARD ALLOWANCES

Eley standard game loads have a nominal observed velocity of 325 m sec (1070 ft sec). Eley high velocity loads have a nominal observed velocity of 340 m sec (1120 ft sec).

One might suppose that the change in velocity would make a noticeable difference to the forward allowance but, as will be seen from the table, the question is one of inches in a forward allowance measured in feet. The difference may for all practical purposes, be ignored.

COMPARISON OF CARTRIDGES

Forward Allowance

Birds crossing at 65 km ph (40 mph)   No. 6 shot

Range	30m	30yd	35m	35yd	40m	40yd	45m	45yd	50m	50yd
Standard Velocity	1.89m	5' 6"	2.26m	6' 8"	2.68m	8' 0"	3.29m	9' 6"	3.97m	11' 1"
High Velocity	1.81m	5' 3"	2.18m	6' 5"	2.58m	7' 8"	3.16m	9' 1"	3.02m	10' 8"

Speed and Distance

Then there is speed and distance – I am afraid that only personal experience and practise can teach you how to handle these. A good shooting instructor can help you on the path, but we are all individuals, with personal visual acuity and reaction times and no two people see lead or forward allowance in exactly the same way. One man's two feet can be another's six! Do you see inches at the barrel or feet at the target? It is a matter of individual perception.

Clockwork

To visualize the lead and angle when practising with clay targets or in the field, imagine a clock face overlaid on the shooting field with you standing on the 6 o'clock.

If the target enters the clock at 3 o'clock and exits at 9 o'clock, it is easy to judge the shot string's interception on its path to be 90 degrees, with the obtuse angle created indicating the amount of lead required.

The great advantage of using the "clock method" is that while the angle of inception is always in transition, changing second by second throughout the target's flight, you can picture your position in relation to the clock face. This allows you to constantly visualize the leads and to shoot in the position best suited to your particular technique and style.

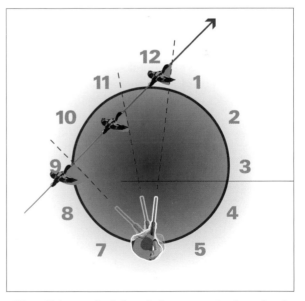

Visualizing a clock face helps recognize how lead changes as the angle to the gun changes.

Practice Targets

Because of the great diversity of game birds in size and speed, try to choose the practice target presentations that replicate the quarry's characteristics as closely as possible.

The high tower at the E.J. Churchill Shooting Grounds.

Simulated grouse butt sequence.

Targets can be set to mimic all forms of wingshooting, from covey rises to driven pheasant off the high tower. Simulated game days at a shooting ground are a perfect pre-season sharpener.

Remember whether shooting sporting clays or using a skeet or trap field, to shoot the targets from the low gun position, with full use of the gun. After all, for a wingshooter, the second barrel is there for a second shot or to dispatch a crippled bird.

Upland Birds or Rough Shooting

There are two main categories of game bird: upland and migratory. The upland bird species are ground game, only flying as a last resort, when forced to do so. They are a minimalist bird, preferring to run on the ground, rather than fly – their meat is light or white, like a chicken's.

Take the bobwhite quail – when flushed, the covey will explode from cover, flying at speeds up to 45 mph straight to the nearest sanctuary where they can hide or continue to run. Quail are shot, on average, between 15 and 25 yards. Shooting distances increase with different species and different flush/flight characteristics. A red grouse or sage grouse, for example, would be taken 25 to 40 yards out. The best place to practise on clay targets for the flushing, upland birds is on the Trap field.

Upland bird shooting. (TERRY ALLEN)

Trap

In its multiple forms, Trap was the first of the clay target games and owes its origins directly to live pigeon shooting where gentlemen placed live pigeons under their top hats to which a length of string was attached. Taking turns, they would stand at a marked distance with their gun at the ready and call "PULL!" The organizer of the event would pull one of the strings, toppling the hat and releasing the pigeon, while the gunner would attempt to shoot it.

Such rudimentary matches, originally designed for money wagers, soon led to drawing up a set of rules. Standardized distances of targets, duration of the game and the type of gun permitted, along with equipment to make the random selection of bird releases, made the sport fair to all participants.

With the eventual ban on or lack of the use of live pigeons, the pigeon clubs began to throw inanimate objects to replicate the flight of the live birds. Trap targets leave a trap, or traps, in front of the line of Guns and travel away. There is a set angle and distance to their flight, with the trap oscillating to present random and more challenging shots. The targets fly directly away from the guns and are both at distance and edge-on when the shot is taken.

Trap is very good practice for the quartering target so often encountered by the upland bird hunter, as trap targets replicate the explosive rise and random flight of quail, chukar and Hungarian partridge. To practise, try to reserve a Trap field yourself and, maintaining a safe field of fire, shoot from the low gun position at various ranges, starting at the trap house and moving back.

In the UK, when walked-up hunting over dogs, we teach a little mantra to time the shot on a flushing bird. First, this ensures a smooth gun mount and second, that the bird is shot at a sufficient distance to be edible, not a mess just fit for the ferrets. "You Are Dead" is the three-beat tempo that guarantees smooth shooting and good eating. A good friend has his own Southern version of this – "Molasses in February" – both work well.

Migratory Birds

Migratory birds are ill-equipped to walk – just look at the mallard duck's ungainly gait. However, they are far more accomplished flyers than the upland bird, capable of covering great distances. Their meat is dark because of their continual flying.

The flight speed of the different species of migratory game birds varies greatly, but on average, it is between 15 and 45 miles per hour. Passing shots at mourning dove and waterfowl are taken anywhere between 20 and 40 yards, but decoyed waterfowl are more often shot within 30 yards.

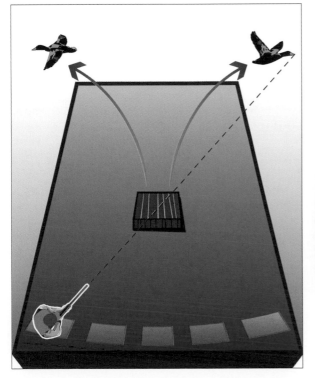

Shooting from a duck blind. (JOHN TAYLOR)

LEFT: The Trap range with its random targets shot from a low gun position offers good practice for upland bird hunting.

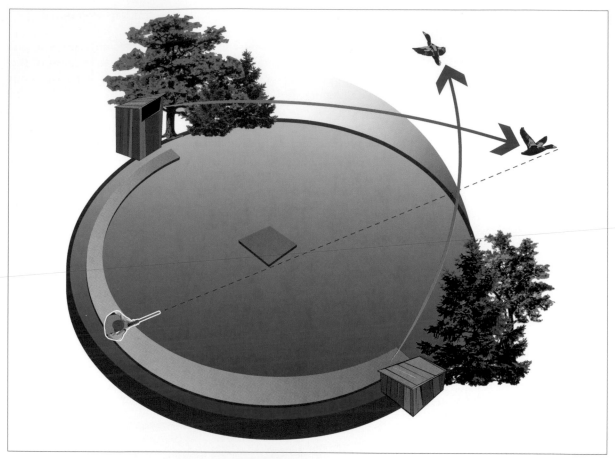

Skeet was originally created as practice for upland bird hunting; when shot from a low gun position, it is still great practice.

Skeet

As a clay shooting game, Skeet offers excellent practice for the migratory and upland bird shooter. Named for the Scandinavian word "to shoot", Skeet evolved from the game of "clock shooting". Twelve stations were set at the12 hours of the clock and the targets were thrown from one tower, simulating every angle the quarry could present to the hunter.

This circle required a very large safety area for shot fall-out so, very quickly, some bright innovator thought to "fold" the field in half. They placed high and low towers at the ends of the half-circle crescent, so now the targets offered every conceivable angle of incoming, outgoing, crossing and quartering target that a bird hunter would encounter in the field.

When shot from the low gun position, Skeet is the ultimate wingshooting practice, as any field scenario can be replicated. For example, quail, partridge and pheasant, when flushed, can fly in any direction so using a random pull target release, Skeet shooting is excellent practice for these flushing birds.

If you are a wildfowler, dove or pigeon shooter, you are often required to shoot from a seated position. To practise this move, take your dove bucket to the Skeet field and shoot one or two rounds from the seated position. Low gun and random pulls are great practice for anyone who shoots from a blind or hunts over dogs.

Shooting Skeet from a dove bucket is great practise for shooting from a seated positon in a hide or blind.

The only practice for high birds is on the high towers. (OPPOSITE: PAUL FIEVEZ AND *ABOVE* BETTWS HALL SPORTING)

Driven Shooting

Partridge and pheasant driven from cover on high bluffs can pass over the line anywhere from 25 to 50 yards and more. Red grouse are shot at a whole range of yardages, ranging from very close (15 yards) to very far (50 yards). The high towers and grouse butts of the Shooting Grounds are the only places to practise these shots.

Sporting Clays

Sporting Clays owes its origins directly to practise for wingshooting. It is distinctive from the other clay target disciplines in that it offers different sizes and shapes of targets, with no set angles, speeds or distances.

For the wingshooter, the game of Sporting Clays has advanced to the point that the increasingly difficult targets demanded by the competitive sporting shooters have little resemblance to a bird in flight. The clay targets are thrown at distances that would never be shot by a wingshooter for fear of leaving a pricked or wounded bird.

Naysayers argue that they would never shoot a live bird at such distances so why practise shooting clay targets at these ranges? The simple answer is, the skills needed to shoot long targets in sporting clays equate to better shooting in the field. Everything needs to be just right, there is no margin for error and a good shot at 50 yards is going to be an even better shot at 25!

Any target, live or inanimate, shot at distance is as often missed off-line as it is in front or behind. The ability to consistently break a 50 yard crossing clay target requires that you start in balance and finish in balance. Also, all of the fundamentals should be in place, techniques practised until perfect, the gun properly fitted, both choke and cartridge combinations right.

It is important that your shooting, regardless of the clay shooting discipline you use for practice, should be done from a low gun position (gun down), as you would shoot in the field. That said, shooting any of the clay target disciplines as practice for wingshooting is going to result in cleaner kills and more birds in the bag.

Ready position for upland bird shooting.

Step into the line of flight and make a smooth move to the target.

Complete the mount to the cheek, not the shoulder, and fire without pause or check.

Chapter 15
Eyes and Vision

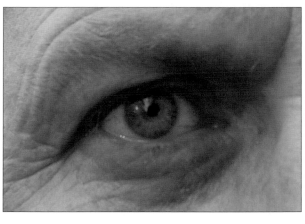

Eyesight is the most essential part of shooting. Your hands are controlled by the brain which receives its instruction from the eyes. As you make a shot, the brain is required to manage over 100 billion neurons – these neural paths are controlled by your vision which in turn controls your arms and body. These paths remain organized for a very short window of time and the shot must be taken when this process is at its peak. This timing is referred to as eye and hand co-ordination, but it is simply the interaction of the eyes and the hands as a single unit.

In our day-to-day life we have very little cause to "hard focus"; our normal vision setting is "panoramic", with no single object in mind. This is because we have no real need for concentrated focusing, which is hard work for both the eyes and the brain.

Try a little experiment to demonstrate this: look up from this book and pick out an object on the opposite side of the room – the centre of a clock or the corner of a picture frame. Zero in on it and attempt to keep intense focus on it for the count of 20. See? You have already quit and relaxed your vision!

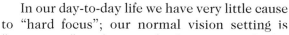
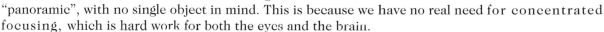
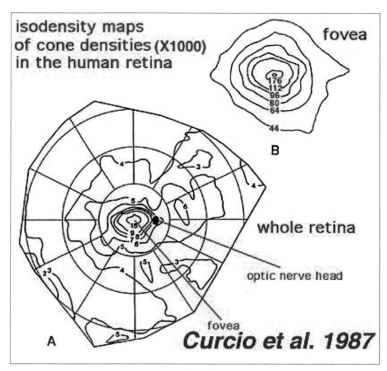

Distribution of rods and cones.

It is extremely hard and some times uncomfortable to hold a "hard focus" on an object for even a few seconds, yet this is the essential skill we need to master if we are to shoot well with any consistency.

Concentration

It takes concentration to maintain focus on a bird on the wing and "hard focus" means keeping both eyes on the bird without being distracted by background, peripheral images, shadows, colours or movement. This concentration is divided into two parts:

1. Saccadic – is the first visual reaction to a moving bird; your eyes locate the target by direction and speed.

2. Pursuit – is the second reaction as your eyes centre in on the bird.

Saccadic and Pursuit work independently. Saccadic cannot centre and Pursuit cannot locate, so it is a balance between the two that is essential to straight shooting. Once the target is centred, if you let your Pursuit reaction lapse into the Saccadic mode, the target becomes lost in your peripheral vision and vice versa.

If we look too hard (stare) in the area we expect the bird to flush, or if it is still out of range and we attempt to centre on it, we reduce our peripheral awareness and the bird literally gets the jump on us. Learning how to look properly for and at the bird is one of the critical fundamentals of shooting well.

The secret to centring on a bird is to know *where* to look and why.

Optical Illusions

The image of a moving target is created by its passage against the background of trees or sky. From this, the eye gathers the information required to locate and centre on the bird. But the motion is always perceived to be behind the target. Until a bird has passed in front of a background or an object, the bird is, in effect, stationary to the eye. The eyes are programmed to detect and react to movement – a defence mechanism – and therefore we naturally look at where the bird has been, not where it is going.

Centring

I have described how the shot cloud disperses into a column approximately three feet wide by eight feet long (Chapter 4, The Shotgun). This shot pattern is what gives us the margin for error in shooting a bird on the wing. If our focus is on the tail of the bird, this margin is considerably reduced because the target is moving *away* from the shot column.

Even with the correct lead, if you don't focus on *the head*, you will always be hitting the back of the bird. If we learn to centre on the bird's head, we achieve two important benefits: first, the bird will appear slower and second, it is now travelling *into* the shot column/pattern, maximizing our chances of success and increasing our margin for error.

When you learn to concentrate on the head of the bird, you will feel more in charge and that you have more time to take your shot. If you look at the back, or the "wake" of the bird, you will feel rushed, falter, fumble and often miss behind.

Visual Hold

We are pedestrians and have pedestrian-paced vision. If you can, visualize an 8mm film projector – the human eye sees the equivalent of 16 frames per second. A flushing bird is moving at 32 frames per second. If we look in the wrong place, the target is seen only every other frame or as a blur. The wrong visual hold defeats the Saccadic process and slows the Pursuit mechanism so you need to discover the point at which you maximize your Saccadic reaction to the bird and ensure swift Pursuit acquisition.

Do not attempt to look hard for the bird – this restricts Saccadic movement. Instead, adopt a "soft focus", looking at nothing in particular, but in the anticipated direction of the bird. Open your eyes wider by lifting your eyebrows – this gives you a twenty-percent increase in light-gathering vision! Light reduction causes vision reduction and makes the bird appear vague and fast flying… the cause of many missed shots.

Opening your eyes wide will result in a marked improvement in your shooting performance.

Eyesight Fitness

The eyesight standard of 20/20 is what we see – vision is the process of *reacting* to what we see. When we are making a shot, the lens of the eye is flexing repeatedly (accommodation) to maintain a sharp focus on the bird and has to make many thousands of adjustments for depth, background and flight.

Different lens tints enhance the birds' colours and suppress the background, improving visual acuity.

This action is comparable to the lens on a motor-ized camera focusing back and forth to achieve a sharp picture. The eye is like a muscle in the body and can be exercised to improve this skill. A few simple exercises each day can strengthen the lens' ability to flex so as to better locate and concentrate focus on a moving bird – the same way you can increase the strength of your arms by exercising your biceps.

The muscles of your eyes can move the eye through 360 degree rotations – left to right, up and down. Though we may have become rather sophisticated animals, we are still, nonetheless, animals. We are omnivores or hunter-gatherers, but in the main, gatherers. As such, our eyes are predisposed to look *down and in*. Most of our everyday activities take place *below* the level of our eyes and the eye muscles for looking down and in are much stronger than those used for looking up and out.

Any activity that requires our eyes to look *up and out* for any length of time is extremely fatiguing. Take, for example, driving a car. This activity uses very similar eye action as is used when shooting. The modern car is effortless to drive and extremely comfortable, yet if you drive for an hour or more, you quickly become tired. This is due to the ongoing contest between the stronger lower eye muscles and the weaker upper eye muscles.

Visual Enhancement

Wingshooting takes place under varying light conditions and backgrounds. Birds are in constant motion against this background and the flutuating light and shadows make it difficult to maintain hard focus on the bird. This creates inaccurate information for the brain to process, and the result is often a missed shooting opportunity.

It has long been recognized that wearing shooting glass lenses in certain colours can enhance the bird under specific light and background conditions. The right coloured lenses can make the difference between a kill and a miss. This is because the eye achieves better definition and depth perception when the pupil is constricted and maximum constriction is achieved by using the brightest colour lenses you have.

For example, vermillion-coloured lenses bring out the buffs and tans of birds against a moderately-bright background, while yellow and orange lens tints work well in overcast or poor light. Brown tints in varying shades are very effective in bright sunshine. All tints offer enhanced contrast and definition, however, the choice is very subjective and often person-specific. Everyone has a degree of colour blindness and it is important to experiment to find the tints that work best for you in various light conditions and with birds of different plumages.

The more light that enters the eye, the better the vision process and the better the eye and hand co-ordination. Any coloured lenses that we use block some part of the light spectrum, actually reducing the amount of light available. You need to redress this by balancing any light loss with enhanced contrast, using the lightest tint possible.

Lenses for shooting glasses should be polarized for ultimate protection from ultra-violet radiation which contributes to the development of cataracts and has been shown to cause degeneration of the retinal pigment epithelium. It has also been discovered that exposure to harmful UV rays can accelerate age-related macular degeneration.

Frames

Regular glasses are designed to place the lens centre directly in line with the pupil. When we lower our head into the correct shooting position, we end up looking off the optical centre of the ordinary spectacle lens. A further problem is that everyday glasses are designed for fashion and looks rather than function; this often means that the frame interferes with or, in the worst case, obscures the vision.

Properly-designed shooting glasses sit high up on the nose and have correctly placed optics so that when the head is lowered into the proper shooting position, the pupil is looking through the optical centre of the lens, slightly above the actual centre. Shooting glasses have lenses that are oversized and frameless, so there is no obstruction between the eyes and the target. The frame arms have padded, curved ear pieces and nose pads to stop the glasses from slipping or being knocked ajar by movement or recoil. This high fit means that they stand slightly off the face and air can flow freely between the lens and the eye, preventing fogging on wet and humid days. The lenses can also be polished with an anti-mist solution.

Eyesight Correction

The choice of eyewear is very important. The type of lens, the frame design and fit can all contribute significantly to a shooter's performance. The lenses for shooting glasses are made from two materials, CR 39 plastic and polycarbonate. In terms of safety, polycarbonate is the best and most effective. The lenses are less than half the weight of glass lenses and polycarbonate has outstanding impact resistance. The polycarbonate lens requires careful processing and is prone to scratching when uncoated. It should always have an anti-scratch finish applied.

A clear lens will only allow 90 percent of the available light to pass through to the eye, with 10 percent being lost in reflection. Anti-glare coatings allow more light to reach the eye and will allow you to see better – especially in poor light conditions. Polarized lenses offer the ultimate in UV protection but more important, eliminate reflections and glare.

The best shooting glasses should include a comfortable and durable frame, tinted and coated lenses, providing protection, increased visual acuity, better depth perception, improved vision and contrast and will help to control eye fatigue.

Prescription Glasses, Contact Lenses and Corrective Surgery

If you require corrective prescription lenses, have only single vision lenses fitted to your shooting glasses. Bi- and Tri-focal lenses cause distortion and the graduated prescription or "Varilux" type cause even more visual problems. As the light passes through the lens it is bent or refracted, so when the head is in the correct shooting position it may not be in the optimum position for the "distance" section of the Bi- or Tri-focal lenses.

If you cannot see the primers of the cartridges in the chambers of an open gun, then you cannot see if the safe is on or off and you should have a small bifocal in your shooting glasses.

Prescription shooting glasses should be ordered through an ophthalmologist who specializes in the shooting sports. They are familiar with the correct head positioning of the corrective "sweet spot" on the lens when the head is mounted on the stock. They also take into consideration the shooter's physique when fitting the frames.

Contact lenses offer distinct advantages compared to the prescription glasses. Contacts project a larger image on the back of the eye and eliminate spectacle distortion. This helps you see your targets sooner, sharper and bigger. If you wear contacts, you can use the standard, non-prescription (less expensive) shooting glasses.

A growing number of people are choosing laser corrective surgery. When doing so, they often opt to have one eye fixed for long sight or distance vision and one for short or close-up vision, to eliminate the requirement for Bi- or Tri-focal prescriptions entirely. This is also done with contact lenses. If you choose to go this route, be sure that the eye for long sight matches the shoulder from which you are shooting.

Points to Remember

- At times we can all listen and not hear, touch and not feel, look without seeing; you must learn to maximize your visual stimulus on every bird.

- The eyes control the body, they synchronize the motor-muscular movements to the target, decide the timing of when to pull the trigger.

- Misses are a result of faulty visual perception, caused by a failure to centre on the bird.

- Learn to zero in and remain locked onto the point of impact – the primary zone – the bird's head – throughout the shooting action.

- The primary zone of the target, the head, is always changing direction, speed, angle and distance and the ability to focus on it is learned with instruction and practice.

Visual reaction time can be improved with eye exercises.

Eye-Vision Exercises

These exercises are simple and the equipment needed is minimal. We begin with some stretching exercises for the eyes.

1. With your eyes closed but relaxed, start by rotating them up and around in a 360 degree circle. Do 5 full rotations, first to the right and then 5 full rotations to the left. Then with your eyes still shut, look up and down 5 times in each direction. Finally, roll your eyes 5 times fully left and right. At first you will find stretching exercises difficult to do, but with practice, they become an excellent preliminary work-out before further shooting exercises.

2. Take a straw and a toothpick and hold them horizontally, one in each hand, at arms' length. Bring them together, inserting the toothpick into the straw. Do this 20 times, 10 times holding the toothpick in your right hand, then 10 times holding the toothpick in your left hand.

3. Thread a tennis ball on a piece of cord. Write 4 numbers on it with a black felt pen. Hang it from a beam or in a door frame. Take a yardstick or a 3 foot dowel and, tapping it, start the ball in motion. Concentrate on one number and, with the stick at arm's length, touch it as it swings and rotates. You may have to start with just your finger and graduate to the stick, as it is a lot trickier than I have made it sound.

4. Take a pen and, holding it vertically at arm's length, look at and concentrate hard on an object aross the room. The pen will appear double in your near-sight (the pen and a ghost image). Now transfer your point of focus to the pen, concentrate hard and the object across the room will double (the original and a ghost image). Repeat as often as you feel comfortable doing so. At first it will only be a few times, but, with practice, you will be able to increase and decrease the separation of the object and the pen and increase the number of times you can perform the exercise.

5. Using a yardstick, put a mark in the middle at the 18 inch mark. Now hold it at this point with one hand and move it out at arm's length. Keeping your head locked rigid, move your eyes to the left and right as far as you can, seeing how far out you can read the numbers on the yardstick. With practice, you will increase the range of eye movement and be able to read the numbers almost to the ends.

6. Take some tennis balls and mark each one with a black felt tip with a single digit number, 1 through 9. Practise with a friend or friends standing 10 to 15 yards apart. Toss the tennis balls, underarm, to each other, and try to look past the actual ball and read the number on it, calling it out during its flight.

The emphasis of all these exercises is on flexible focus, both near and far. All will help improve **accommodation**, **focus** and **centring**, increasing your ability to locate and shoot the bird. We all have a given amount of eye and hand co-ordination – the best shots have, by natural acquisition or diligent practise, sharper visual acuity. The ability to focus sharply can be learned, improved and ultimately mastered, but it requires constant practice.

Chapter 16
Lady Shots

The majority of men have a preconceived idea of their inherent sporting ability. They believe they are born with the gift of superlative hand and eye co-ordination making them a *"Natural"* when it comes to driving a car, striking a golf ball or, of course, shooting a shotgun! Instruction is usually a last resort, taken only after every permutation of gun and gear has been exhausted and even then, they expect a pinch of fairy dust or a magic pill will provide an instant fix.

Ladies, on the other hand, approach learning any new skill with a more open mind. They are inquisitive and, having *no* preconceived ideas, they just want to know how things work and to understand what is required to complete the task asked of them.

Simply put, men want to shoot and only listen when they miss, women want to listen, understand, then shoot and hit the target.

As an instructor, gunfitter, gunmaker and sporting agent, it is refreshing to see more and more of the "Fairer Sex" in the field, on the clay ground and at the pattern plate. While their introduction to the shooting sports may come from a parent, partner or boyfriend, their initial foray is often unnecessarily difficult and far too many ladies are put off by an unsuccessful and/or painful start.

The Right Start

This difficult entry is easily avoided with an understanding of the extra – or rather different – challenges the majority of women face at the outset and how to overcome them. The first introduction to shooting should be enjoyable, educational and, most important, successful.

Successfully shooting a shotgun requires basic hand and eye co-ordination, the same skills needed to catch a ball. And ladies' successful participation is not determined by who can lift the most weight, run faster, jump higher or hit a ball further. Shooting depends on rhythm and timing and as ladies usually have a more *"natural"* timing, so in the field or on the shooting ground they can give the men more than a run for their money. Given the right start, with the right equipment, some practical instruction, and the determination to practise, there is no reason why women cannot shoot as well, if not better than, men.

Growing up, most boys have a toy gun, and, if from a shooting family, this toy will, with age and a sense of responsibility, be replaced by an air (BB) gun, then eventually, a small-gauge shotgun. This early experience with guns gives men an advantage when they begin formal shooting – they are already familiar with the noise, recoil and weight when handling and shooting a shotgun.

Only a small percentage of women have these opportunities. While lately more girls are joining their brothers in the sport, the majority of lady shooters still come to shooting in their late teens or older and may have a natural apprehension of shotguns.

Even if it is used recreationally like a tennis racquet or golf club, a shotgun is still a loud, heavy, lethal weapon and can be intimidating. This apprehension is the first hurdle to jump, and, if done correctly, will lay the foundation for a smooth introduction to and steady progress in the sport.

The first step might be to begin as a spectator – accompanying friends or family in the field or for practice on the shooting grounds. Without the

Practising at Sporting Clays.

pressure of having to shoot, the lady beginner has the opportunity to observe the safety and etiquette required and become familiar with different types of shooting, i.e., walked-up over dogs, decoyed, driven, pass shooting or practice at clay targets. As an observer, she can get used to the noise and activity and have time to ask questions about all the aspects of the sport that the more experienced shot takes for granted.

Shooting Instruction for Ladies

As I make my living as a shooting instructor, I may be biased, but I highly recommend qualified instruction for the beginner, but especially when the beginner is a lady. A good instructor/loader accompanying a lady on her first one or two outings in the field will instill confidence, allowing her to relax and concentrate on her shooting.

As always, safety and safe gun handling is the first priority! Under supervision, with an unloaded shotgun, the lady shooter should learn its parts, their function, and how to open and close the gun. Next, she should move on to loading the shotgun using snap caps (dummy cartridges), then firing it, and unloading it.

At this time, she must also learn about safe gun handling and the Rules of Wing and Field Shooting, and be shown the basic moves needed to shoot a simple target. In the field, she should learn to have an awareness of fellow shots, guides, beaters, pickers-up and dogs and to recognize the safe lines and areas of fire. This knowledge will help her overcome the natural apprehension felt when first learning to shoot.

Though the fundamentals of straight shooting apply equally to men and women, ladies face several shooting challenges that are different from men. First and foremost is their body size and shape which impacts on gun choice, clothing, and equipment. Ladies have different eye dominance issues which can, among other things, have an impact on perceived lead. So eye dominance should be established and any fixes required should be carried out before progressing further.

Women and Eye Dominance

Women are multi-taskers, usually able to carry out several activities at one time. Nature pre-programmed them this way to be able to cope with nursing and raising children while still maintaining the "flight or fight" survival awareness.

In the brain, the corpus callosum is a network of nerves that transmits

Shooting from the ready position on the skeet field.

messages between the right and left halves of the brain. It is better integrated in women than in men, enabling women to use both sides of the brain at one time and is the reason why more women are ambidextrous than men. However, this "message integration" has a downside: approximately 70 to 90 percent of women's eyes are cross dominant or have central vision.

It is essential that eye dominance be checked and then double checked. In a perfect world, if a person is right-handed, they would be right eye dominant. However, especially in women, this is often not the case.

If her eye dominance is opposite the shoulder she would like to shoot off, there are two options to correct this discrepancy. First, she can swap shooting shoulders to align her shoulder with the dominant eye, which, with a beginner, is always the best long-term option. Second, she can obscure the dominant eye, allowing her to shoot off the preferred shoulder, although obscuring one eye can interfere with spatial vision.

If the diagnosis is central or fluctuating vision, then the only option is to obscure one eye to ensure the gun shoots where she looks.

The most simple and effective cure for cross dominance and/or central vision is to place a small piece of opaque tape on the lens of the shooting glasses over the dominant eye. This should be applied so that when her head is on the stock, ready to take the shot, the tape covers the dominant eye

Pheasant hunting in Dakota. (TERRY ALLEN)

in the centre of the pupil. The advantage to this method is that until the shot is ready to be taken, the brain is receiving binocular signals and can better identify the target in space and distance.

Shooting 101

Once the lady is familiar with the shotgun and knows how to open and close it, and how to load it using "snap caps" (dummy cartridges), she needs to learn the correct stance and posture to create the body shape needed to mount her shotgun correctly. During her first shooting lesson the gun can be premounted, but in subsequent lessons, the gun should be mounted from the low gun position. The gun mount is best practised at home, by slowly and smoothly lifting the unloaded gun, with both hands working in sync, and placing it under the cheek bone. This ensures that when the stock is correctly placed in the cheek, it is correctly placed in the shoulder pocket.

The next step is learning how to shoot a moving target. The initial explanation of target shooting should be as simple as possible and when the instructor is confident that his client understands what is being asked of her, she can be taken to the range for her first live-firing experience. The initial targets should be easy so, from the outset, the student should be breaking clays consistently and comfortably. Further, the instructor should always let her finish the lesson after a series of successfully broken targets.

Gun Selection

A 20 bore over and under shotgun in combination with a light cartridge is a great choice for the first lessons for a lady. The reduced weight and lower recoil will allow her to concentrate on the correct movement and to hard-focus on the target. (A word of caution: don't let her better half talk her into using his 12 bore side by side for her first lesson – it is a sure recipe for bruises and frustration.)

Later, as her shooting progresses and her strength will allow, a light 12 gauge with a suitably light cartridge can be substituted for the 20 gauge. The margin for error in a 12 gauge is so much greater than with a 20 and success is so important for the beginner. If she is indeed "bitten by the bug" and progresses to shooting high driven birds, the step up to a 12 gauge is inevitable.

Dallas Divas at the end of a quail shoot.

Dove shooting in Argentina.

Gun Weight

"It's so heavy!" is one of the most common comments I hear on a lady's first lesson. Because of the weight of the gun, women and other shooters of small stature tend to lean backwards, pushing their hips forward, using their upper body to counter (cantilever) and support the gun's weight instead of bending forward at the waist and taking the weight of the gun in their outstretched arms.

The length of the gun also has an impact on its perceived weight. If the stock is too long, the weight of the gun is pushed farther from the axis of the body, increasing this subconscious need to push the hips forward and transfer more weight to the back foot to counter-balance the weight of the gun.

Good Gun Mount = Extra Targets

Proper posture is required to absorb recoil, create better access to the cheek bone and create a good pocket for the gun in the shoulder in the gun mount. This calls for a slight inclination or angling of the body towards the target. Simply shifting the hips backward and bending slightly at the waist achieves the proper posture. Exercises aimed specifically at developing the arms and upper body areas used in the shooting action will help. These will increase strength and teach the lady shooter to mount the gun firmly and consistently into the proper place in her cheek and shoulder.

Get a five-pound dumbbell and, holding it in the left hand (if a right-shoulder shooter), extend the arm to the natural shooting position and begin tracing lines and shapes until the muscles begin to complain.

Keep one dumbbell in the office and another at home and repeat this exercise as often as possible, whenever there are a few minutes, while on the phone or watching television.

This exercise will increase the strength in the leading hand, ensure a better gun mount, give her more control of the gun and help her to establish the all-important eye–target relationship. In a proper gun mount, she should be able to let go of the unloaded gun with her right hand and the gun should not move, being totally supported by the left hand.

Taking a high pheasant in Clovelly.

Another tip for the lady shooter: when shooting gun down, in the ready position hold the gunstock an inch or two off or away from the body. This way she will avoid hitting her chest and her gun mount will be unimpeded and much smoother.

Cartridge Choice

Recoil is controlled by the combination of the gun's weight and cartridge velocity. She should use the heaviest gun that can be comfortably controlled with the most efficient softest-shooting cartridge.

She should start with low pressure cartridge, either ¾ or ⅞ths of an ounce load. This combination results in little recoil and maximum comfort, allowing her total concentration on breaking targets.

Gun Fit for a Lady

Overall, gunstocks are built to fit men, so some alteration is required to make them comfortable for most ladies to shoot. Stock fit for ladies is not simply a matter of a shorter stock, as there are other obvious differences in body shape between the sexes. Ladies have a different skeletal shape from men. They are lighter and more petite; everything is scaled down, including bone length, diameter and muscle mass. This means ladies move differently – compare the actions of a man and a woman throwing a ball.

These differences impact on a woman's choice of gun, its fit and the gun mounting action. Compared to men, most women have high cheek bones and a long neck which require a gun to have a high comb to achieve proper alignment of the eye and rib without her having to drop or roll her head. The Monte Carlo configuration is ideal for the majority of ladies, who typically have less distance between the cheek bone and eye socket than men.

The thick grips and forward trigger placements of some guns are not suitable for ladies' smaller hands. A slimmer, semi-pistol grip, like a Prince of Wales, is best for proper control and comfort.

The shape and soft tissue of a woman's chest require careful adjustment to the pitch (angle of the rear portion of the butt that contacts the shoulder) on the stock. Too much pitch and all of the recoil forces are concentrated through the toe (bottom of the butt) of the gun. Not only is this painful and bruising, but can result in twisting or canting the gun or, worse, placing the butt of the stock out onto the biceps. This fitting problem can be further compounded by the adjuster or buckle on the bra strap. This clip is often exactly where the toe of the gun rests, adding to the discomfort.

A minimum of 6 to 8 degrees of pitch is recommended, plus a sports bra with no strap adjustments and a recoil pad to further displace recoil. While it is not possible to lay down any hard and fast rules, years of gun fitting have given me these yardstick dimensions for the average lady shooter:

Length of Pull: 12¾ inches to 14½ inches with negative pitch of six to eight degrees.

Drop: at precisely where the face (cheek bone) contacts the top of the comb – 1⅝ inches, give or take ⅛ inch.

Cast: ⅛ inch at the heel, ⅜ inch at the toe.

Recoil Reaction

Recoil anxiety is always an element of many ladies' early experiences or lessons. The *anticipation* of recoil can cause as many flinches and trigger freezes as the *actual* recoil. The control of recoil is achieved by a suitable gun that is properly fitted, lighter cartridge selection, good ear protection, correct posture, good positioning of the hands for control and grip, and a solid gun mount. Repeated dry firing with snap caps (dummy cartridges) can help cure recoil anticipation and encourage smooth trigger pulls.

The G.R.I.T.S (Girls Really Into Shooting) group in Argentina being coached in wingshooting. Note the Krieghoff K20, perfect for high volume bird shooting.

Lead

I cannot recall where I read it or who wrote it, but I remember this remark caused quite a debate among instructors. The statement was: "Women see lead at the barrel, whereas men see it at the target." There is no doubt that, regardless of gender, we each have our own individual perceptions of lead or forward allowance, and learning it is an essential ingredient of successful shooting. I cannot say that women see lead in a different way than men, but I have found that they need a little more help in understanding what they *are* seeing.

Trying to describe what you see to another person, particularly one just beginning to shoot, is tough. With ladies, I have found a simple method that appears to work and is easily understood.

I start out working with a simple incoming target, like a Low-House Station Two on the Skeet field. Now, *I* know the picture that breaks this target. I have the lady shoot the target and, regardless of the miss or hit, ask her what she saw. I do this while showing a to-scale target at the end of the muzzle. I then ask her to adjust the picture to match the one she saw. One or two shots in this way, and I know how she sees lead. Whether it is in inches at the barrel or feet at the target, this becomes her individual unit of lead.

I then ask her to picture something that is comparable in length to what she perceived. This can be anything from a box of shells to a flat of cartridges. From then on, helping the shooter to learn her individual picturing is easy. I just ask her to increase or decrease the forward allowance by her own perception of lead, such as "give it two boxes" on the next shot or "reduce it to one flat" on another.

Clothing and Accessories

Most shooting clothing is designed to fit men. All too often ladies' clothing is the same cut as men's only in smaller sizes and brighter colours. Many designers make no allowance for the fit required for women to be comfortable and to perform at their best. Take a typical man's shooting vest: it is big in the shoulders, adequate across the chest, then falling straight to the hips – this does not in any way accommodate the shape of the female form. Poor fit at the waist and torso means that surplus cloth is gathered under the armpits when a lady attempts to mount the gun, making it snag or hang up. This male orientation in design is apparent in guns, earmuffs, earplugs and shooting glasses too.

However, there are now several companies that, recognizing the different needs of the lady shooter, offer clothing designed specifically for women. In a pinch, if you are good with a needle and thread, you can restyle an off-the-rack vest or jacket to fit better by removing the surplus material – even the humble safety pin can work wonders.

For a lady shooter, a simple pair of earplugs that fits can be difficult to find – earmuffs, gloves and shooting glasses equally so. By persistence and not compromising on quality, it is possible to find those shooting accessories that offer the best fit and the most comfort. Custom fit ear protection is available from companies like ESP, EAR and Green Leopard. Shooting glasses can be ordered in a variety of frame sizes from Morgan Optical specializing in the Randolph Ranger line or from Pilla Hi Def.

There are now many specialist companies like MizMac, owned by ladies and offering clothing and accessories designed by and for the lady shooter. Taking the hint from The Really Wild Company, known for combining fashion and function, the major brands like Musto, Berreta and Orvis now sell properly designed ladies' shooting attire.

A Final Word for Lady Shooters

A lady can shoot on an even playing field with men if she has the following: a structured introduction to the shooting sports, an understanding of the fundamentals, the correct gun, properly fitted, a soft-shooting cartridge, a commitment to exercising, and time to shoot enough to learn a smooth and controlled move to the target.

Stance, posture and gun mount are the nuts and bolts of straight shooting so ladies, lighter on their feet than men, can easily quick-step their way to shooting success.

The G.R.I.T.S Group (Girls Really Into Shooting) introduces ladies into the shooting sports.

Chapter 17
Young Shots

Every parent or grandparent knows the pleasure of sharing their passion for a hobby with their children or grandchildren. Time spent together, passing on experience and knowledge, creates memories that will last a lifetime.

The enthusiastic Game Shot is usually quick to encourage his children to join him in his favourite sport. However, in his enthusiasm, he must be careful not to push an unwilling child into an activity in which they have little interest or to start them too early when size and strength are inadequate to handle and shoot a shotgun safely.

Before you begin to teach your child to shoot, first be sure that he or she really wants to learn to shoot. Today's children have learned to expect instant gratification from a multitude of recreational activities – the internet, video games, from friends and, of course, television. Often, if there is not instant success in a new activity, a child can easily become an unwilling participant. I have occasionally instructed children who are only trying to shoot to keep their parents happy – it is not a pleasant experience for any involved.

Once you are sure your child is excited by and committed to learning to shoot, you have to make your toughest decision: are you a good enough instructor to teach your child yourself or should you take them to a professional?

If you feel you are not really qualified, you need to consider taking your child to a Shooting School or, in the UK, to one of the BASC Young Shot Days. As an instructor, one of the highest compliments that I can receive is to be asked to teach a client's child to shoot. A child's big grin in response to that first crushed target is a sight that is hard to beat!

From the first lesson, the fundamentals of straight shooting need to be taught. If this is not done, poor form will be the result and, once ingrained, that poor form will place a ceiling on consistency and progress for the life of that shooter.

The early lessons should be short, simple and fun but, most important, successful!

Safety Always Comes First!

Safe shooting includes etiquette and gun handling. Begin with a simple explanation of how a shotgun works, how to correctly open, load and close the gun. Then demonstrate the correct placement of the trigger finger – off the trigger on the trigger guard until the moment the shot is taken.

Next describe the correct sequence of making a shot: as the gun is mounted, the safety is pushed off, the trigger finger moves from the guard to the trigger and the shot is taken.

Waiting for the drive to start. (PAUL FIEVEZ)

The introduction of snap caps allows dry-runs of the full shooting cycle of loading, firing and opening a shotgun safely. Emphasize that the 'safe' is simply a trigger block and even when on, can malfunction, allowing the gun to discharge accidentally. The correct handling and loading of the gun, always keeping it pointed in a safe direction, is an essential part of safe shooting.

The First Rule of Safe Shooting:
Treat all guns as if they are loaded. A shotgun should always be open to prove this, but even when known to be empty, it is prudent to treat every gun as if were loaded.

The Second Rule of Safe Shooting:
Never point a gun, loaded or unloaded, in an unsafe direction.

This excellent advice should be hung in every gunroom. It sums up safe shooting in the field succinctly and, most important for a youngster, in a fun, easily understood manner.

This poem was written many years ago by Mark Beaufoy, an English hunter, when he presented his son with his first gun. Mr. Beaufoy's fine training and enthusiasm stayed with his sons all their lives. His youngest son, who lost his right arm in World War I, continued to hunt and shoot for many years thereafter.

The poem is reprinted with the kind permission of the author's granddaughter, Mrs Prue M. Guild of Athole Cottage, Kirkton, Hawick, Roxburghshire, Scotland.

"A Father's Advice" by H.M. Beaufoy

If a sportsmen true you'd be
Listen carefully to me;

Never, never let your gun
Pointed be at anyone;
That it may unloaded be
Matters not the least to me.

When a hedge or fence you cross,
Though of time it cause a loss,
From your gun the cartridge take
For the greater safety sake.

If twixt you and neighbouring gun
Bird may fly or beast may run.
Let this maxim e'er be thine:
"Follow not across the line."

Stops and beaters, oft unseen,
Lurk behind some leafy screen;
Calm and steady always be:
"Never shoot where you can't see."

Keep your place and silent be,
Game can hear and game can see;
Don't be greedy, better spared
Is a pheasant, than one shared.

You may kill, or you may miss,
But at all times think of this ....
"All the pheasants ever bred
Won't repay for one man dead."

Helping with the picking up. (PAUL FIEVEZ)

Supervision at all times

Never, ever leave a Young Shooter alone, even for a minute, while in the field or at the shooting grounds. There are dangerous out-of-bounds areas and, on the shooting grounds, potentially dangerous mechanical equipment is everywhere. Children are inquisitive by nature so it is imperative to keep them with you at all times!

And last, but most important, *always* put only one shell in the gun at one time and always keep possession of all other cartridges to control the shooting safely.

Etiquette

Etiquette is simply good manners, recognition and respect for the quarry being hunted, its habitat and the countryside in general.

Equipment

Progress in any sport goes hand in glove with the best equipment for the job. For a beginner, the requirements are simple: a suitable gun and low pressure cartridges, essential ear and eye protection and clothing in which to shoot comfortably.

Resist the temptation to purchase a high-end gun and expensive equipment until it is really needed. A high-priced shotgun will not knock down one more bird or break one single extra target than an inexpensive gun, but sound fundamentals will.

The shooting industry caters to the average-sized man in both guns and clothing. Just like the Shooting Lady, Young Shots face many challenges when it comes to finding a gun and equipment that fits and works best for them. Clothing should be chosen for fit and to allow an unimpeded gun mount. Ear protection is mandatory and eye protection should be equally so, be it in the field or on the clay ground. One errant pellet or shard of clay can cause the loss of an eye and unprotected hearing is very quickly damaged.

What Is the Best Age to Start?

More accurately stated, the question should be… what is the best size to start shooting? Regardless of the age of the child, they should weigh around 100 pounds to be able to handle a shotgun safely. I have had 8-year-olds who could do so and 12-year-olds who could not. There are no hard and fast rules on age, but there are definite criteria when it comes to size and strength.

Children need encouragement to progress and this comes from success. They need to have the wherewithal to understand the task being asked of them and have sufficient strength to control and swing a shotgun safely and consistently. All of these elements are required to achieve this success.

There is nothing worse than seeing a young person leaning back, trembling with effort, trying to support a too-heavy gun, or attempting to shoot an unsuitable target. Discomfort and missing will quickly create frustration and disillusionment with the sport, and a return to something at which they are already successful.

I would encourage patience in both you and your child. Wait to shoot together until he or she is of sufficient size, strength and wit to do so successfully. It would be better to take your time allowing them to accompany you when you shoot, learning safety, proper gun handling and field etiquette. They may begin to practise using an airgun with the sights removed – shooting at balloons, tennis balls or static clay targets against a safe background. These exercises guarantee success, are great fun and can be used to instil safe gun handling and shooting skills and to develop the shooting muscle groups prior to progressing to shooting a shotgun.

A 28 gauge makes an excellent first gun.

Eye Dominance in Children

It is worth noting that eye dominance in adolescents is a work in progress and can fluctuate into their teenage years. In a perfect world, they would learn to shoot off the shoulder matching the dominant eye, allowing the correct practise of shooting with both eyes open. However, thorough testing and continued monitoring are needed to quickly address the situation if any cross dominance issues arise. Where there is no definitive dominant eye, I would suggest shooting off the shoulder of their dominant hand and obscuring the cross dominant eye with a piece of opaque foil on their shooting glasses.

What About Gun Fit?

Gun fit for children is an essential element and will evolve with growth and shooting progress. A poorly fitted gun and excessive recoil are the first hurdles to clear on the path to straight shooting. A manageable gun weight, low-pressure cartridges and open chokes in a gun that fits will make their first experiences an enjoyable success and will go a long way to creating a lifetime passion for shooting.

With regard to gun fit, children have the same requirements as adults – the gun must fit to hit – it must shoot where they look. Children grow at an alarming rate so, even though their gun fit dimensions will be constantly changing through adolescence, each alteration should be for a good period. Just like eye dominance, gun fit should be checked and rectified as needed on a regular basis.

When the gun is initially shortened to the correct length, the wood that is removed should be kept and cut into half-inch slices. This way, as the child grows and extra length is required, the slices can be replaced, one at a time, and will exactly match the size and grain of the stock.

Alterations to cast and drop are simply achieved by bending the stock using heat lamps and hot oil. Though it might look odd on a game gun, an adjustable stock would be excellent to make periodic alterations to suit a growing youngster.

Shortening the stock can make the gun barrel heavy, cumbersome and unwieldy but this problem can be easily rectified by putting a matching lead weight in the stock.

Which Is the Best Gun for the Beginner?

There is a direct relationship between the weight of the gun in the smaller gauges (.410, 28 and 20) and the size of the pattern and shot string that they throw. The lightweight .410 is the easiest shotgun for a child to handle but the hardest with which to hit a target – it is a gauge for the expert shot, not the beginner.

If the child's strength will allow, a 28 or 20 bore offers a better gun weight-to-pattern ratio. As his or her strength increases, and as soon as the child can competently control and swing a 12 gauge, then let them have one – the 12 gauge is the king in both range and pattern.

Recoil is one of the biggest challenges that faces the Young Gun. Recoil is controlled, not by shooting a small gauge, but by the cartridge selection, the type of gun, its weight and fit. A side by side, for example, has two phases of recoil, to the back and to the side, while an over and under has only one – in a single direct line. Though this may upset the traditionalist, the over and under is a far easier gun for the beginner to learn with and is more comfortable to shoot.

I usually recommend a short-barrelled 28 gauge over and under with a KICK-EEZ rubber recoil pad as the best gun for the beginner. This gauge, in combination with a low pressure cartridge in a light load of ¾ of an ounce, gives the beginner a gun with minimum recoil, manageable weight and a good margin for error and hence, success.

Small hands need smaller grips to be able to reach the trigger comfortably. A competent gunsmith, in addition to reducing the length of pull, can reduce the grip and forend, making them more suitable for small hands. There are special "Youth Model" shotguns made for the USA market, but these are all semi-automatics. It is a shame that one of the big makers does not make a "Youth Model" over and under for this fast-growing market.

Perfect Practice

The best place to practise a gun mount is indoors, in front of a mirror. Repeating the fundamentals of stance and footwork, posture and head position, using their empty gun, the child can practise the "mount and move" to the target.

Beretta Youth Model semi-automatic is an excellent gun to start a child; light in both weight and recoil and with good stock dimensions for a youth.

By concentrating on good form, you are putting in place the building blocks for their good technique. They do not need to shoot a great deal to develop this – practising a little and often is the secret with Young Guns.

Keep it fun – do not overload them with technicalities. They do not need to know about chokes and cartridges or other trivia, but they *do* need success. Keep lessons short and be ever watchful for fatigue, usually demonstrated by sloppy gun handling as muscles tire. Practise the fundamentals, emphasizing footwork, stance, good posture and head position. Practise the gun mount and move to the target. Use a drawing board to explain the basics of hitting a moving target and, when understood, begin with easy targets.

The first target is as important as the gun and cartridge. It should be slow and reasonably close, like a springing teal, going away or, best of all, an incoming target that requires a small amount of lead and teaches proper shotgunning. A straight-away target, though easier to hit, teaches aiming – and that is a hard habit to correct when moving on to driven shooting.

Building Confidence

There are two possible outcomes of a first lesson: frustration and disappointment, which gives little encouragement to continue, or success and enjoyment, which will hopefully ignite their interest in shooting.

Be sure to finish every session with a success. If youthful strength and co-ordination will not allow the shooting of a moving target, I will start the beginner out on stationary clay targets set on edge along a bank at different ranges. At a young age, an exploding target, whether stationary or in flight, is great fun and will allow you to engage their interest and work on the fundamentals earlier. Ending each session with a broken target ensures a boost of confidence and instills the desire to shoot again.

When you take your child into the field, be sure that they are warm enough. Outfit them with the correct footwear and clothing to ensure this. Kids burn energy, so always be sure to have a snack or a sweet on hand for those lulls in shooting when the opportunity is offered to take a break and recharge their batteries. When not shooting, let them participate fully in the shoot by helping with decoys, spotting or working the dog.

Children and the Law

The UK Firearms Act of 1968 imposes no minimum age for the granting of a Shotgun Certificate. The Act has been amended on several occasions since it became law but without any change to this provision.

Even if a young person is granted a Shotgun Certificate, he or she is not allowed to use a shotgun before the age of 15 except under the supervision of an adult 21 years of age or older. This exception addresses any objections which might be based on concerns over the age of criminal responsibility. A new amendment states that a young person cannot buy or hire a shotgun or purchase amunition until he is 18.

When considering a young applicant, Chief Officers apply the following criteria:

1. Is the young person of adequate stature to use a shotgun safely?

2. Do they understand the basic rules of safe gun handling and can they demonstrate them?

3. Will he receive proper support and training from his immediate social circle?

If the answer to all of these questions is YES, then the Chief Officer knows that granting a certificate to the young person in question poses no danger to public safety or to the peace.

Young Shots and The Future

It is our challenge to make shooting as much or more fun than the other games and sports to which children have access. Their diligent practise and your patience will soon see that great day when they join you in the line or blind for the first time.

The shooting sports are under threat from an expanding urban lifestyle which fuels political efforts to stop the shooting. It is the continuing introduction of Young Shots that is the life blood of our sport – they are the future of the shooting sports.

The smile that says it all.

Chapter 18
Gun Maintenance

It's the first day of the season and your dog is locked on point. You are walking into position when the bird bursts from cover, wings whirring to match the rhythm of your heart! Early season nerves make you a little jittery, but you fall back on experience and your off-season practise and, stepping into the line, you move and mount the muzzles to the bird. As the stock reaches your cheek and shoulder pocket, you brush the gun gently out in front, overthrowing the muzzles, and with that fleeting glimpse of daylight between gun and bird, you instinctively pull the trigger and *"Click!"*

There is nothing more frustrating than a gun malfunction at any time during the season and it *always* seems to happen at the worst times, effectively putting an end to the hunt or the whole day.

It doesn't matter if the shotgun is new or old, factory-made or "best" gun; they can and will go wrong. So, what can you do to avoid these situations? The simple answer is *"an ounce of prevention is better than a pound of cure"*.

The UK is a small country with a gunsmith in almost every village, so it is traditional that, at the end of the game season, the serious shot sends his or her guns to their local gunsmith for inspection and a "strip and clean". In the US, the number of gunsmiths may be adequate, but they are not always close by and the size of the country plus the cost of shipping makes getting your gun to them, post-season, a bit more difficult. Nevertheless, I urge you to take the same preventive maintenance measures described, especially for older or vintage guns.

The locks being cleaned and inspected during an annual strip and clean.

The Annual Strip and Clean

For a proper "strip and clean", the gunsmith first inspects the barrels for dents, dings, loose ribs, pitting or rust. All of these problems – the results of wear and tear – if caught in time, can be remedied. The dents can be raised, barrels honed, ribs re-laid and the barrels re-blacked.

The gunsmith then removes the stock and forend to inspect for any cracks that might not be apparent from the outside and checks for soft spots from over-oiling. The outside of the stock is inspected for hair-line cracks, particularly in the hand and horns. The chequering should not be worn smooth but should be crisp and sharp (essential for safe gun handling).

The action and locks are disassembled and the parts inspected for wear; the bent and sears are checked to ensure they are correctly seated – if not, they could cause an accidental discharge. Trigger pulls are checked for the correct poundage and regulated if needed. Ejectors are checked, regulated and timed and the safety should be operating correctly.

It is amazing what can be discovered inside an action. Dried oil, rust, powder residue and extremely small pieces of wood from the interior of the stock head – even a piece of feather has been found. Any of this debris can contribute to the unsafe operation or be the cause of those "mystery malfunctions".

Shotgun parts interact like a watch movement and so even the slightest amount of debris can cause a malfunction. Springs may weaken if they are kept compressed for long periods of time. Replacement parts are often hand-made, and they may be made of different steel or incorrectly hardened, causing them to burr or to burr their counterpart, but often the discrepancies are just the wear and tear of age and use. A gun made "between the wars" will have been used for 80 plus seasons!

The majority of modern over and under shotguns have captive firing pins contained within coiled springs. They are literally bomb-proof! If the firing pin breaks, the coiled spring holds it in place and if the spring breaks, the firing pin does the same. It is not unusual for a gun that has fired tens of thousands of rounds to be taken apart for a strip and clean and find either a spring or a firing pin broken but have the gun still functioning flawlessly. It will be interesting to see how the modern over and under, with its machined parts and modern metallurgy, will fare after a comparable eight decades of shooting.

Once your shotgun is checked over, the gunsmith will advise you of any remedial work that needs to be carried out to lock, stock and barrels or if the gun is in sound condition. The action and locks will be thoroughly cleaned and lubricated, the gun reassembled and test fired, cleaned a second time and finally, stored, ready for collection. The average price for this annual service is £90 ($150) for a boxlock and £120 ($250) for a sidelock plus any remedial work required. But your peace of mind, knowing your gun will work when you pull the trigger, is priceless.

Prevention is better than the cure.

A comprehensive cleaning kit is a wise investment.

Now that you have gotten your gun "clicking and ticking", the next step is to keep it that way.

Field Cleaning

Every shot you take lights a fire in the chamber, creating heat and moisture. The moisture gets trapped against the barrel walls by the burnt powder residue. This combines with the plastic fouling and lead residue created by the wad and shot scrubbing along the barrel at great heat and high velocity. If this fouling is not thoroughly removed, the trapped moisture will corrode and rust the bores.

As soon as shooting has ceased, make sure your gun is unloaded then wipe it all over with an oiled cloth. I like to pull a snake bore or run a rod through it at the same time, to begin removing the bore surface moisture and fouling.

External corrosion has three causes: handling, moisture and storage. A large component of perspiration (sweat) is salt and salt causes rust. If you have handled a gun on a hot day, you need to be sure to wipe it off with the same thoroughness as if it were wet. You should wipe off your gun immediately, every time you use it!

If your gun has been shot in the rain, wipe it off and place it in a case or gunslip for the minimum amount of time, then take it out as soon as possible, wipe it once again and then let it dry for several hours. This allows any residual water to "sweat out" before the normal cleaning regime is carried out. If a wet gun has been placed in a case or slip, these need to be thoroughly dried as well.

Safe-approved storage, which should have a dehumidifier such as the "Golden Rod".

When you arrive home or to your hotel or lodge, remember that when you take a gun from the cold outside to the warm indoors, condensation is created, so your first action should be to remove the gun from its case or slip and wipe it off again. If possible, never leave the gun in its case or slip overnight; if any moisture is present it will accelerate corrosion.

Never leave your guns in gunslips or cases for prolonged periods of time. They should be stored dry, with a light coating of oil, in a gun safe with a de-humidifier installed (or at least a sack of silica crystals) to remove any moisture created by condensation. If your guns are not in regular use, they should periodically be removed, inspected and wiped over again.

The Essential Gun Cleaning Kit

1. Cleaning rod, bronze brush, jag, wool mop, patches of the correct bore size for the gun.

2. Bore cleaning solvent.

3. Gun oil, serving two purposes: lubrication and protective coating.

4. Clean lint-free cloths.

5. Small brushes (toothbrush and nail brush).

6. Cotton buds and a medium-sized feather.

7. Kitchen roll.

8. Jar of WD 40.

9. Snake bore of the correct bore/gauge size.

10. Choke and action grease.

Cleaning Your Gun

Before you begin cleaning, always check that the gun is unloaded. Next, dismantle it into its component parts of stock, action, barrels and forend and remove multi-chokes, if they are fitted. (These can be placed in a jar of WD 40 overnight.)

Spray barrel bores with bore solvent or dip the brush in the solvent jar. Using the rod, run the brush through the barrels from the breech to the muzzles several times. Next, use balled kitchen roll or patches with the jag to remove residue and to dry the bores. Use clean material with each pass, until the paper or patch emerges clean. (After soaking, multi-chokes are cleaned in the same manner.)

Taking a small brush, a cotton bud or a feather, clean all loose debris from between the ribs, ejectors and action. Check that all screws and pins are correctly positioned and tight. These can become loose or even drop out in use.

Using the rod and mop, wipe all metal surfaces, including the internal bores, with a light coating of gun oil. Multi-choke tubes require a thin smear of gun grease applied to their ends before re-installation. A small amount of gun grease should also be applied to all bearing parts of the action and forend.

The chequering of both stock and forend can be brushed clean using the nail brush. Then wipe off the woodwork and oil or polish with the stock care product appropriate for the finish. The gun is then reassembled and placed in safe (and dry) storage.

Note: Before using again, always run a rod and patch through the bores to remove oil residue.

Just as you take care of your car, your shotgun needs regular service and lubrication to give reliable performance. A consistent cleaning and maintenance regime requires a little time and effort but will ensure the reliability, safe functioning and long life of your shotgun.

Chapter 19

Travelling With Shotguns

There are always concerns when travelling with shotguns, whether you are shooting at home or abroad. The legal requirements for transport via cars, trains, boats and aeroplanes, as well as for storage when in transit in hotels and lodges, are many and varied. To keep it simple, I am going to separate the advice by country.

United Kingdom (UK)

To possess a shotgun in the UK, you must have a Shotgun Certificate. You must be age 17 or over to be issued a Shotgun Certificate. If you are aged less than 17, you may still get a Shotgun Certificate as long as you have your parents' or guardians' signed permission. You must be aged 18 or over to purchase ammunition.

Be sure to have all permits, licenses and travel documents before travelling.

Travelling from the UK to the EU

If you are the holder of a UK Shotgun Certificate and you wish to take your weapons abroad within the European Union (EU), you will need a European Firearms Passport. This is issued free of charge upon written application to your Firearms Licensing Office. You need to specify the shotguns you wish to take and include descriptions and serial numbers. Even with this European Firearms Passport, some EU countries require additional documents. Always check with the country's Embassy or Consulate to determine what is required. Your hunting outfitter or agent should be able to assist you in this process.

Note: Holders of British Firearm and Shotgun Certificates, who wish to take their firearms to Northern Ireland, should be aware that a valid Certificate of Approval from the Chief Constable of the Police Service of Northern Ireland is required in addition to their UK Shotgun Certificate.

Travelling from the UK and the EU to the United States of America

To travel with your shotgun from Europe and UK to the USA, you will need to apply to the Bureau of Alcohol, Tobacco, Firearms and Explosives (ATF) for a Temporary Importation Form 6. To begin this process, you will need an invitation from your host or the event you are attending declaring the purpose and dates of your visit. This is a simple and straightforward process, but I advise you apply several months in advance of your travel date to allow ample time for processing.

At check-in at your point of departure, you declare the shotgun. It is a legal requirement in the USA, that prior to arrival in the USA, a firearm must have been declared and inspected, and a signed declaration placed in the firearm case. Once this process has been done, a security guard will take you and your shotgun through customs where the serial number will be checked against your Shotgun Certificate, then taken to the aeroplane.

On arrival in the USA, your shotgun will come out on the luggage carousel with your baggage. You will then proceed to customs, declare the shotgun and produce the Temporary Importation Form 6. The serial number will be checked and you will proceed to the Transportation Security Agency (TSA) who will review your ATF Form 6 and check the declaration paper work in your case. They may ask to see your UK Shotgun Certificate or your European Firearms Passport, in addition to your regular Passport.

When flying abroad, always allow extra time for check-in and customs. Don't make any connecting flights closer than 2 hours from the time you arrive. And always check in two to three hours before your initial flight is scheduled to depart.

Note: Prior to making your reservations, contact the airline, train or ferry/boat company to check that they do allow passengers to carry shotguns.

Travelling from the UK and the EU to Canada, Central America, Eastern Europe, South America, Africa and Asia

Each country has its own set of rules, regulations and requirements regarding visitors coming to shoot game. Your sporting agent or outfitter will advise you, provide the necessary documents and meet you at customs when you enter the country to facilitate and expedite your entrance. There is a fee for licenses and permits and often an airport transit fee, in and out. Again, your agent or outfitter will notify you of these in advance of your arrival.

The United States of America (USA)

In the USA, most states do not require that the owner of a firearm have a Shotgun Registration Certificate, although some do. Visitors to a state with such requirements will usually only need their identification and a Visitors Hunting License for that state. The host, outfitter or agent of the event or shooting venue will advise, in advance, what is required.

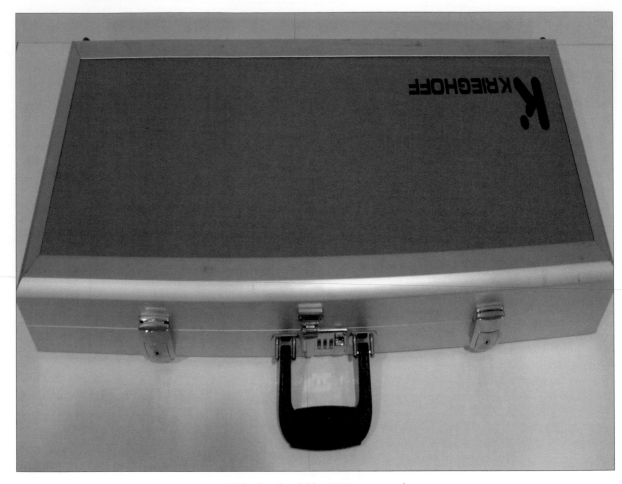

All locks should be TSA approved.

Travelling from the USA to the UK

Visitors from the USA to the UK require a Visitor's Shotgun Permit (in the UK) and shooting insurance. Either your sporting agent will apply for this on your behalf, or you can apply online to the Clay Pigeon Shooting Association (www.cpsa.co.uk) or the British Association of Shooting and Conservation (www.basc.org.uk). The Visitor's Shotgun Permit specifies the dates you will be shooting in the UK, but can be valid for up to one year. The permit will apply to the shotgun you intend to travel with into the UK, and also allow you to purchase cartridges and, if requested, permission to buy a shotgun during your visit.

Prior to your departure from the USA, the shotgun that you intend to travel with has to be taken to your local customs house where you must obtain a Form 4457. This document shows that you own the shotgun and did not purchase it abroad. When you bring the shotgun back into the USA, you will be required to declare the shotgun at customs and present the Form 4457.

Upon entering the UK, your shotgun will be taken to customs by the baggage handlers, you will collect the rest of your baggage, proceed to customs and present your UK Visitor's Shotgun Permit. The gun's serial number will be checked and you will be on your way. When returning to the USA, you declare the shotgun at check-in, a security guard will be called and he will take you through customs where the same process is carried out and the shotgun is taken by the guard to the aeroplane.

Travelling from the USA to Canada, Central America, the EU, Eastern Europe, South America, Africa and Asia

When shooting elsewhere in Canada, Central America, the EU, Eastern Europe, South America, Africa and Asia, your outfitter or sporting agent will apply for the necessary permits and meet you at the airport and assist you through customs. In every country there is a fee for the licenses and permits, and often some form of airport tax or duty. Again, your sporting agent or outfitter is the best source of information and means of acquiring the documents necessary to expedite your visit, both entering and leaving the country.

Transporting a Shotgun

Travelling by Automobile

When transporting a shotgun in a car, it should be in its case or slip, concealed from sight in a locked boot or trunk. If it cannot be concealed, the locked case or the gun should be secured to the car by a cable and the car should have an alarm/immobilizer fitted. If the shotgun is to be left unattended in a vehicle, I recommend that the forend be removed and carried on your person.

Storage in a Hotel or Lodge

It is important that the hotel or lodge where you are has secure storage and, ideally (in the UK) are Shotgun Certificate holders. If they are not, the owner could be found in unlawful possession of a shotgun. If they are not Shotgun Certificate holders, in addition to the locked case, you should use your own security device such as a cable, trigger and/or breech locks to secure the shotgun.

The Tuffpak™ holds 4 guns in breakdown slips and is incredibly strong. Wheels and telescoping handle make it easy to transport both guns and kit.

Shotgun Travel Cases

I always advise that for any type of travel, the shotgun should be packed in a sturdy, locked case. The travelling shotgun case must fulfil several requirements – it needs to protect and secure the shotgun and also be of sufficient strength and resilience to survive rough handling.

I recommend a break-down case for any shotgun, as the chances for damage are greatly reduced and, on inspection, there can be no question that the gun is empty. There are many excellent travel cases from which to choose and your choice can be determined by the number of guns being transported, weight, convenience and simply personal taste.

Americase (www.americase.com) makes a great series of very durable aluminum travel cases. I have used these often, and they are particularly good for shipping guns. There are many other travel case companies with their own set of advantages and advocates, but I am writing based on my personal experience.

When transporting one or more shotguns, my choice is the Tuffpak™ (www.tuffpak.com). Originally designed and developed to transport cameras and tripods for the film industry, the Tuffpak™ shell is rotationally moulded from high-density cross-linked plastic. Rotational moulding produces an extremely durable, lightweight case that can withstand even the roughest baggage handlers. The Tuffpak™ comes in both full-length and compact models. The latter is my favourite as it can carry up to 4 shotguns, broken down, in their gunslips in discreet security. It is also light and rolls effortlessly. When carrying fewer than 4 guns, your hunting clothing and equipment fits in easily. It is the very best case I have ever used and have taken it to three continents and never had a gun get damaged or go missing.

Insurance

In addition to trip, personal medical and cancellation insurance, I recommend that you insure your shotguns against damage or loss when travelling at home or abroad.

The more familiar and experienced you become visiting the various locations and countries, shooting at new and exciting hunting destinations, the more comfortable you will feel when it comes to travelling with shotguns.

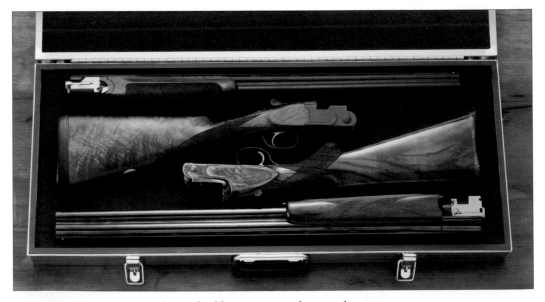

Orvis double gun case, robust and secure.

Chapter 20

Glossary of Shotgun and Wingshooting Terms

Shotgun Terms

Action: The moving parts of a shotgun where the cartridge is loaded, fired and ejected.

Barrel Selector: The mechanism that allows the selection of which barrel fires first on a single trigger shotgun.

Barrel Blacking: The controlled rusting process that creates the black/blue colour that protects the gun barrels.

Bents: Notches or "bents" inside the action which are engaged by the sprung sear, locking the hammers to keep them from moving forward until the trigger is pulled.

Bore: The internal diameter or nominal boring of a shotgun barrel, the measurement of which is referred to as its gauge. (the exception is the .410 which is a calibre – see Gauge).

Boxlock: The lock design in which the action components are contained within the body of the action, recognized by its square, box-like shape.

Break Action: Any shotgun that is hinged so that, on opening, the barrels drop, exposing the chambers for loading and ejecting the cartridges.

Breech: The end of the muzzles that meets the action face.

Butt: The surface of the end of the stock that contacts the shoulder pocket.

Chamber: The breech end of the barrel, sized for the correct cartridge to match the gauge and proof of a shotgun.

Choke: A controlled restriction at the muzzles designed to control the effective range of the pellets of a shotgun cartridge. Chokes can be either fixed (off-line) or removable (multi-chokes).

Comb: The top edge of the stock where the cheek meets for proper eye–rib alignment.

Ejector/Extractor: The mechanism which trips springs to eject the spent shell or lifts the spent shell for manual extraction.

Fixed Action: Any shotgun that cannot be hinged at the action: Pump, Semi-automatic and Bolt-action shotguns.

Forend: The woodwork that is fitted under the barrels to provide grip, control and to protect the hand from heat.

Gauge: The nominal boring of a shotgun, determined by the number of lead spheres made from a pound of lead. The exception is the .410 which is actually a calibre – it contains 67 balls of lead in the shell and hence is a 67 gauge.

Grip: Also referred to as "the Hand", it is the place on the stock where the trigger hand grips the gun.

Intercepting Sear: The second sear in the action that "intercepts" the hammer to stop it from falling, thereby preventing accidental discharges should the gun be dropped or its mechanism jarred. Only by pulling the trigger are both the first and second (intercepting) sears moved out of the way simultaneously, allowing the gun to fire.

Muzzle: The end of the barrels where the choke is fitted and the pattern is created.

Over and Under: A shotgun with superposed barrels, one stacked on top of the other.

Pattern: The quality (hardness) of the shot and the amount of choke determine the down-range pattern of the shot pellets, traditionally defined as a 70% pellet count within a 30 inch circle at 40 yards.

Pump: A shotgun that is loaded and ejected by the manual operation of a slide forward and back, which loads and ejects the cartridge.

Recoil: The reactive backwards force of the shotgun upon firing.

Safety: There are two types. Automatic: the safety is automatically placed "on" when the shotgun is opened. Manual: the safety catch or button is consciously applied or set "on" or taken "off".

Semi-automatic: A shotgun action where the pressure created by firing works the mechanism to eject and reload a second shell. Note: Semi-auto actions have reduced recoil because of the shock absorber effect of the gas pressure.

Shot/Pellet: Shot pellets contained in the shells or cartridges are made of lead, steel or non-toxic materials. The shot spheres are made in different sizes and loads to match the quarry being hunted.

Side by Side: A traditional break-action shotgun which has both barrels aligned horizontally, or "side by side".

Top Lever: The lever at the top of the action which operates the mechanism that allows the shotgun to be opened.

Wingshooting Terms

Beater: The quality of a driven shoot is directly proportional to the quality of its beaters. It would be impossible to have driven shooting without the line of beaters. Working in a line under the direction of the keeper they beat the coppices, spinneys and cover crops to drive and flush the birds over the waiting line of Guns.

Bird Boy: In South America, a Gun is allocated a Bird Boy for the duration of his stay. The Bird Boy escorts the shooter to his peg, carries the gun, brings cartridges and refreshments, spots birds,

cleans the gun at the end of the day and generally does what he can to ensure a good shooting experience.

Flankers: The flankers, also referred to as flaggers, use flags to keep the birds from breaking out of the sides of the drive or from turning back into the cover. The clever positioning of flankers, both stationary and mobile, helps to guide and direct the birds in the desired direction.

Gamekeeper: The Gamekeeper's job is, traditionally, to prevent poaching on his employer's land. While poacher prevention is still part of the Gamekeeper's job, today it encompasses the management of large tracts of land to maintain and protect the habitat for raising and releasing game birds.

Guide: The professional who guides you while hunting, the Guide has an in-depth knowledge of the quarry and its habitat as well as the shotgun, equipment and dogs most suitable for the type of hunting. A good guide ensures a safe and successful day in the field.

Gun: The name or term given to an individual shooting in a line; hence the expression "a line of Guns".

Loader: In driven shooting, when a shooter is using a pair of guns, the Loader stands behind and passes the loaded gun, takes the empty gun, re-loads it, passing it back and taking the now-empty gun in turn. If the shooter is using a single gun, the Loader stands to the side and stuffs the empty gun as required. In Spain, the Loader sits in front of the Gun, loading and passing the gun from a seated position.

Outfitter: See Sporting Agent.

Pegs: Canes, posts, sticks or individual butts positioned 35 to 40 yards apart in a line facing the direction of shooting. The team of Guns draws their peg position prior to the beginning of the shoot.

Picker-up: The Picker-up is responsible for swiftly

Pickers-up.

retrieving shot birds and humanely dispatching any wounded birds as quickly as possible. Their job is essential in any shooting, but in driven game shooting where large numbers of birds are shot, it is even more so. Pickers-up are placed at the rear of the shooting line and use dogs of a variety of breeds and numbers.

Roving Syndicate: A team of Guns that prefers to shoot together in different locations and in various countries will purchase a Season's shooting as a group or Syndicate.

Secretario/Spotter: (Spain) The Secretario sits behind the Gun at his peg and counts the shot birds and marks their position to ensure that all are retrieved. When shooting with a team of individual Guns, the Secretario keeps accurate track of the bag for his Gun – this is vital when the Gun may be paying for overages.

Shoot Captain: Whether it is your host, his appointed deputy or agent, the Shoot Captain will brief you on safety, the quarry and supervise the choosing of pegs. During the day he will marshal the team of Guns to ensure the day runs smoothly.

Sporting Agent: A Sporting Agent is someone who buys, manages and sells shooting. It could range from whole estates to single days for Syndicates or single Guns. They are experts in their field and offer further services such has liability and shoot cancellation insurance. They will also provide advice on travel, clothing, equipment and organize the necessary permits and licenses required for shooting in the country being visited.

Syndicate: A group of sportsmen that purchases the shooting rights for an estate, either outright or for a number of days per season. Their advertising will often offer shooting for a "Full Gun", referring to a Gun who is willing to take the full season's shooting or a "Half Gun", where two Guns will share the season's shooting and the cost.

Under or Beat Keeper: On larger estates requiring more than one keeper, the Head Keeper will be supported by an Under Keeper or several Beat Keepers who have specific responsibilities for certain drives.

Bibliography

Adams, Cyril S. and Braden, Robert S., *Lock, Stock and Barrel*, Safari Press, Long Beach, CA, 1996

Askins, Charles, *Wing and Trap Shooting*, Outing Publishing, New York, NY, 1911

Barnes, Mike, *The Game Shooting Handbook*, The Crowood Press, Wiltshire, UK, 2005

Basic Shotgun Instruction, National Rifle Association, Washington, D.C., 1962

Barsness, John, *Shotguns for Wingshooting*, Krause Publications, Iola, WI, 1999

Batley, John, *The Pigeon Shooter*, Quiller, Shrewsbury, UK, 2004

Bingham, Derek, *Driven Game Shooting*, Unwin Hyman Ltd., London, UK, 1989

Blagdon, *Shooting. With Game and Gun Room Notes*, Read Country Books, Warwickshire, UK, 2005

Black's Wing & Clay, Grand View Media Group, Birmingham, AL, 2011

Book for Dangerous Men, The Field and Barbour, London, UK, 2008

Boothroyd, Geoffrey and Boothroyd, Susan, *Boothroyds' Revised Dictionary of British Gunmakers*, Sand Lake Press, Amity, OR, 1997

Bowlen, Bruce, *The Orvis Wingshooting Handbook*, Lyons and Buford, New York, NY, 1984

Brander, Michael, *A Concise Guide to Game Shooting*, The Sportsman's Press, Wiltshire, UK, 1986

Brindle, John, *Shotgun Shooting*, Nimrod Book Services, Hants, UK, 1985

Brister, Bob, *Shotgunning: The Art and Science*, New Win Publishing, Inc., Clinton, NJ, 1976

British Proof Authorities, *Notes on the Proofs of Shotguns and Other Small Arms*, The Worshipful Company of Gunmakers of The City of London, the Proof House, Commercial Road, London and The Guardians of the Birmingham Proof House, The Gun Barrel Proof House, Banbury Street, Birmingham

Brown, Nigel, *British Gunmakers Volume One,* Quiller, Shrewsbury Buckingham, Nash, *Mr.*

Buck: The *Autobiography of Nash Buckingham*, Dyrk Halstead and Steve Smith, Country Sport Press, Traverse City, MI, 1990

Burrard, Major Sir Gerald BT., *In The Gunroom*, Herbert Jenkins Ltd. London, UK, 1964
– *The Modern Shotgun Volumes 1, 11 & 111*, Ashford Press Publishing, Hants, UK, 1985

Carlisle, Dan and Adams, Dolph, *Taking More Birds: A Practical Guide to Greater Success at Sporting Clays and Wingshooting*, Lyons and Buford, New York, NY, 1993

Carter, Art, *The Sporting Craftsmen*, Country Sports Press, New Albany, OH, 1994

Catchpole, Giles and Parry, Bryn, *Shooting Types*, Quiller, Shrewsbury, UK, 2003

Churchill, Robert, *How to Shoot*, Geoffrey Bles, London, UK, 1935
– *Shotgun Book*, Alfred A. Knopf, New York, NY, 1955
– *Game Shooting*, Michael Joseph Ltd., London, UK, 1955

Cradock, Chris, *Cradock on Shotguns*, B.T. Batsford Ltd., London, UK, 1989

Curtis, Captain Paul A., *Guns and Gunning*, The Penn Publishing Company, Philadelphia, PA, 1941

Dallas, Donald, *Boss & Co.*, Quiller, Shrewsbury, UK, 2005

Davies, Ken, *The Better Shot*, Quiller, London, UK, 1992

DeVinne, Charles, DVM, *The Orvis Field Guide to First Aid for Sporting Dogs*, Willow Creek Press, Minocqua, WI, 2000

Dorsey, Chris, *The World's Greatest Wingshooting Destinations*, Sycamore Island Books, Boulder, CO, 2002

Downing, Graham, *Shooting for Beginners*, Quiller, Shrewsbury, UK, 1996

Drought, Captain J. B., *A Shot in the Making*, Herbert Jenkins Ltd, London, UK, 1937

DU Pocket Guide, Ducks Unlimited, Memphis, TN, 2004

Eley Book of Shooting Technique, The, Chancerel Publishers Ltd., London, UK, 1978

Evans, George, *The Best of Nash Buckingham*, Winchester Press, New York, NY, 1973

Gage, Rex, *Game Shooting with Rex Gage*, Percival Marshall Ltd., London, UK, 1977

Grant, David, and Venters, Vic, *The Best of British*, Quiller, Shrewsbury, UK, 2010

Handbook of Shooting: The Sporting Shotgun, British Association of Shooting and Conservation, Quiller, Shrewsbury, UK, 2000

Hastings, MacDonald, *How to Shoot Straight*, A. Barnes and Company, Newark, NJ, 1970

Hearn, Arthur, *Shooting and Gunfitting*, Herbert Jenkins, London, UK, 1930

Hoskins, Ben, *The Nature of Game*, Quiller, London, UK, 1994

Hudson, David, *Pheasant Shooting*, Quiller, Shrewsbury, UK, 2005

Hunt, Lynn Bogue, *An Artist's Game Bag*, The Derrydale Press, Lyons, MS, 1990

Johnson, Peter and Wannenburgh, Alf, *The World of Shooting*, Photographex, Inc., Lausanne, Switzerland, 1987

Knight, Richard Alden, *Mastering the Shotgun*, E.P. Dutton, New York, NY, 1975

Lancaster, Charles, *The Art of Shooting*, McCorquodale & Company, London, UK, 1954

Little, Crawford, *Pheasant Shooting*, Unwin Hyman Ltd., London, UK, 1989

Macdonald, Glynn, *Alexander Technique*, Element Books Ltd., Shaftesbury, Dorset, UK, 1998

Marshall-Ball, Robin, *The Sporting Shotgun: A User's Handbook*, Quiller, 2003

Martin, Brian P., *The Great Shoots*, Quiller
– *The Glorious Grouse*, David and Charles, Publishing, London, UK 1990

Martin, Dr. Wayne F., *An Insight to Sports: Featuring Trap Shooting and Golf*, Sports Vision Inc., Seattle, WA, 1987

Masters, Don, *The House of Churchill*, Safari Press, Long Beach, CA, 2002

McCawley, E.S. Jr., *Shotguns & Shooting*, Van Norstrand Reingold Company, New York, NY, 1965

McIntosh, Michael, *Best Guns*, Countrysport Press, Camden, ME, 1989
– and David Trevallion, *Shotgun Technicana*, Countrysport Press, Camden, ME, 2002
– with Jan Roorsenburg, *The Best of Holland & Holland*, Safari Press, Long Beach, CA, 2003

Modern Bird Hunting, North American Hunting Club, Minneapolis, MN, 1990

Montague, A. Andrew, *Successful Shotgun Shooting*, Winchester Press, New York, NY, 1971, Derrydale Press, Lanham, MD, 2000

Muderlak, Ed, *Parker Brothers Knight of the Trigger*, Old Reliable Publishing, Davis, IL, 2002

Mulak, Steven, *Good Shot*, Stackpole Books, Mechanicsburg, PA, 2008

Nickerson, Sir Joseph, *A Shooting Man's Creed*, Quiller, Shrewsbury, UK, 2004

Norman, Geoffrey, *The Orvis Book of Upland Bird Shooting*, Winchester Press, Piscataway, NY, 1985

Oberfell, George G. and Thompson, Charles E., *The Mysteries of Shotgun Patterns*, Oklahoma State University Press, Stillwater, OK, 1957

O'Connor, Jack, *The Shotgun Book*, Alfred A. Knopf, Inc., New York, NY, 1965
– *The Complete Book of Shooting*, Outdoor Life, New York, NY, 1965

Parker, Eric, *The Lonsdale Anthology of Sporting Prose and Verse*, Seeley, Service & Company Ltd, London, UK, 1932

Parry, Bryn, *101 Shooting Excuses*, Quiller, Shrewsbury, UK, 2005

Percy, Lord James, *Hot Tips for Hot Shots*, Barbour and The Field, London, UK, 2005

Pollard, Major Hugh B.C., *Shotguns Their History and Development*, Read Country Books, Warwickshire, UK, 2005

Purdey, T.D.S. and Purdey, Captain J.A, *The Shotgun*, Adam and Charles Black, London, UK, 1962

Reynolds, Mike with Barnes, Mike, *Shooting Made Easy*, The Crowood Press, Marlborough, Wiltshire, UK, 1989

Rose, Michael, *Guncraft: Clay and Game Shooting*, Chancerel Publishers Ltd, London, UK, 1978

Ruffer, Major Jonathan E.M., *The Art of Good Shooting*, David and Charles Publishers Ltd., Devon, UK, 1972

Schroder, Piffa, *Fair Game*, Ashford Press Publishing, Southampton, UK 1988

Sheldon, Colonel Harold P., *Tranquility*, The Countryman Press, New York, NY, 1945
– *Tranquility Revisited*, The Countryman Press, New York, NY, 1945
– *Tranquility Regained*, The Countryman Press, New York, NY, 1945

Shotgun Shooting, British Field Sports Society, E.P. Publishing Ltd., 1972

Smith, Steve, *Hunting Upland Gamebirds*, Stackpole Books, Harrisburg, PA, 1987

Stadt, Ronald W., *Winchester Shotguns and Shotshells*, Armory Publications, Tacoma, WA, 1984

Stanbury, Percy and Carlisle, G. L., *Shotgun Marksmanship*, Herbert Jenkins Ltd., London, UK, 1965
– *Shotgun and Shooter*, Barrie and Jenkins Ltd., London, UK, 1970

Stanford, John Keith, *The Twelfth & After*, Quiller, London, UK, 1944, 1985
– *Guns Wanted*, Charles Scribner's Sons, New York, NY, 1949

Sullivan, John C., Jr., *Waterfowling on the Chesapeake 1819–1936*, Johns Hopkins University Press, Baltimore, MD, 2003

Sussex, East, *The Shot-gun and Its Uses*, Simpkin, Marshall, Hamilton, Kent and Company Ltd., London, UK, 1995

Tarrant, Bill and Editors of *Field and Stream*, *The Field and Stream Upland Bird Hunting Handbook*, The Lyons Press, New York, NY, 1999

Tate, Douglas, *British Gun Engraving*, Safari Press, Long Beach, CA 2000

Taylor, John, *The Shotgun Encyclopedia*, Safari Press, Long Beach, CA, 2001
– *Shotshells and Ballistics*, Safari Press, Long Beach, CA, 2003

Teasdale-Bucknell, G.T., *Experts on Guns and Shooting*, Ashford Press Publishing, Southampton, UK, 1986

Timberdoodle Days, The Timberdoodle Club, Sherwin Dodge Printers, Temple, NH, 2002

Waitzkin, Josh, *The Art of Learning*, Free Press, New York, NY, 2007

Weiland, Terry, *Spanish Best*, Countrysport Press, Camden, ME, 2001
– *Vintage British Shotguns*, Country Sport Press, Camden, ME, 2008

Willett, Roderick, *Modern Game Shooting*, Seeley, Service & Company, London, UK, 1975

Williams, Ben O., *American Wingshooting*, Willow Creek Press, Minocqua, WI, 1998

Yardley, Michael, *Gunfitting: The Quest for Perfection*, Quiller, UK, 2006
– *Positive Shooting*, The Crowood Press, Marlborough, Wiltshire, UK, 1994
– *The Shotgun: A Shooting Instructor's Handbook*, Quiller, UK, 2001

Zutz, Don, *Modern Waterfowling, Guns and Gunning*, Stoeger Publishing Company, South Hackensack, NJ, 1985
– *The Double Shotgun*, Winchester Press, New York, NY, 1985
– *Shotgunning: Trend in Transition*, Wolfe Publishing, Prescott, AZ, 1989
– *Shotgun Stuff*, Shotgun Sports Inc., Auburn, CA, 1991
– *Grand Old Shotguns*, Further Adventures, Inc., Auburn, CA, 1995

Periodicals

Fieldsports
Bourne Publishing Group (Stamford) Ltd
Roebuck House
33 Broad Street, Stamford
Lincs PE9 1RB
www.fieldsportsmagazine.com

Shooting Gazette
PO Box 225
Stamford
Lincs PE9 2HS
www.shootinggazette.co.uk

Shooting Sportsman
PO Box 1357
Camden
Maine 04843
www.shootingsportsman.com

Shooting Times and Country Magazine
9th Floor, Blue Fin Building
110 Southwark Street
London SE1 0SU
www.shootingtimes.co.uk

Shotgun Sports
PO Box 6810
Auburn
California 95604
www.shotgunsports.com

Sporting Clays
5211 South Washington Avenue
Titusville
Florida 32780
USA
www.sportingclays.net

Sporting Gun
IPC Magazines Ltd
Kings Reach Tower
Stamford Street
London SE1 9LS
www.sportinggun.co.uk

The Field
Blue Fin Building
110 Southwark Street
London SE1 0SU
www.thefield.co.uk

The Upland Almanac
PO Box 70
Fairfax
Vermont 05454
www.uplandalmanac.com

Wingshooting and Conservation Organizations

British Association of Shooting and Conservation
Marton Mill
Rossett
Wrexham LL12 0HL
UK
www.basc.org.uk

Countryside Alliance
The Old Town Hall
367 Kennington Road
London SE11 4PT
UK
www.countryside-alliance.org.uk

Ducks Unlimited
1 Waterfowl Way
Memphis
TN 38020
USA
www.ducks.org

Game Conservancy
Burgate Manor
Fordingbridge
Hampshire SP6 1EF
UK
www.gwct.org.uk

Pheasants Forever
1783 Buerkle Circle
St Paul, MN 55110
USA
www.pheasantsforever.org

Quail Unlimited
31 Quail Run
Edgefield, SC 29824
UK
www.qu.org

The Ruffed Grouse Society
451 McCormick Road
Coraopolis, PA 15108
www.ruffedgrousesociety.org

Professional Organizations

Association of Professional Shooting Instructors
www.apsi.co.uk

Guild of Shooting Instructors
www.shootinginstructors.co.uk

The Institute of Clay Shooting Instructors
Fairview
Church End
Main Road
Parson Drive
Cambridge PE13 4LF, UK
www.icsi.org.uk

Index

Page numbers in *italic* refer to captions and illustrations

(TERRY ALLEN)